WRITING
New Adult
FICTION

WRITER'S DIGEST
BOOKS

WritersDigest.*com*
Cincinnati, Ohio

DEBORAH HALVERSON

For more resources for writers, visit www.writersdigest.com.

18 17 16 15 14   5 4 3 2 1

Distributed in Canada by Fraser Direct
100 Armstrong Avenue
Georgetown, Ontario, Canada L7G 5S4
Tel: (905) 877-4411

Distributed in the U.K. and Europe by F+W Media International
Brunel House, Newton Abbot, Devon, TQ12 4PU, England
Tel: (+44) 1626-323200, Fax: (+44) 1626-323319
E-mail: postmaster@davidandcharles.co.uk

Distributed in Australia by Capricorn Link
P.O. Box 704, Windsor, NSW 2756 Australia
Tel: (02) 4577-3555

ISBN-13: 978-1-59963-800-3

Edited by Rachel Randall and Melissa Wuske
Designed by Claudean Wheeler
Cover photo by solominviktor/Fotolia.com
Production coordinated by Debbie Thomas

DEDICATION

For Michael, my new adult hottie turned life-long love.

ACKNOWLEDGMENTS

The author wishes to thank these generous authors, editors, and agents for sharing their experiences and expertise in interviews for this book: Jennifer L. Armentrout (writing NA fiction as J. Lynn), Amanda Bergeron, Carrie Butler, Jill Corcoran, Sylvia Day, Jaycee DeLorenzo, Kristina DeMichele, Stacey Donaghy, Karen Grove, Juliana Haygert, L.G. Kelso, Summer Lane, Trisha Leigh (writing NA fiction as Lyla Payne), Robin Ludwig, Kevan Lyon, Molly McAdams, Jen McConnel, Sara Megibow, Lynn Rush, Victoria H. Smith, Denise Grover Swank, Suzie Townsend, Tammara Webber, Dan Weiss, and E.J. Wesley.

ABOUT THE AUTHOR

DEBORAH HALVERSON spent a decade editing young adult and middle-grade fiction and picture books for Harcourt Children's Books before climbing over the desk to try out the author chair on the other side. She's now the award-winning author of *Writing Young Adult Fiction for Dummies*, the teen novels *Honk If You Hate Me* and *Big Mouth*, three books in Rubicon's Remix series for struggling readers, and the picture book *Letters to Santa*.

Deborah is also the founder of the popular writers' advice website DearEditor.com, a writing teacher for groups and institutions, and an advisory board member for UC San Diego Extension's Specialized Certificate in Children's Book Writing and Illustration. She's a frequent speaker at writers' conferences—her annual state of the market keynote is a much-anticipated part of the SCBWI Summer Conference, which draws more than 1,300 writers for young people every summer—and on radio programs and in classrooms such as UC Berkeley and Stanford University, where her *Writing Young Adult Fiction for Dummies* has been an assigned textbook.

Deborah now freelance edits fiction and nonfiction for both published authors and writers seeking their first book deals. Books she's edited have garnered top industry awards, and many of the aspiring writers she's coached have landed agent representation and lucrative book deals. She enjoys editing adult fiction and nonfiction but specializes in Young Adult and New Adult fiction. For more about Deborah, her books, and her editorial guidance, visit www. DeborahHalverson.com.

CONTRIBUTORS

ALANA ALBERTSON: "Beyond the Book: Creating Your Own Audio Book" (Chapter 13). Alana is former president of both Romance Writers of America's Young Adult and Chick Lit chapters. She's the author of two New Adult series, Dancing Under the Stars and Invincible, and the New Adult short story "Snow Queen." Alana also writes Young Adult fiction. (www.AlanaAlbertson.com)

SYLVIA DAY: Foreword. Sylvia is the No. 1 *New York Times* and No. 1 international best-selling author of over a dozen award-winning novels. Two of her novels—*Bared to You* and *Reflected in You*, both in the New Adult fiction Crossfire series—took spots among the top ten best-selling books of 2012 on year-end sales round-ups throughout the world. Sylvia served as the 22nd president of Romance Writers of America. (www.SylviaDay.com)

KAREN GROVE: "Breaking Into the Traditional Market" (Chapter 14), with Nicole Steinhaus. Karen is Senior Editor and Editorial Director of Embrace, Entangled Publishing's New Adult fiction imprint. She's been an editor for almost thirty years, working with authors at Harcourt and then Houghton Mifflin Harcourt before launching the New Adult Fiction imprint Embrace. The majority of Karen's books have earned starred reviews from major review journals and such prestigious awards as the National Book Award, Michael L. Printz Honor, multiple Edgar Allan Poe Awards (Mystery Writers of America), and a RITA Award (Romance Writers of America). (www.entangledpublishing.com/category/new-adult)

ROBIN LUDWIG: "Author Branding Through Cover Design" (Chapter 13). Robin is an award-winning book cover designer and president of Robin Ludwig Design, serving clients with design and print services while specializing in book cover and graphic design services for authors and book industry clients worldwide. She was a finalist for Best Cover Design Fiction for the 2012 Indie Book Awards. (www.gobookcoverdesign.com)

KEVAN LYON: "What It Means to Look for 'Fresh'" (Chapter 14). Kevan is a literary agent and partner with Marsal Lyon Literary Agency. She has more than twenty years in the publishing business, including wholesale, retail, and distribution. Kevan handles women's fiction, with an emphasis on commercial women's fiction, Young Adult and New Adult fiction, and all genres of romance. Her list includes *The New York Times* and *USA Today* best-selling authors Jennifer L. Armentrout, Jennifer Probst, Kristen Proby, Molly McAdams, A.L. Jackson, Laura Griffin, among others. (www.MarsalLyonLiteraryAgency.com)

MOLLY MCADAMS: "Giving Chase a Voice" (Chapter 3). Molly is the *New York Times* and *USA Today* best-selling author of the New Adult contemporary romance series Taking Chances and Forgiving Lies, as well as other novels and novellas for New Adult readers. (www.MollyMcAdams.com)

NICOLE STEINHAUS: "Breaking Into the Traditional Market" (Chapter 14), with Karen Grove. Nicole is Assistant Editor at Embrace, Entangled Publishing's New Adult fiction imprint. Writing as Brooklyn Skye, she is also the author of Amazon's best-selling New Adult contemporary romance *Stripped*. (www.brooklyn skye.wordpress.com, www.entangledpublishing.com/category/new-adult)

TABLE OF CONTENTS

FOREWORD: Sylvia Day 1

INTRODUCTION: Three Cheers for Emerging Adults! 3

CHAPTER 1: Mastering the New Adult Market......................................8

CHAPTER 2: Creating Your Premise, NA-Style 24

CHAPTER 3: Crafting a Youthful Yet Sophisticated Voice and Sensibility.......... 36

CHAPTER 4: Filling Your Fiction With Characters Who Act Their Age 57

CHAPTER 5: How to Talk Like a New Adult 88

CHAPTER 6: Strategizing an NA Storyline That's Fresh and Wholly You.......... 108

CHAPTER 7: Structuring a Satisfying Storyline 120

CHAPTER 8: Writing a Seamless Story From Beginning to End..........................131

CHAPTER 9: Cranking Up the Conflict, Tension, and Pacing in Your NA Fiction 145

CHAPTER 10: Love and Sex in the Age of Experimentation 153

CHAPTER 11: Building a World Around the New Adult Experience 176

CHAPTER 12: Revising in a Speed-Driven Market 187

CHAPTER 13: Self-Publishing Your New Adult Fiction.....................................208

CHAPTER 14: Casting Your Lot With a Traditional Publisher 235

CHAPTER 15: Marketing Your New Adult Fiction ... and Yourself 261

INDEX.. 278

Foreword

BY SYLVIA DAY

When I began writing the story that became the global bestseller *Bared to You*, there was no New Adult subgenre of fiction. I had no idea my tale of a recent college graduate tackling adulthood and her first mature relationship was tapping into a particular niche. I knew only that my heroine was on her own for the first time, making new mistakes while trying to learn from her old ones.

In many ways, I was embarking on a new chapter along with my heroine.

In picking up *Writing New Adult Fiction*, you, too, are turning to a new page in your writing career. Trying new things and taking risks is very much a part of being a successful entrepreneur, and educating yourself about the avenues you wish to explore is one of the most important aspects of career building. I commend you for performing your due diligence. By compiling the appropriate knowledge base to begin your story with confidence, you are contributing to your own success.

Take what you learn in the pages that follow, then adapt the knowledge to suit your story and style. Let the information work for you. Learn the rules so you can break them. You will lead your New Adult characters on a similar journey of discovery and adaptation. It's a path we can all relate to, which is why the genre resonates with so many readers, regardless of age and background.

I have long said that we as readers fall in love with characters not for the things they get right, but for the things they get wrong. I hope you will give yourself the same latitude.

You are not writing another version of an existing story. You are writing *your* story, and that means you will be taking a road not yet traveled. You may get lost, you will certainly hit bumps in the road, you might have to turn around or take detours. Deborah's advice and guidance will help you spot the landmarks, but forgive yourself for any misadventures. Careers aren't built on successes; they're built on the lessons you learn from your failures.

But you won't fail. You'll write the next great New Adult novel, and I look forward to reading it.

Sylvia Day

Three Cheers for Emerging Adults!

*T*hey're not full-blown grownups yet, but they're pretty darn close. They're not teenagers anymore, but they're not done growing up. They're in-between, relatively unfettered by the rules or expectations of either group. Finally—*finally!*—they can do what they want, when they want, where they want, how they want. That's freedom! That's independence! That's scary stuff.

That's the experience of the eighteen- to twenty-five-year-olds whom psychologists have dubbed "emerging adults." (That sounds like psychologists, doesn't it?) This seven-year phase of development is as distinct as childhood, teenhood, and adulthood—and so crucially different from each one. This post-teen, pre-adult phase is marked by identity exploration, instability, self-focus, and possibilities. Oh, the possibilities.

Emerging adults—or as fiction writers refer to them (and how this book will from now on), new adults—are shedding the roles and relationships that defined them as teens, when they received guidance, support, resources, and imposed structure. Now they're forging new relationships in which they decide what goes, constructing new social circles in which power is shared or mutual. These young people are operating in a lifestyle fairly oozing in its transitory nature, so the commitments, roles, and relationships are understood to be temporary.

They are also awash in a sense of brass rings screaming to be grabbed. New adults have a stunning breadth of opportunities to explore in love and work before they have to commit to a life partner and path—something they know they'll do eventually but which they feel little compunction to do at this particular moment, thank you very much. New adults are optimistic. Things are unstable and stresses high, sure, but they know it'll work out for them even if it doesn't for other people. They're quite aware that stability comes when you commit to the responsibilities of true adulthood—careers and marriages and partnerships and parenthood—and for the most part, they look forward to that. The new adult phase is marked by intense identity exploration and experimentation, making it fraught with both possibility and instability, with high expectations and shattered realities. Freedom from oversight is also freedom to screw up big time—and that makes for glorious fiction gold.

For some new adults, life is just too much. For most, it's an emotionally charged time. And for all, it's full of *big firsts*. First serious love relationships, where you're no longer the tentative teen wondering what love feels like but are instead working out what traits in a lover sync with the new, self-actualized you. First career explorations, where your job focus changes from pulling in cash or rent money to laying down the foundations of a future career. First financial challenges … first true understanding of what it means to be responsible for yourself … first time you've walked the rope without a safety net. Life-changing choices and consequences are the "emerging adult experience," and that's New Adult fiction.

"I'm not writing for *a certain age group but* about *a certain age group."*—**TAMMARA WEBBER**, *New York Times* and *USA Today* best-selling author of *Easy* and the Between the Lines series

---

REFLECTING THE NA LIFE IN FICTION

We all want to read stories that reflect our own existence, and new adults are no different. They need their own stories that reflect their own experience. Not young adult or "YA" fiction. And not adult fiction. *New Adult* fiction. NA. What is NA fiction, and how do you write stories that are distinctly NA? How can you explore the themes, characters, and issues you want to explore while giving NA readers stories in which they see themselves and feel truly entertained or enriched for the experience? This book answers those questions, digging into the new adult mind-set and experience and teaching you how to use trusted writing techniques and strategies in ways that allow you to create a wholly, distinctly, satisfyingly NA story.

Your job as an NA writer is extra challenging *and extra fun* because you're not aiming to please just yourself or readers between ages eighteen and twenty-five. New Adult fiction also enjoys a readership of people older than twenty-five who totally qualify as full-grown, psychologist-approved "adults." We're talking readers in their thirties and forties who are well established with spouses, children, and careers. These *crossover readers*—the same ones who helped boost YA lit to the top of the trade fiction profit spectrum starting with the Harry Potter and Twilight series—love themselves some NA, too.

With such a wide audience range and no "Age Appropriate" limits on content, you can explore life through your fiction in a way that YA writers can't. NA fiction goes further than teen fiction, showing young people struggling through situations where the stakes are higher and the consequences longer term. New adults are doing their darnedest to deal with things on their own, taking their first big steps toward becoming the grown-ups they want to be, and New Adult fiction mirrors this in the choices the characters make and the type of situations they face. And it can mean, sometimes, more sex. Eighty percent of American college students are doing the premarital hubba-hubba, after all. Exploring your identity involves probing your sexuality, and new adults finally have the time, unfettered access, and social acceptance to probe as often and as experimentally as floats their boats. That's where the NA category takes some heat. "Sexed-up fiction for teens," NBC Today News declared. "Sounds like pornos to me," one children's book agent quipped while onstage at a national book conference. And so NA writers have had to defend their fiction as being about *more* than its often-explicit love scenes.

It really is more. This book is about the diversity of the NA realm. Diversity in plots. Diversity in settings and themes, and in character goals and circumstances. Fiction reflects its audience's experiences and needs, and there's extreme diversity within the new adult experience. It's not all wild, casual sex in the dorms. Forty percent of Americans don't go straight into college after high school. They join the full-time work force. They join the military. They get married and start families. Some struggle for work, some join the Peace Corps to satisfy their need to give to others while they find themselves, some flounder at home with Mom and Dad or on their own. The full new adult spectrum gets explored in New Adult fiction.

I'VE GOT YOUR BACK

This book will show you how to mine this rich phase of life for your fiction. While the elements of storytelling are the same for New Adult fiction as they are for standard teen and adult fiction, NA writers must come at those elements with a unique mind-set. After all, this category has its own expectations, quirks, and a very opinionated audience. In this book, I identify and teach actionable techniques to create the distinct sensibility of the New Adult mind-set and craft an appealingly youthful narrative voice and storyline. I'll also help you sculpt your themes, settings, characterizations, and dialogue with the NA reader in mind.

Teaching these skills means breaking storytelling down into elements that in reality are intertwined and interdependent, but as long as you keep the concept of "variety" in mind and strive to mix and match elements while you draft your stories, the seams between those elements will disappear and you'll stop thinking of techniques in isolation. Interweaving elements and focusing on effect rather than executing techniques will become second nature for you.

If you're totally new to writing, you'll find this a comprehensive book that'll usher you from great idea to fabulous final draft and beyond into publishing and promoting. And for those of you who have been writing for a long time, I aim to remind you of things you've forgotten as you've plugged away in your writer's cave, as well as to surprise you with other things you might never have considered, particularly in regards to NA's distinct readership. I've organized this book so that you can dip in and out of it as each manuscript demands. Perhaps you're aiming to launch your craft to the next level? I've kept that in mind, too. Years of work with best-selling authors and top award winners has shown me that the best writers keep their pencils sharp by consciously working on their craft. If you have a finished manuscript on your hands, you'll be able to use this book to evaluate that draft, spotting weaknesses that you can then improve and strengths that you can hone for an even more satisfying story.

I do all of this with the unqualified declaration that this book is not about rules but rather about embodying the NA mind-set and experience in words and stories that are true to your very personal style and vision. Just as new adults feel unfettered by the rules and expectations of teenhood and adulthood, New Adult fiction evolved as a realm for storytellers who take the path that feels right to them rather than the path that's approved by the powers that be.

"NA has freedom to break the rules because more NAs are self-published." — **JENNIFER L. ARMENTROUT**, publishing NA fiction as J. Lynn, best-selling author of the Wait for You series

---

My teaching includes frequent discussions of the marketplace and publishing industry. Writer. Businessperson. Marketer. You need to do all of it well, and to help you do that I've brought in others who've traveled this path already—a slew of authors and agents and publishers and publicity pros. You'll recognize some of the names from the bestseller lists, while others may be new to you as up-and-comers, behind-the-scenes experts, and notable advocates for NA. All shared their insights with me in off-the-cuff interviews, snippets of which I've peppered throughout this book, and some generously contributed full inserts devoted to particular elements of NA writing, publishing, and marketing. I can tell you that across the board, these amazing experts have important common ground: They care about NA writers and readers and the future of NA fiction. They're all delighted to be there for you as you realize your New Adult fiction dreams, through this book and their own websites and social media, which they fill with craft tips and news about NA fiction happenings and cheers for fellow writers. NA is marking itself as a diverse and profoundly supportive community. Welcome to the fold, and happy writing.

CHAPTER 1

Mastering the New Adult Market

To publish is to be in business, and every businessperson should understand the market in which they participate. For us that means plopping the word *revolution* on the table. Because, make no mistake, that's what the emergence of NA fiction is: a people's revolution, starring writers and readers. Which makes you a revolutionary. You're writing in a category that the reigning powers of publishing did not sanction until readers who shared your interest forced them to acknowledge their needs. In interview after interview, pioneering authors of NA fiction told me they were just writing what they wanted to read, and what they wanted to read were stories about the soul-soaring and soul-crushing experiences of young people living, loving, and learning in those years after high school but before marriage, career, and kids. NA is indeed a fiction of the reader, by the reader, and for the reader.

Most of this book is about the art and craft of storytelling, because that's what ultimately melts readers' butter—and ours, too. We all crave killer stories. But if you're planning to publish your story, you're going into business either for yourself or with a publishing company, and you need to work out how you fit into this scheme. In this chapter I'll explain NA's unique marketplace and lay it against the larger publishing landscape. I'll distinguish NA from fiction for teens and fiction for adults, shine the spotlight on NA readers and their expectations, and give you insight into the blooming NA community of authors, readers, and industry players. Along the way, I'll regale you with the tale of how this revolution unfolded.

WHERE NA CAME FROM AND WHERE IT'S GOING

It's not often that a new category emerges in the publishing industry, and *speed* isn't the word to describe the emergence when it happens. It took Young Adult fiction over fifty years and a split into YA and MG (middle-grade) subcategories to become the industry juggernaut it is today. In every way, the volcanic emergence of the New Adult fiction category in 2012 defies precedent.

The NA genesis story can be summed up simply: It started with writers.

In true grassroots fashion, writers—many of them new adults themselves—yearned for stories that reflect the lives of people immediately following high school graduation, and when they didn't find those stories in bookstores, they started writing them. It wasn't a wholly new urge. I'd seen a number of manuscripts featuring college-aged protagonists in my years with a children's trade fiction division in the 1990s and early 2000s as writers tried to place these manuscripts with publishers of Young Adult fiction. But the publishers stuck tight to the notion that high school graduation marked the YA ceiling. Young Adult fiction was about the twelve- to eighteen-year-old experience, period. The prevailing belief was that once readers graduated from high school themselves, they moved on to their college-assigned reading or to novels for adults. Bookstores believed they'd have no customers for NA books, and without those bookstores buying the books from publishers, publishers had little incentive to produce them. This, of course, was in the days before e-books and up through the early days of publishing's digital revolution.

One editor, Dan Weiss of St. Martin's Press, tried to carve a place for these wayward eighteen-plus stories in 2009 and coined the term "New Adult fiction." Alas, without bookstore support, Weiss failed to score the breakout book needed to force the rest of the publishing industry to acknowledge the new fiction.

A year or so after Weiss's efforts, with the Twilight series having locked in the fervent loyalty of the crossover readers who'd discovered the YA category via Harry Potter, there was a sense of things coming to a head. Teen fiction seemed to be pushing at its upper limits, trying to punch a hole in its ceiling. What about the lives of teens after high school? What about their experiences in college, when grownups aren't around to tell them who to be, how to be, where to be, and when to be there? You wouldn't find that in adult fiction categories any more than you'd find it on the YA shelves. The gap was starting to show.

"I didn't make a conscious decision to write 'New Adult.' I wrote about the kinds of experiences that happened to me or to people I knew in college. I like my books to be real, so I put a lot of myself into them. That's how they ended up being New Adult. Then I read Easy *and* Beautiful Disaster *and realized that other people wrote for the college age, too."*—**MOLLY MCADAMS**, author of the best-selling novel *Taking Chances* and other NA novels

---

Authors like Molly McAdams, Tammara Webber, and Jamie McGuire stepped into that gap and, exhibiting the very optimism, experimentation, and high expectations that mark the New Adult mind-set, published their books themselves. The digital publishing revolution had reached the point where the technology for self-publishing e-books was accessible and affordable to everybody, and e-reading devices were commonplace. They struck gold. Not only were there readers for the books, there were *lots* of readers. Ignoring conventional wisdom and acting on their own creative impulses, the authors had proven that college-aged people were eager for books that reflected their experiences.

In the stroke that rendered this emergence truly volcanic, the timing of this communion of writers and readers coincided with the maturation of social media and the culture-rocking *Fifty Shades of Grey*, hailed as one of the first NAs, published in May 2011 and selling 44 million copies by late 2012 (first published by small indie publisher The Writer's Coffee Shop, then by Random House in 2013). New adults and crossover readers are very active online and very vocal when they like something. It was the perfect storm. Fan word of mouth drove sales of self-published NA fiction through the roof, fast and loud. By the end of 2012, Goodreads.com had logged 14,000 New Adult titles, NA books were hitting bestseller lists, and the world had taken notice. Articles examining the NA fiction phenomenon appeared in mainstream media such as *The New York Times*, NBC News, *New York Magazine*, *The Guardian*, *Publishers Weekly*, *School Library Journal*, *The Huffington Post*, Jezebel.com, and MediaBistro's Galley Cat. Ladies and gentlemen, NA fiction was in the building.

Traditional publishers took notice. In a rush of headline-worthy deals, they signed self-publishing standouts like Sylvia Day, whose *Bared to You*, the first book in her NA Crossfire series, was already a bestseller through her own efforts. *New York Times* best-selling authors Tammara Webber, Jessica Park, Jennifer Probst, and Jennifer L. Armentrout (writing her NA fiction as J. Lynn) landed high-profile deals, too. By the end of 2012, publishers were rolling out their own New Adult imprints, with Random House and Entangled both announcing their dedicated New Adult lines, Flirt and Entangled Embrace, in December of that year.

REVOLUTION DOESN'T HAPPEN WITHOUT A FIGHT

Even as the fans cheered and begged for sequels and editors signed big sellers, many within publishing still pooh-poohed this category that had emerged without their blessing or oversight. They called "New Adult" a marketing label, explaining that it was a useful term for positioning this "sexed-up YA" fare for those readers who'd just finished *Fifty Shades of Grey* and now craved more sexually explicit books about young people. Other publishing people saw the larger potential of this fiction but considered it a subgenre of YA. For them, publishing NA fiction through their children's/YA trade fiction divisions as "mature YA" would allow them to hang on to those crossover readers who'd helped turn YA into a publishing juggernaut.

This debate was a dynamic step in developing a strong, definable category. Young Adult fiction had gone through the same hesitancy. There still lingered a sense within the industry that children's divisions were quaint side endeavors when I arrived on-scene in 1995, a couple of years before the first Harry Potter book was published. One children's book publisher told me about feeling indulged at a high-level meeting with VPs of the other divisions, as if she were a precious child seated at the adult table. With the phenomenal multimedia success of Harry Potter, Twilight, and The Hunger Games, plus the growing awareness that Young Adult fiction offered rich and very skilled storytelling, YA removed the booster from its seat. In fact, in many ways and due to factors including the negative impact that e-book growth had on adult trade divisions' bottom lines in the early 2000s, YA moved to the head of the table.

It makes sense that many publishers have been interested in publishing NA through their children's book divisions. NA themes can look at first blush like an extension of YA themes. Other publishers, though, see the more mature content and mind-set as being just too far beyond teen and tween fiction to be a true partner there, instead embracing that mature content and publishing NA through their adult divisions, as William Morrow (an imprint of HarperCollins) decided to do.

But NA is not simply "mature YA", or "sexed-up YA", or YA anything. New adults have left the teen experience behind in a significant way, with its intensely structured life of reporting to school in the morning and being shuffled about by bells and grown-ups for the rest of the day. Post-graduation realities have these young people developing a new mind-set, devising their own structure (or operating without it entirely), forming new goals, and trying to shape themselves to be truly independent adults. They may consult their parents, and younger NAs still have a big decision-making learning curve ahead of them, but they are the ones doing that decision-making. They want it. They are looking forward in life, not looking back to their teen years. New adults view their world and their place in it through a new lens, and that's what readers and writers of New Adult fiction explore. I'll delve more deeply into the ways that the new adult mind-set and perspective differs from that of teens and adults in Chapters 3 and 4, which focus on the NA sensibility and on creating believable NA characters.

New Adult fiction surely isn't hype—we know that now. Publishers don't create imprints for hype. Staffing, launching, and running imprints is a serious financial endeavor. And over time, NA has grown big and is moving independently from other fiction categories, so it can't be dismissed as a mere marketing term. Publishers have been vital in this growth, injecting legitimacy and credibility, and helping cull and cultivate the immense volume of NA being published for those readers who prefer such filters. But this unique writer-reader-spawned, self-publishing-driven category depends most on its community of writers, bloggers, and readers for its growth. The majority of NA readers are plenty happy to continue going right to the source for their NA fiction—to you, the writer. This category has grown organically and will continue to do so as NA writers flesh out the genres and offer readers fresh storylines about the vast and varied new adult experience.

The people's revolution continues.

WHAT NA IS AND WHAT IT ISN'T

What exactly makes a manuscript "New Adult" fiction, anyway? Is casting a protagonist between ages eighteen and twenty-five in the leading role enough?

No way, José.

As with most things literary, writing NA fiction isn't as simple as accounting for one feature, even its main one. Dropping some luscious sex scenes into the story won't bump it into NA territory, either. The characteristics that distinguish NA fiction from teen fiction and fiction for adults reflect the perspective, sensibility, and interests of young people at this very distinct phase of life. That's what NA readers respond to, and they're quick to object through social media and in bookstore comment sections when an NA offering doesn't feel truly NA.

"I've seen a lot of people thinking they're writing NA because the characters are between eighteen and twenty-five years old. However, their stories are either adult stories with young characters—they don't have that underlying theme of growing wings and developing identity; or they are young adult stories— YA themes but with lots of sex. Neither of these are what I consider NA. New Adult is not just age or sex, it's an underlying theme of finding one's place in the adult world." **—KAREN GROVE,** Editorial Director, Entangled Embrace

NA'S INGREDIENTS

The new adult phase is a spectrum representing young people who are moving from fresh-out-of-high school all the way to those experiencing their first post-college, career-oriented jobs. NA fiction embraces all of it. As with YA fiction, where a book about a fourteen-year-old high school freshman will showcase a less developed maturity and more youthful sensibility than a book about an eighteen-year-old high school senior, NA offers story opportunities across a deliciously wide spectrum. Further enriching this publishing category, every genre has full access to that spectrum: A necromancer on his first assignment without his father is at a different point of discovery in his new adult phase than a necromancer who's been waking the dead on his own for a couple of years now but feels like he hasn't yet found *his* calling in life—and he has no idea what that calling could be.

With this understanding that a significant range of maturity exists in this seven-year span, here are nine traits that together distinguish NA fiction from teen fiction or fiction for adults. All of these will be examined from many different angles and to many different ends as we dig into the writing of your NA story.

1. Main Characters in the NA Age Range

NA stories star eighteen- to twenty-five-year-olds who haven't yet defined themselves enough to settle into marriage, career, and children, the three markers of adulthood. Protagonists on the older end of the spectrum may be revising the plans they thought they'd laid out so carefully, which is why the early careerists fit in the NA realm. There's still a ton of self-definition and exploring to be done, giving plenty of opportunity for inner conflict and stress.

2. Themes Related to Identity Establishment

New adults are figuring out who they are, separate from their families and the identities many feel were foisted upon them as children and teens. Therefore, NA characters are embroiled in the act of self-definition. It has them exploring and experimenting, sometimes leaping and sometimes cowering, through their plots. NA narratives often include conscious thought about the protagonists' need to know who they *really* are and what they *really* want in life now that they get their say. This active exploration is laced with both desperation and hope, which of course sets up delicious opportunities for fictional drama.

3. Independence as a Story Driver

"Free at last!" could be the rallying cry for new adults, particularly the youngest ones. The sense of finally grabbing the bull by the horns pervades most NA stories—which can be at various times exciting and terrifying, successful or disastrous. There's a strong strain of self-determination in NA fiction as characters take responsibility for themselves, their actions, their problems. They may embrace this responsibility or struggle against it, and it fits into any story regardless of genre and specific plotline. NA protagonists are always empowered to resolve their own problems, even those who choose to consult with their peers or parents. Ultimately, the responsibility is on them to make the call and take the action.

4. A Self-Focused Perspective

The quest to work out their own identities, combined with their newfound self-determination, focuses new adults on their own needs, wants, dreams, and interests. That self-focus permeates the narrative sensibility of NA stories and affects character behavior. Characters are "self-centered" not because they are uncaring of others but because this is likely the one time in their lives when their only responsibility is themselves. Note that self*ishness* may be a flaw of specific characters here and there, just as in any work of fiction, but as a group, NA's Good Guy characters exhibit compassion for others. NA characterizations, relationships, and plot choices are heavily influenced by this perspective.

5. Heightened Sense of Change and Instability

The new adult phase of life is marked by change, making it a very unstable time. Even good change requires reassessments, rearrangements, and uncertainty. Factor into that the absence of daily structure that has regulated the previous eighteen-plus years of their existence and you've got serious stress roiling the NA gut. These stories throw a lot of change at their characters and channel their stress into worsening conflict and bad decisions.

6. Clash of High Expectations and Harsh Reality

New adults are an optimistic bunch, at least in terms of their own lives. They generally have a positive outlook for themselves, believing things will work out well for them even if their outlook for the rest of the world is grim. That means they are ripe for a crushing blow and harsh realities. NA stories tap into the conflict and tension that results from this clash, making their optimistic characters aim big but miss even bigger.

7. Peer-Heavy Social Circles

In NA fiction, a social circle of peers often acts as the protagonist's post-teen "family," sharing intimate details and experiences with the main character, serving as social and moral barometers, and in some cases being present on a daily basis, as with roommates or co-workers. Generally these peers have similar interests. Even those new adults who "stay behind" to live with Mom and Dad after high school end up forming new social circles as their friends move on. Parents are out of the picture, or nearly so, in NA fiction. In some stories the new adult may consult the parents, but Mom and Dad's power over the young person is diminished or gone, especially as the new adult's financial independence grows. Some NA fiction features parents unable to let go, causing the new adult to struggle for freedom.

8. Significant Romances

Almost invariably, the NA novel includes a romantic storyline, whether as the primary plot or as a secondary thread. New adult characters are beyond the first-love, in-the-moment romances of teen fiction. These new relationships are intense, usually include sex, and are as much about the protagonist's self-discovery as they are about the object of their affections. Less "Does he love me?" and more "Do I love him? What do I love about him? How do I feel about myself when I'm with him?" The sex scenes are often explicit, although they don't have to be. Romance is such a prime element of NA fiction that I go whole hog with it in Chapter 10, "Love and Sex in the Age of Experimentation."

9. NA-Relevant Circumstances

NA fiction examines universal themes through situations and circumstances that are believable within the new adult experience and within the logic of the fictional world. Examples include temporary living arrangements, short-term jobs, fluid social circles, unfamiliar activities and settings, and financial stress. Chapter 6 is dedicated to helping you develop circumstances for your characters that NA readers can relate to and that offer you superb opportunities for spinning a fresh and distinct storyline.

You can come at these universal NA elements from countless angles, through a myriad of combinations and degrees of emphasis, with either positive or negative spins. NA fiction is a rich realm for a storyteller.

NA GENRE ROLL CALL

I keep calling New Adult fiction a "category." That's important. A publishing *category* tells you the general topic, in this case the experience of new adults. Categories are then broken down into kinds of stories—*genres*. NA genres include dystopian, contemporary romance, paranormal, and historical (more below), but really there's no limit to the kind of story through which you can explore the lives of young people living, loving, learning, and struggling in that gap between late adolescence and adulthood. You can even mash up the genres, throwing some paranormal elements into your historical fiction about a young person struggling in the Confederate South, for example. There's ample room for this new category of fiction to expand its offerings and to mature, bringing in new voices, fans, and creativity.

Contemporary romance has been the most dominant NA genre, but *dominant* has never meant *only*. As NA continues to grow, more books are being published into nonromance genres, although their storylines still incorporate romance in some way. Here's a rundown of the most-published NA genres.

- **CONTEMPORARY ROMANCE.** Romance stories first and foremost, set in modern-day settings and circumstances, with the protagonist's primary struggle being the search for fulfillment through a romantic partner. Happily Ever After endings with promises of marriage and family aren't required; more often, these stories end with the couple together and strong, fulfilled both in their love for each other and in their discoveries about themselves. Examples: Sylvia Day's *Bared to You*; Jessica Park's *Flat-Out Love*; J. Lynn's *Wait for You*; Jay Crownover's *Rule*; Abbi Glines's *The Vincent Boys*; Jamie McGuire's *Beautiful Disaster*.
- **CONTEMPORARY REALISTIC (OR CONTEMPORARY).** New adults struggling to define identity in modern-day settings and circumstances—most commonly in college but also frequently in major cities where the focus is on hip lifestyles and career-launching. Unlike contemporary romance, the love storyline takes a back seat to a more primary conflict for the protag-

onist. Examples: Markus Zusak's *I Am the Messenger*; Amy Efaw's *Battle Dress*; Denise Grover Swank's *Twenty-Eight and a Half Wishes*; Rainbow Rowell's *Fangirl*.

- **SPECULATIVE.** An umbrella label for all fantastical genres. The following prevail in the NA market, but there are many other varieties of speculative fiction and there's a lot of mixing and mashing of speculative elements, as with Ilona Andrews's popular Kate Daniels series, which takes place in a world that's suffered a magic-related apocalypse and includes advanced technology and mythical monsters with its magical spells.

  - **PARANORMAL.** Real-life characters and settings touched by supernatural elements like magic or magical creatures. Demons, werewolves, and winged creatures are common. The menacing atmosphere and psychological fear mongering of horror fiction is often a part of NA paranormal novels, though it is not required. Examples: Carrie Butler's Mark of Nexus series (paranormal romance); Alyssa Rose Ivy's The Crescent Chronicles series (supernatural); Lynn Rush's *Wasteland* (paranormal romance/time travel). E.J. Wesley's *Blood Fugue* stands as an example of a paranormal/horror/action *novella*, a shorter alternative to the full-length novel and prevalent in the NA category.

  - **SCIENCE FICTION/DYSTOPIAN/APOCALYPTIC.** Science fiction has many subgenres, such as genetic engineering and alternate worlds, but NA's offerings seem to coalesce around time travel, dystopian/post-apocalyptic, and futuristic stories. To distinguish between post-apocalyptic and dystopian, imagine civilization surviving its near end (usually through human-deployed weaponry) versus being totally gone to pot (again through man's inhumanity to man). Examples: Summer Lane's Collapse series (post-apocalyptic); Ernest Cline's *Ready Player One* (futuristic science fiction); Aubrie Dionne's A New Dawn series (science fiction/romance); Julie Cross's Tempest series (science fiction/time travel/thriller).

  - **FANTASY.** Stories that are magical or in other ways supernatural. Subgenres include high fantasy, dark fantasy, gothic novels, parallel worlds, urban fantasy, and fictional landscapes that are in some way fantastical. Paranormal is fantasy, but it's so dominant in NA that I singled it out above. Examples: Carrie Vaughn's *After the Golden Age* (fantasy/super-heroes); Samantha Young's *Slumber* (fantasy romance/fairy tale retelling); Juliana Haygert's The Everlast Trilogy (futuristic urban fantasy).

- **HISTORICAL/HISTORICAL ROMANCE.** Stories featuring characters in past eras like the Roaring '20s, or experiencing historical events like President Lincoln's assassination. Far-flung locales and cultures add to the appeal of this genre. If the story is primarily one of romance, then the genre is specified as "historical romance." The cutoff era for historical fiction is a point of debate, so I recommend applying this label to any story set through the 1980s and being clear about the specific time period in all your descriptions of the book. True blue historical fiction fans probably want dramatically different clothing and lifestyles than they'd find in anything after the 1970s. Examples: Melanie Harlow's *Speak Easy* (historical); Allison Rushby's *The Heiresses* (historical romance; serial novellas).

THE THRIVING NA COMMUNITY

An active, supportive community of writers, readers, industry experts, and bloggers/reviewers has grown around New Adult fiction. Most of their interaction takes place online, through social media and blogs, so you can be a part of this community no matter where you live. I'll get into that interaction and its networking potential in Chapter 15, "Marketing Your New Adult Fiction … and Yourself."

NA READERS ARE NA CHEERLEADERS

NA authors, editors, agents, and bloggers generally agree that the audience for New Adult fiction is primarily the same full-fledged-adult crossover audience that took YA to the top of the industry, with college-aged readers coming in second and some advanced teen readers bringing up the rear. These claims have yet to be confirmed by official researchers, but a report by the publishing market research firm Bowker in September 2012 gives us a good look at these "crossover" readers. Bowker determined that over half of the people buying YA books were eighteen years old or older, and that most of them were purchasing those books for their own reading pleasure, not to gift to a teen. The largest segment of these eighteen-plus-ers was the thirty- to forty-four-year-olds. That's a lot of "older" people reading stories about young people in less settled phases of life than their own. Simple escapism is often cited as a reason for their reading choice, as well as a nostalgia for a time in life without the full weight of adult responsibilities. Authors and editors continue to learn about the NA audience through the same writer-reader online interaction that fueled the category's initial growth.

NA readers of all ages interact with authors online, fall in love with characters, and speak freely about what they like and don't like. They don't shy from making suggestions and requests. Molly McAdams specifically wrote the sequel *Stealing Harper* at the mass urging of fans of her *Taking Chances*. NA readers want to connect deeply with their lead characters, and when they do, they let it be known. They hold contests on social media sites where they vote on the sexiest NA hottie. They write fan fiction. And they spread word of their favorite NA books and authors with gusto.

Many NA readers are also bloggers and book reviewers. The blogs act as online gathering places for readers to talk all things NA. Some blogs are dedicated to full-length book reviews, a vital contribution for a category filled with self-published books that aren't likely to get mainstream media book reviews. Bloggers also support authors directly by hosting blog tours and doing book giveaways. I'll cover bloggers extensively in my marketing chapter.

YOUR FELLOW WRITERS

NA writers span the gamut of the writing spectrum, from those trying their hands at fiction for the first time to published veterans. Many are new adults themselves, while others are solidly among the crossover audience age, even topping it. They often write in other categories and across genres, particularly adult category romance and Young Adult fiction (frequently paranormal YA). Jennifer L. Armentrout publishes her YA paranormal/urban fantasy fiction under her full name but her sexier adult and New Adult romance as J. Lynn to keep the lines clear for her readers.

New Adult writers are just as active online as their readers, keeping up their end of the avid writer-reader communion that marks NA fiction. Note that it isn't just the up-and-comers doing this interacting. Sylvia Day, who was already RWA president and successful author of a slew of novels when she self-published the first book in her Crossfire NA series, is constantly online with her peeps, and she updates her blog and maintains her website content herself. Her tweets and blog posts sound like her because it *is* her doing the tweeting and the blogging. Readers love that their NA authors are this accessible and "real." The writers engage with each other online, too, talking craft and business through the blogs, Twitter #*NAlit* chats, and various individual efforts. With the same grassroots spirit that sparked the NA revolution in the first place, they support and promote each other and NA fiction as a category even as they write and promote their own books.

PUBLISHERS AND AGENTS BRING EXPERTISE TO THE TABLE

Publishers are helping to define and grow the category as well, bringing to bear their editorial acumen, marketing power, and distribution channels. Independent publishing experts, such as freelance editors, interior and cover designers, and publicists, also play a significant role as self-published New Adult writers aim for quality in content and promotional strategy. NA authors may sign with a traditional publisher, self-publish, or balance a hybrid career where they do both. Literary agents fit into all three choices as they manage author rights with publishers and those seeking film, audio, or foreign rights, guide authors' long-term writing careers, and sell manuscripts to publishers that don't have open submission policies. I'll go into great detail about the experts' roles and how they fit your publishing choices in my chapters about publishing with traditional houses, self-publishing, and marketing. Remember, to publish is to be in business, and knowing your marketplace means knowing the full breadth of your options and making the best-informed decisions you can for each book and for your overall writing career.

INDUSTRY INSIGHT: "IT WASN'T A CATEGORY THEN, BUT I KNEW IT WAS THERE." AN INTERVIEW WITH DAN WEISS

Dan Weiss, packager of Francine Pascal's 1980s hit Sweet Valley High and Sweet Valley University series, was excited about a new series his packaging company was developing with Francine Pascal called Fearless. Fearless pushed the envelope of the then intensely rigid YA market, running its seventeen-year-old protagonist through a gauntlet of violence, romance, philosophy, and solitude. Weiss knew there was an older market for Fearless and pressed Simon & Schuster to publish it as an adult novel series. Despite S&S's decision to send it into the world as a YA series, Dan saw that as the beginning of what he knew would be a new kind of publishing, one he would eventually dub New Adult fiction.

In 2009, Dan Weiss had just joined St. Martin's Press as an editor. He hadn't forgotten his experience with Simon & Schuster and the Fearless books and felt the time was now right to publish fiction about college-aged protagonists for college-aged readers. His recent experience running the SparkNotes online study site for junior and senior high schoolers and college students gave him a great deal of data about the market, and so he knew the college crowd was still reading Young Adult books, only dipping into adult fiction for the bestsellers. This was contrary to the industry-wide belief that college students were only reading their school-assigned textbooks or had moved on to books for grownups. "My experience says the market follows the audience when it comes to young people but then can quickly catch up," he says. He set about catching the market up to the college crowd.

Dan had a hunch that books written specifically for that college-aged readership, about their experiences and time of life, could be published at St. Martin's. Needing a label for this new kind of fiction, he called it New Adult fiction and had his assistant announce a contest on his blog. That blog post defined the category.

When I interviewed Dan in May 2013, he broke his definition of New Adult fiction into three parts:

"One, perspective. A new adult might be suffering the same trials as the young adult, but it's about perspective. YA is tunnel-visioned. In the NA mind, the perspective about the character's own situation is distinct. They've been through this before, in a way—it's not new—but it has a new context.

"Two, sexuality. Sexual awakenings or sexual independence that an adult might experiment with. This aspect is important. Is New Adult really YA with sex? No. It's more. It's about understanding and experimenting with yourself.

"Three, a readership that is looking back on its younger years. More passionate, more sensual, more dramatic than their actual lives where they are now, at thirty-ish, with young children, doing the day to day, and needing to escape."

In that visionary St. Martin's NA contest, Dan received a lot of submissions from writers who'd been writing New Adult fiction without having a label for it or, in most cases, even thinking there was a market for it. They just had to write the stories that were burning inside them. St. Martin's published a few of these entries in their Griffin imprint, a paperback line in their adult trade fiction division. Alas, the books lacked the retail outlets to forge a new space in the market. "Where do we shelve something called 'New Adult fiction?'" retailers said as they passed on the books during sales calls. The fiction would have to wait for the technological revolution that bypassed physical bookstores completely, allowing readers to discover these novels online and download them, no retail shelves required. That wouldn't happen for another couple of years, but Weiss had laid the scaffolding for the category that was to come. New Adult fiction had a name and an identity, and a community of writers and readers embraced it and set out to make it their own.

Dan Weiss is the former publisher at large at St. Martin's Press.

CHAPTER 2

Creating Your Premise, NA-Style

People have been writing stories about falling in love for hundreds of years. And they've been writing stories about trust issues for hundreds of years, and about finding happiness amid poverty for hundreds of years, and so on. Basic themes get recycled because humans are always intrigued by them. Your challenge as a writer is to put together a set of fictional variables that, when blended into specific characters, concept, conflicts, and circumstances, make your story a fresh and intriguing presentation of your chosen theme. That unique collection of story elements is the *premise* for your story. If readers like what your premise offers, you're well on your road to happy readers, and that's a powerful force to have behind you. Seriously, when NA readers love a book, their social media pom-poming is off the charts. Summing up your premise in a single alluring sentence, called a "hook statement," can help you write that book.

In this chapter I help you develop your idea into a pom-pom-worthy premise using a hook statement as your development tool. I walk you through this premise-building process and show you how you can then use your finished hook to write the story you conceptualized. If you've already finished a draft of your story, writing a hook for that story is a keen way to evaluate the manuscript and make sure you've delivered something distinct and fresh. And then—because by golly this hook thing just keeps on giving—you can use your hook to pitch your finished novel to agents, editors, and readers, ultimately arming those cheering readers with the perfect sound bite to plug right into their social networks.

LEAD WITH THE RIGHT HOOK

A successful premise starts with a core idea. That idea might be a theme you want to explore, like falling in love, or it might be a single image in your head, like a young woman standing on a ledge with a trophy in one hand and a Samurai sword in the other. Or maybe it's a concept, such as Joe Normal saving the President of the United States from assassination. Those are all cool ideas, but you can't dive into your first draft armed only with that. Where would you begin? Who would you put in that first scene, and what would they be doing? You need at least a sense of your main character and conflict, the main themes or issues you'll explore, and the general context of the story, like the era or locale or life circumstances that form the stage for your fiction. You need to develop that core idea into a story premise, and an excellent way to do that is to try to describe your premise in a twenty-five- to forty-word hook statement.

USING A HOOK TO DEVELOP IDEAS INTO PREMISES

A hook statement, or simply a *hook*, describes what the story's about, how it fits into the NA marketplace, and what makes it stand out from all the other books in that market, all in a single sentence. You're best served crafting your hook as soon as you start working with that cool idea of yours. It's an awful feeling to find yourself, after spending weeks, months, or even years writing hundreds of pages, with a full manuscript that's so indistinct it leaves beta readers going, "Okay … but so what?" The story is just *there*. They can't point to anything really wrong about it because it's well written craft-wise; they just know it's not rocking their boat.

How do you pitch an indistinct story to readers when you go to publish and promote it? *It's a love story! … It's a demon story! … It's a first-year-in-college story!* Yeah, but so what? There are plenty of love stories out there. And demon stories. And first-year-in-college stories. What's different about *your* love story? What makes these lives worth reading about? "Ordinary people with extraordinary lives is fresh"—that's how Harlequin's Vice President of Series Editorial Dianne Moggy urged listeners in a 2013 *Publishers Weekly* webcast to reach for "fresh" angles in a romance. Articulating your main conflict and the distinct elements of your tale from the get-go can help you make sure you've got "extraordinary" covered.

Hook-writing is the perfect exercise for challenging yourself to work out unusual but believable and intriguing details for your story. If I handed the above ideas to three different NA writers and worked through the hook-writing process with them, we'd end up with three very different premises. Check out these hook statements, which are variations of the Joe Normal assassination idea I brainstormed above:

> A shy Georgetown student saves the President from a backpack bomb during a campus visit, gaining head-spinning access to dinners at the White House, parties in DC mansions, and the hottest guy on Earth—the president's twenty-three-year-old son. (35 words; contemporary romance)

> A chef's apprentice at the Waldorf-Astoria who'd rather study Mozart is assigned to serve FDR on a secret train below the hotel, where he's shocked to find a beautiful chambermaid being set up as the patsy for an assassination attempt. (40 words; historical thriller romance)

Both of these hooks start with the same idea, yet the specific details tell us that we've got very different kinds of stories focused on very different themes. Yet both are clearly NA in their protagonist's ages, concerns, and life circumstances. Finally, both set their universal NA themes among a set of variables that are distinct and feel new for the market. No same ol', same ol' here.

USING YOUR HOOK TO WRITE YOUR BOOK

If you develop your hook early in your project—ideally while you're developing your idea into a full concept—you've got a powerful tool to juice your creativity and keep it on track through the arduous writing process. Articulating your stories' primary elements centers your brain and aims your creative juices without boxing you in with details. Your hook proclaims the essence of the story you want to tell, without any of the nitty-gritty details that are better left for discovery either in prewriting, outlining, or actual story writing. The hook is your compass, not your map.

Pointing yourself toward a goal with your story keeps you on task when those inevitable tangents beckon. Yes, you *could* explore the life of that secondary character before he walked into your story because it probably was a really cool life and you'd have a super time poking around in it. But that's not your story. Your story is about your main character and *her* journey. Or, how about those times when you're trying to cram all these groovy details into your story because, honestly and truly, they really would have direct impact on your main character—only, they're burying the main thread of the story as surely as any avalanche. Or, how about that really awesome scene you just wrote that you totally love but that doesn't further the story in any significant way—do you keep it? How do you figure out what's a must and what's fluff or flat-out too much? Your hook is your beacon in the mist, keeping you on course when tangents sing like sirens and details sock in the story. In fact, I recommend printing up your hook when it's done and posting it above your computer so that you can re-center yourself any time you're feeling overwhelmed or lost just by looking up. *Ah yes, THAT's the story I want to tell. Take a hike, tangent!*

USING YOUR HOOK TO SELL YOUR BOOK

Because it accounts for the market and readership, your hook will be a vital tool after you finish writing your book, too. A strong hook articulates the main conflict of your story and highlights its distinguishing elements in a single sentence that will pique one's interest as surely as any marketing pitch. That's what a hook is, in essence—a pitch. You're letting everyone know who among the New Adult readership will be interested in your story and what exactly makes it different from all the other stories in that market space. *This is the kind of story you like to read and it's different from other books in this great way and so you should choose this one!*

Don't confuse a hook with a *tagline*, the pithy phrase that graces the front cover of books, setting a mood or enticing the reader but not revealing what specific thing is special about the story. Tags are useful packaging elements that work in tandem with the cover image and the title to catch readers' eyes.

Imagine this tagline with a cover image of a sexy couple holding bloodied hands and looking at each other with starry eyes, a combination that is sure to give pause to anyone seeing it:

> She came to college for a degree, she left with a murderer.

Immediately readers are wondering: *He's a murderer yet she loves him? He's a murderer yet he's capable of this kind of adoration? I've got to know more!* Sometimes taglines aren't even full sentences, such as *Boys and their toys. …*

Now imagine that murderer book listed on the author's website or on an online retailer website, with this hook statement accompanying that intriguing cover image:

> A naïve girl in her first year at the New York Film Academy falls for an intense, sexy senior whose eerie portrayal of Jack the Ripper in his student film has the school abuzz—and terrified.

That's a great way to grab that initial interest and yank it closer, bringing the reader's eyes to the expanded description that you'd set below it. Reeling 'em in, step by step.

Note that there's a difference between the hook and that expanded description, which would be the *jacket flap blurb* or *back-cover blurb* on a bound book. The expanded description is a mini-summary meant to highlight full storylines. Readers can't plug that long description into their social media if they like the book, and sometimes those can be so detailed on a website that potential readers have to really work through them to figure out the main premise of the book. Make things easy for your readers: Lead your book listings with your concise, compelling hook.

I'll talk more about how these sell copy elements work together in the marketing section. For now, know that your hard work on your hook will pay off at every level of your publishing endeavor.

WRITE YOUR HOOK

I break the hook-writing process into four parts that reflect the four elements of a strong hook—character, theme, core conflict and goal, and context. To help illustrate the process, I'll craft a hook of my own as we move through the process together. If you've already started writing your manuscript, stop and craft a hook for the story now to make sure you've got everything covered. If you're totally done with a full draft, write a hook to help you identify any holes or weaknesses in your concept; you need to know if your story is *just there*. At the end of this process, you can move forward with your novel in confidence that you have a fresh and marketable book on your hands.

Here are basic principles to keep in mind as we work through those parts:

- **CHARACTER AND CONFLICT GET TOP BILLING.** Those are your biggest carrots because those are what readers care about the most.

- **BREVITY IS BOSS.** This is a brief articulation of your vision—as few as twenty-five words, if you can swing it, making it Tweetable.
- **AVOID HYPERBOLE.** "… and saves the world as we know it" may sound catchy, but expansive phrases like that are so overused in American pop culture that people's brains barely register the words. They don't reveal anything specific about your book, anyway.
- **SPECIFICITY IS YOUR FRIEND.** Being specific forces you to analyze your premise and gives readers something tangible to latch onto. "Jack the Ripper" evokes a stronger set of associations than "a serial killer."
- **TONE TEASES.** You'll start drafting your hook with statements about your key elements, then you'll massage the words and phrasing into a tight sentence that captures the tone of your story—scary, lighthearted, etc.

HOOK-WRITING IN FOUR PARTS

My sample hook will evolve as I explain the parts of the hook—character, theme, primary conflict and goal, and additional context—but you don't have to work through these parts sequentially when you draft your own hook. After all, your initial idea may not be a character.

Character

Most readers start telling their friends about the book they're enjoying by saying, "It's about this guy who …" Start your hook by giving context to "this guy." What is his circumstance in life? Is he a college guy? A discharged Marine? A cowboy turned city slicker? Rich? Broke? Cocky? Shy? When you work in your theme and core conflict, he'll come more clearly into focus, but do include an evocative clue about what makes this guy unique as soon as you introduce him. Pick a trait or circumstance that plays into his big conflict for the book. This is particularly powerful if it's clear that this character trait will somehow exacerbate the main conflict. The start of my hook:

> A cocky rich guy …

Theme

We've introduced the character; now let's reveal the internal battle he's going to have by hinting or even directly stating the theme. Regardless of their specific circumstances, new adults experience a range of universal issues and concerns, like *instability, identity establishment, first meaningful love,* and *wisdom from failure.* I covered new adult concerns in Chapter 1, and you'll find more in Chapter 6, "Strategizing an NA Storyline That's Fresh and Wholly You." Your NA character will grow through his struggles, eventually attaining a place of increased stability or wisdom, happiness or success. In a high-concept book, where a mass-appeal idea is so dominant it makes the characters feel almost incidental (often the case with mass-market thriller fiction), you probably wouldn't get into the theme in your hook. You'd just state the external conflict, such as a meteor about to crash into Earth and needing to be deflected or destroyed. But NA fiction is usually character-focused even when there's a lot of action, so that's not likely to be your scenario. In my earlier examples about a presidential assassination, the nineteenth-century boy is dealing with a frustrated dream (to study music instead of slaving in a kitchen), and the modern girl must navigate overwhelming new social circles in the most powerful city on Earth. Both suggest that love will be a theme in the book, too.

How about that cocky rich guy in my sample hook? That guy needs to learn compassion and humility and to reset his personal philosophy. He's been that rich kid who got whatever he wanted with zero effort for far too long. It's time for him to see the realities the rest of the world deals with. We'll tie that theme in as we craft the primary conflict.

Primary Conflict and Goal

What will your character's big problem be? What thing does he want so much that he's willing to push through the monumental problems you've got planned for him? This is where your book will truly get its fresh spin. It's an ideal time to ask yourself the powerful question, What if …? *What if such-and-such happened? What if so-and-so did this? Okay …* then *what?* What basic set-up can you create to push your character out of his comfort zone, forcing him to act and react until things reach a climactic level of broken?

My rich guy could learn humility by being forced to join the Army, or by being forced to volunteer in a hospital, or by being forced to be a Big Brother and seeing what life is like without a rich daddy around. *Force* is an important word here. I'm going to make him do something that's against his nature or hard for him and that he doesn't want to do. That's conflict, and conflict leads to increasing problems and growing stress, or *tension,* which is a storytelling element that drives the story forward. I'm going to force my rich guy to live homeless for six months in order to get his inheritance while his buddies party at college. His friends aren't the main problem, but there's potential for extra story conflict in his relationship with them because they get to do what he's being denied.

So my guy's goal is to get that inheritance, and he's going to push through his discomfort and conflict to get it. How will that goal work out for him? At the moment, that's not my concern—I'll find out when I'm outlining or prewriting or writing the story itself. It's enough to know his conflict and goal for now and to have a feel for the themes that'll be winding through his journey. So:

> A cocky rich guy is forced to live homeless for six months in order to get his inheritance.

In NA fiction there's usually a romantic storyline woven in. This is the step to account for that. Introduce the romantic partner, preferably by showing how the romantic relationship will add more conflict. Conflict fills romantic relationships in fiction, after all—it's not all chocolate and roses. Let me give my guy a girl:

> A cocky rich guy who is forced to live homeless for six months to get his inheritance risks it all to live a double life when he meets a beautiful journalism major—who happens to be investigating his homeless camp for her newspaper internship.

The potential for tension just shot way up, didn't it? What would that girl think of him if she learned his deception? That he's shallow? That he's mocking those less fortunate? Would she discover his deception? Would there be close calls? Would she dump him for lying to her? What if she thought he made her look like a fool? If the romantic in you doesn't think the idea of losing inheritance is a strong enough motivator for his keeping up the deception in the face of true love, you could make him risk more than his inheritance. Perhaps he dreams of a future political career, and an article showing him living homeless would totally torpedo that. Maybe the money was his *original* motivation, but now he chooses to lie for the sake of the homeless people he's befriended.

Context

This is the moment when you add vital information, such as the era if this is historical fiction, or the locale if it matters to the story. In my presidential assassination story, readers need insight into how Joe Normal could come close enough to the President to prevent an assassination, so in the first example I added that my female student goes to Georgetown University, which is in Washington, DC. For the historical fiction example, I named the character's place of employment, the Waldorf-Astoria, and revealed that it has a secret entrance and an underground train platform. Naming the president as Franklin Delano Roosevelt sets the story in the 1930s.

What vital contextual information do you need to call out in your hook? Age is sometimes necessary, as with my example mentioning the President's hot son since he could have been any age. Identifying the girl as a Georgetown University student is enough age specificity for her, underscored by her link to a 23-year-old love interest. In my rich homeless guy hook, I suggest his age through association with his college-aged love interest. If you decided to give him political aspirations, perhaps the city would be an important factor to mention, too.

This step is also where you do your massaging, taking the hook beyond a statement of facts to something tight and tantalizing. You can choose evocative words that create a mood or inject judgment, as I do with *cocky* in the rich guy hook. The word *risk* in that hook implies danger and empowers the character, suggesting he's bold enough (or perhaps desperate enough?) to risk that danger. If you're going for a playful story vibe, you might work in words like *flub* or *goof* in place of *risk*. You can add flavor with specifics, as I did when I put the woman on the ledge with a Samurai sword instead of just "a sword." You can use an em-dash in your hook as I've done a few times to deliver a punch line-type of surprise. This is also the time to shave your hook, replacing two-word phrases with a single word, for example. Brevity forces you to be clear, compels you to choose evocative words that sync with the overall tone of your story, and increases the likelihood that happy readers will cut and paste your powerful hook into their social media.

STRATEGIZING A SERIES BY WRITING A HOOK

Remember how I said hooks just keep on giving? Well, here's another hook gift: You can use a hook to develop, write, and pitch a series, too. Series are popular with NA readers, who appreciate extra adventures with beloved characters.

"Readers really like to return to the world. From a marketing standpoint it's great to have a series in there." —**AMANDA BERGERON**, Editor at William Morrow and Avon (imprints of HarperCollins)

Go through the hook-writing process for the series, and then for each book within the series. Keep the following thoughts in mind as you do so.

A SERIES NEEDS ITS OWN GOAL

Just as you need a goal for a single book, you need a goal for a whole series. There must always be the sense of forward progression, with the characters moving toward something specific and learning things about themselves along the way. This makes the series feel like one big unit, giving it an overall sense of cohesiveness. Make sure the series hook and each book's hook reflect this unifying goal.

A SERIES IS DRIVEN BY A CHARACTER OR RELATIONSHIP

It's certainly possible to write a series wherein each book is entirely self-contained, with the main character being the linking factor. This approach works wonderfully for adult category mystery series, such as Sue Grafton's Alphabet Series, in which P.I. Kinsey Millhone solves a new crime in each book. But that's not the usual approach for the New Adult category.

More common in NA is the series that sports alternating points of view from book to book, with the girlfriend being the point-of-view character in Book 1 and the boyfriend being the point-of-view character in Book 2, for example. With this approach, each new point of view should reveal new information and insights so that readers get the feeling of moving forward, both in their understanding of the characters and in the growth of the romantic relationship in the series. You must be especially mindful of this if your second book is revisiting the events of Book 1 from the other character's point of view. Otherwise, you're essentially asking readers to reread the same book, and that will likely bore them.

You can identify your character's most basic need at this point in her life and then roll your series arc out of that. If you've got a romantic couple who share the series as co-stars, have the series arc be their mutual growth, as Sylvia Day does with her Crossfire series, which has man and woman taking turns dealing with their childhood traumas even as they move forward (shakily) as a couple. The series hook will indicate shifting POV, and each book's hook will tell readers who the key character is in that book.

A STRONG SERIES KEEPS THE STORY FRESH WITHIN THE SERIES

New revelations, new relationships, expanded old relationships, new problems to solve. Whether you're returning to a previous event or moving forward to completely new events, push the story and character beyond the parameters of the storyline in the previous book. Your protagonist conquered the emotional aftermath of a traumatic event suffered in her high school years? Then have her face a new trauma or problem that forces her to reaffirm her new emotional strength. Or, have her offer her newfound strength to Boyfriend in his time of need, only to have him reject her out of fear or pride or independence or whatever. Life is about continually building and testing our skills with new challenges.

HOOKING STORIES ON PASSION INSTEAD OF TREND

One of the biggest weaknesses your hook can have is focusing more on current trends than your passions as an author. The drive to tell stories is behind every word a writer lays on the page. Even so, most writers dream of selling enough books to develop a fan base and a long-term writing career. With that need poking at you, it sure can be tempting to write whatever kinds of stories are sizzling up the bestseller lists at the moment.

That's dangerous thinking.

Writing to market trends can lead to a story that's already been told a million times, only with different character names. That book can then land in a market already glutted with those stories, where readers either overlook it or pass on it because they're already moving on to the next trend. On top of that, writing to trends can lead to you tiring of the story before you're even done writing it because it's not the story you would've written had you not aimed at that trend. That's hardly conducive to a long-term career.

Instead of writing to trends, develop your stories to capitalize on your passions. This will keep you enthusiastic and productive through the entire writing process, and it will launch you into your promotion phase with equal passion about telling everyone what makes your book special. There are plenty of universal themes, mind-sets, and experiences in the new adult experience for you to tap into as you develop an original story that plenty of readers can connect with, sink into, and get passionate about with you. So let's talk about finding your passion.

- **KNOW WHAT REVS YOUR ENGINES.** Identifying your tastes as a reader helps you know the direction you should proceed in developing your idea into a full concept. Do you lose yourself in novels that linger in protagonists' psyches? Dive into your own protagonist's psyche, then. Take a long, sudsy bath in it. If that's what gets your reader juices flowing, it'll get your storyteller juices flowing.

- **KNOW HOW YOU PROCESS YOUR WORLD.** Do you dwell on the things people say, or do you focus on their movements and behavior? Do you notice the ambiance of places, imagining how that will affect the mood of people as they move through those spaces? When you identify your own way of filtering the world, you can run your stories through those filters.

- **KNOW WHY YOU ARE WRITING.** Understanding what you want from writing and why you write will help you develop the things you're passionate about in your current work-in-progress. What makes your blood boil or your knees knock in real life? What drives you to write? Tap into that to develop your body of work. That can mean specializing in a genre or branding yourself as someone who explores certain themes, such as misfits trying to fit in, or underdogs who triumph, across a variety of genres.

- **KNOW YOUR COMFORT ZONES.** The flip side of writing what impassions you is staying away from that which makes you squeamish. Explicit sex scenes, for example. New Adult fiction runs the gamut with its handling of sensual material. If you're not comfortable with the sexy scenes, don't write them, because they'll sound clunky and be anything but sexy. Same with cussing, and with violence, and with any element you might be tempted to write because you think the market wants it.

CHAPTER 3

Crafting a Youthful Yet Sophisticated Voice and Sensibility

*L*ife is a big head game, and new adults are rising to a new level of play. These young people have more sophistication than they did in high school. Maturity isn't so much their purpose anymore as is racking up life experience that'll hone their maturation. They're now developing *wisdom*. This shift into wisdom acquisition affects how they process the world and their place in it; it gives them the confidence to form their own opinions and worldview instead of automatically parroting or rebelling against those of their parents. And, making things über-interesting, it manifests itself in how they articulate their unique perspectives. Our young people are developing a sensibility and voice of their own. As a writer of their stories, you get to frolic in that moiling headspace with them.

"YA is 'Who am I?' NA is 'What do I do with that information now?'" —JEN MCCONNEL, author of *The Secret of Isobel Key*

All stories have a *narrative sensibility*. That is, the narration exhibits a distinct intellectual and emotional quality, such as thoughtful or jaded. When you combine that with the *narrative voice*—which comes from the words you pick and the way you style them into sentences and paragraphs—you get a novel with a distinct personality. It's like the novel has a *feel* to it. Some novels have first-person narrators, giving readers the direct voice and sensibility of a specific character. Multiple first-person narrators each have their own voices and sensibilities so that they feel and sound different from each other.

In this chapter you will focus on imbuing your story with a communal new adult sensibility even as you create a distinct voice for your narrator. Many factors play into narrative sensibility and voice, so I'll use words like *blending* and *sculpting* a lot. Do keep in mind that while we'll examine the elements that contribute to both sensibility and voice under our microscope individually in this chapter, separating everything strand by strand, you'll work them all together for a final flowing narrative tapestry that gives readers a general *feel* for your particular book. When the manuscript is finished, your readers won't see your stitches.

MOLDING YOUR NARRATIVE SENSIBILITY, NA-STYLE

When you write NA fiction, you bring to bear the communal sensibility of new adults. People in that phase of life are moving from hopeful expectation to hardcore reality, and from anticipating independence to living that independence even as they now anticipate the responsibilities of career, marriage, children, and full financial independence. They're done with one phase but not yet part of another. Being in between and heavy into experimentation, exploration, and change keeps them unstable, and that absolutely affects their sensibility.

NA fiction sensibility differs distinctly from that of YA fiction. Teen fiction generally has a palpable sense of anticipating independence, with the narrative often conveying frustration or even having a flat-out angry or rebellious tone as the characters bump against invisible ceilings and walls. They actively strain against structure and rules and all that stuff that clamps around their lives like a merciless vice. With their limited life experience, teens' sense of their place in the world tends to reach beyond optimism to the point of being grandiose. Their reactions to circumstances and opinions about others reflect that extreme way of viewing life: *Mom is going to kill me. … I want to die. … This is the best day of my life ever. … Shane and I are forever.* NA fiction retains some of that optimism but is tempered by actual experience with an imperfect reality. New adults know independence isn't all it's cracked up to be. They were earnest during their teen years, certainly, but things feel doused with more seriousness now as their entry into adulthood is more obvious and imminent. New adult uncertainty replaces teen insecurity as experience kicks in, sometimes painfully. They are less egocentric than teens, and more able to see other people's points of view.

Many NA writers talk about ages eighteen to twenty-five as being a time of "serious" firsts—not the first love, but the first serious relationship; not the first job, but the first job that is going to lead to a career. In contrast, the adult sense of having responsibility for others and settling into their choices feels very different from the more experimental, less structured, and thus less stable new adulthood. Adult fiction generally demonstrates more wisdom than NA, more self-awareness and self-diagnosis, and often has a sense of trying to fix something or fill holes as characters work through their conflicts. New adults are just developing their fix-it skills and still have a strong sense that the sky's the limit once they succeed.

"The viewpoint must be youthful and without the benefit of years of experience, yet old enough to have developed a stronger sense of identity and responsibility than a teen. After all, these protagonists are experiencing many of these things for the first time." —**KAREN GROVE**, Editorial Director, Entangled Embrace

---

In this section, I'll talk about strategies for cultivating new adult undertones even as you design a very personal sensibility. Be aware that it's easy to fall prey to a kind of two-pronged tunnel vision focusing on love and on work (which includes education, during which you prepare for a career) as you ponder a new adult's focus. But those are only two of the three pillars of adulthood. The third is *worldview*, with your young character establishing her specific political philosophy, faith, morals, and general outlook on life. Worldview gives NA fiction elbow room to continue its evolution beyond the falling-in-love-during-college story. Whatever your genre or storyline, your narrative sensibility should reveal a protagonist who is working to establish his worldview.

CULTIVATING NEW ADULT UNDERTONES

Here I'll lay out a host of techniques that you can employ to shape a distinctly NA narrative voice. By picking and choosing among these techniques and combining them in different ways, each narrator you create can have a distinct narrative voice. This will matter as you move from novel to novel, or from character to character in a novel or series that includes multiple point-of-view characters.

Convey Stress

Stress affects people's moods, temperament, and personality. New adulthood, with all its changes, is a major time of stress. Show your narrative character discounting smart decisions in favor of shortcuts that alleviate stress even as those shortcuts cause greater problems. Imagine a narrative that shows the character considering the wisdom of going to bed early so she can get up early to deal with the problem that's stressing her out, but then that narrative becomes pessimistic about the upcoming morning until the girl gets so revved up that she just says, "Screw it!" and grabs a bottle of bourbon. People tend to be snappish when they're stressed. They may take the path of least resistance. Their logic may be compromised as they judge things based on emotion and mood.

Convey Self-Focus, Not Selfishness

New adults get a pass from society when it comes to indulging their explorations and experimentations. They are allowed, even expected, to do what they want, when they want, because everyone knows the day is fast approaching when they have to commit to a life path where they must consider the needs of others ahead of their own. This is the free time they were so looking for, so let them navel gaze without fearing that they'll appear selfish. As long as they demonstrate compassion for others in their words, deeds, and thoughts, they will be self-*focused*, not self*ish*. That distinction is important for likability and authenticity. New adults are lovely, compassionate people who just happen to be in a phase of life when they can indulge their interests—within the confines of time, finances, and opportunities, of course. In fact, while new adults may be less politically minded than their parents, they volunteer more, showing their optimism regarding their role in the world.

Lace Their Sensibility With Personal Optimism

New adults can be a cynical lot with regards to politics and religious institutions, yet they believe they can create a good and satisfying life for themselves and those they love. A 2012 Clark University poll of 1,029 eighteen- to twenty-nine-year-olds reported nearly nine out of ten of those young people agreed with the statement "I am confident that eventually I will get what I want out of life." Eighty-three percent agreed that "at this time of my life, it still seems like anything is possible." Seventy-seven percent gave a thumbs-up to the statement "I believe that, overall, my life will be better than my parents' lives have been." And these weren't just the college kids talking—respondents from lower socio-economic backgrounds were even more likely to agree with those statements. This self-optimism is an important universal trait to tap into when it comes to getting your protagonists to climb those mountains you put in front of them. The protagonist in any kind of fiction may be pushed by circumstances, but as the star of the book, she needs to have a sense that she truly can survive or make a difference through her efforts. Heroes and heroines aged eighteen to twenty-five automatically come with that feature installed; you get to turn it on, tease it, provoke it, and generally have a field day making it prove itself over and over.

Write Within the Crash of Expectations Against Reality

Show unrealistically high expectations in your point-of-view character's thought process, even when the outward reality looks grim. She can certainly acknowledge that things are bad, but make it clear that she feels she can forge onward. Perseverance is a manifestation of high expectations, as is voicing optimistic outcomes that don't seem likely in the face of what readers can see happening in the plot. Perhaps other characters will even directly challenge your character's optimism, forcing her to defend it even if doubt creeps in. Then, when your plot hits her with the harsh reality or consequences, the character can reel. Writing that reeling will be awfully fun.

Expose Inexperience in Their Decision-Making

It's a scientific fact that our prefrontal cortex, the part of our brain that helps us control impulses and plan and organize our behavior to reach a goal, isn't done developing until age twenty-five for guys, age twenty-three for girls. In fact, only half of the brain development that kicks into gear at the onset of puberty is done by age eighteen. Because that development includes activating the brain's reward system, young people are more likely than adults to engage in uncertain situations to see if they can gain something from it. Being free of the constraints of parental supervision and school structure allows these young people to decide and do risky things, the cost being car wrecks, crime, etc.

As clear as the plot path toward your character's goal may seem in your adult head, write the narration so that it shows the character discounting consequences, downplaying them, or simply not considering them until after they've suffered the consequences of their actions. Part of their journey toward a higher state of enlightenment is dealing with consequences, so go ahead and show that your character's decision-making skills are still faulty, at least in the beginning of the story. This will help your plotting, as you'll be setting up your characters for conflicts and problems, giving them opportunities to learn from and overcome adversity. Readers may guess at consequences and get tense and fearful about them, but allow your characters to step in messes of their own making because they simply didn't consider consequences or they figured that bad things only happen to other people.

Show the Process of Evaluation, of Trial and Error
Go ahead and make experimentation not only a part of your young characters' behavior in the plot but also something that they automatically assign to situations in their heads. A "What the hey, it's temporary!" mental shrug can reveal that state of mind. You can show them actively assessing their choices with a line of thinking that their decision doesn't commit them to a life path. The consequences that flow out of their trial-and-error are just the ticket for pushing your plot forward and your characters beyond their comfort zones. When you pile risk-taking tendencies and inexperienced decision-making on top of a stressed-out new adult, you get lots of opportunities to show a mind-set that is on edge.

"Life experiences ... Readers want to see a thought process that doesn't sound like a child or like a jaded adult." —JAYCEE **DELORENZO**, NA Alley founder and author of *The Truths About Dating and Mating*

Remove Structure and Immediate Accountability

There are oodles of opportunities for conflict and bad decisions as young people take the reins of their lives. Nobody's in their face each day trying to wind them up and set them on course, or running around them with bubble wrap trying to protect them from the consequences of their own actions. Sink or swim, it's all on them. Their choices, their consequences. Their responsibility.

Their life.

Remember the prefrontal cortex business. All those things we freak out over with teens—car accidents and crime and crazy behavior—are in fact issues with eighteen- to twenty-five-year-olds who have opportunities to get into more of these situations thanks to their independence from parents. Again, it's that idea that things are just *bigger*, with a deeper impact on life. That, of course, means lots more opportunities for dramatic plot moments and conflict-creating events. Bring it on!

Write with a Sense of Defiance

Even if it's a struggle to handle their own problems without parental guidance, new adults generally want to do so. Emphasize things in the narrative that demonstrate your characters wanting to make their own go of it. Show them considering options and choosing the option that puts their fate in their own hands—even when it's not the best option. Let them express frustration with rules or authorities that stifle them.

Exhibit Ambivalence to Adult Responsibilities

Many new adults flat-out dread their upcoming adulthood, not wanting to give up their spontaneity and the notion that anything is possible. Others yearn for it as strongly as teens yearned for post-high school freedom. They all understand that adulthood is "out there," that they will have to face it one day, but they generally don't want that day to be now. The younger your new adult, the more applicable this mind-set may be. Figure out where your narrator or protagonist lands in that spectrum and then reflect that in how she thinks about the responsibilities she does face. Might she snap at a roomie who's jelled his hair for a party when she has to tie her curly locks into a bun for the bank fundraiser dinner with the stodgy bank president—even if this chance to rub elbows with that president could make or break her career?

Would she sit on a plane headed for some terrible obligatory paranormal spy assignment, staring longingly at the silly rom-com movie that a peer laughs at so freely across the aisle? You can play actions against thoughts to let us know where your new adult character stands regarding her ambivalence toward responsibility.

Reveal Vulnerabilities

Vulnerability is crucial for the new adult sensibility. This is an uncertain time of life, and these young people are experimental risk-takers with only partially grown brains. This makes them vulnerable physically and emotionally. Identity issues are prominent in this period, as is the anxiety attached to making these big life decisions in love, work, and worldview. It's a lot of pressure to find a great-paying job that is satisfying in both enjoyment and identity fit. Some people even refer to new adulthood's identity struggles as a "quarter-life crisis." Mental health problems often kick in during these years as a result of the stressors. Depression, substance abuse … all of this is compounded in characters who are emerging into this independent time from a challenging adolescence, perhaps one that involved foster care, juvenile detention, or disabilities. Some young people get intensely unsettled by all the uncertainty and instability. As a result, characters may think about and react to situations and people as if they are under attack or feel the need to be defensive.

Show Them Actively Divorcing from Teenhood

New adults become increasingly conscious that they have a past and a future, while teens can get so bogged down in the present that they forget how different they were as children. As your new adult characters encounter new things and develop new interests and skills, they can actively evaluate their abilities, interests, and the childhood influences that are playing a part in their new passions. They get to reinvent themselves, discarding those things from teenhood and childhood that they didn't like. Or, at least, they can attempt to. They can be conscious that they have moved on, seeing where they have come but knowing they have the potential to break from that past. They are conscious of becoming more grown up. Your characters can use this knowledge to explore possible futures as they work to eventually make enduring choices regarding love and work.

Show Awareness of Growing Maturity

New Adult fiction can be viewed as an advanced coming-of-age story, or perhaps a modern coming-of-age story for a society in which young people tend to come of age later. New adults are more mature than teens and thus learn to understand themselves and others better than they did in their teen years. If the human brain isn't done growing until age twenty-five, then new adults are on the upper end of their cognitive development. It's okay to let your characters be aware of their own maturation. Self-awareness is greater in the new adult phase than the teen phase, so show it. Of course, since girls' brains tend to reach maturation a couple of years earlier than guys, your girl characters can express more maturity and self-awareness than their love interests. Or, you can hook up those girls with guys who are a couple of years older than they are, a common device in NA fiction.

Contrast Survival With Moving On

Because your new adult characters are becoming more self-aware, you have the opportunity to write personal journeys through which the character redefines what it means to survive a trauma—a rape, for instance, or physical abuse. As a teen, just getting through that ordeal is "survival." As a new adult, surviving means finally moving on or reaching some sort of peace with or acceptance of the trauma. Many NA novelists build passionate stories of healing thanks to this shift in perspective.

SCULPTING YOUR NARRATIVE VOICE

Now we'll explore how you match the narrative mind-set we've just surveyed with words that express it, creating a *voice* for your narrative. Whereas our discussion of narrative sensibility focused on understanding the way a new adult processes events and relationships, I'm now going to focus on techniques that'll help you codify that sensibility for readers, from word selection to sentence structure and paragraphing to choosing a point of view.

"The words I choose and the thoughts behind the characters and their actions are chosen carefully for this [NA] audience, just as

with YA. You have to be able to capture the voice and thought processes of someone that age." —JENNIFER L. ARMENTROUT, writing as J. Lynn, author of the Wait for You series

CHOOSING YOUR POINT OF VIEW

New Adult fiction doesn't have any rules about point of view, but first person is by far the most common point of view, and frequently you have multiple narrators alternating chapters. *First-person point of view* has you writing from inside the head of your narrating character using the *I* and *me* pronouns. This gives you direct access to that character's internal dialogue, basically turning the narration into a transcript of that character's observations, opinions, and judgments. Many consider this the most candid point of view, allowing you to reveal everything your character thinks. Often it feels to the reader as if the narrator is actually talking to her, as in a conversation, and so it can feel personal and emotional. The downside is that you're limited to telling readers only what that character can witness. A dual first-person point of view narrative, with two people taking turns telling the story, can get you around that problem.

A first-person narrative tends to have a lot of direct statements as we get a narrator basically stating his mind to us readers. Be careful, though: A character who narrates his own feelings (as in "I feel sad" or "I was so ticked off!") risks being too obvious and can sound too self-aware and forced, especially at times when we don't want him analyzing his behavior and feelings but just want him to act on those. It's good to have some self-awareness since we're talking about wizening new adults rather than teens, but these are young people still on the lower end of the wisdom scale. Self-awareness is a huge tip-off of age. That's where the old writer's adage "Show, don't tell" can be a tool to find balance. If you show the feelings in action, you don't need to have your narrator narrate them. It also avoids a common reader complaint about first-person narration: feeling trapped inside the character's head.

Don't let fear of intimacy keep you outside a particular character's head. If you think the best person to tell the tale is a young male when you're an older female, then try it out. Nothing lost but a little time, yet so much to gain in finding out if it's right or not.

Third-person point of view uses the pronouns *he, she,* and *they.* This point of view can be all-seeing and all-knowing (*third-person omniscient,* or simply *omniscient*), letting you head-hop from character to character within a chapter. Or it can be limited to only what the protagonists in that scene can witness or know (*third-person limited*). This is a good choice if you prefer the freedom of describing things outside of what your point-of-view character can see and know, and if you're okay with the risk that readers may feel one step removed from the narrating character. That said, in this point of view, you can still jump into a character's internal thoughts if you want to. You just need to signal that jump with italics and/or a change of tense:

> Dawren raced across the heliopad. *I'm dead meat.* Every muscle in his legs screamed, but he knew he couldn't slow down. She'd made it clear that lateness meant ejection from the airlock, and he had no reason to doubt her sincerity.

Note that I don't write "he thought" after *I'm dead meat.* If you use italics, you don't need that dialogue tag. Readers know he's thinking that line. The tense shift from past to present also signals it. Third person is a great choice if you want a reserved narrator to hold back and make readers guess more.

Don't be afraid to experiment with your point of view. Write a scene or chapter or even a couple of chapters from one point of view, and get a feel for how the rough draft is playing out. If you're sensing anything but total conviction that you've chosen perfectly, write a scene in the other POV and see how it feels to you. You may discover that you're not comfortable writing like a twenty-four-year-old man when you're a thirty-year-old woman. Forcing a narrative point of view will only result in a narrative that *feels* forced.

NA fiction loves *multiple points of view.* In particular, there's a distinct trend in NA of alternating his-and-hers first-person point-of-view chapters, especially in romance plots. (Check out the sidebar in this chapter for tips on how to pull off multiple points of view.) This trend seems to be a middle ground between adult and YA stylings: In adult romance, the third-person dual point of view is common. In Young Adult fiction, the first-person single POV is common. NA seems to straddle that, much in the same way new adulthood is the phase between adolescence and adulthood.

"NA is voice and characters—that's what carries the day and what people talk about. They talk about the names of the characters rather than the name of the book. So it often makes sense to come at the emotion of the story from both points of view."
—**AMANDA BERGERON**, Editor at William Morrow and Avon (imprints of HarperCollins)

But don't use multiple points of view simply because it seems to be "the NA way." Plenty of fabulous NAs feature only one point-of-view narrator. Only use multiple narrators if switching points of view is truly right for your story, because with it comes the extra challenge of developing distinct voices for each character, right down to sentence styling, phrasing, and tone. You'd choose multiple narrators to:

- inject conflict by having two characters report the same event differently, with neither one lying (just ask police how often witness statements contradict)
- inject conflict into your story by having two characters processing the same event to different ends that require different actions
- give readers the chance to connect intimately with multiple characters
- work in information that a single narrator couldn't know
- provide alternate insights or opinions

Each POV shift should deliver new information, insights, or opinions that add depth to the story, not just pages, otherwise you're merely rehashing the same scene, making the shift feel repetitive rather than revelatory. Reward your readers; don't put them on a repeat loop. As you consider whether multiple POVs is the right device for your story, consider that there are other ways to show readers what's going on in another character's head, like his actions, his body language, his words, his choices. What will an additional perspective add to the story? What new information can that character consistently bring to the story to make the extra switching rewarding? Chapter 4 is filled with character ideas.

It would be prudent to ask if your reader even *needs* to know what's going on in that other character's head. In real life, we can't know exactly what's going on in our closest friends' heads or our spouse's head. So much of the miscommunication and trouble in life stems from that blind spot, and miscommunication is fiction's friend. If we want our readers to truly experience this adventure alongside our protagonist, perhaps readers should be just as blind to what others are thinking, just as reliant on guessing, observing, and judging. Perhaps knowing *exactly* what *all* the key characters are thinking renders the reader a passive observer instead of an interactive reader.

When choosing your point of view, consider not POV popularity but rather who the best character is to tell your story. Experiment until you find the right vantage point (or vantage points) for your story.

CRAFT CLOSE-UP: EXECUTING MULTIPLE POINTS OF VIEW

Here are tips for switching between narrators smoothly and strategically so as not to jolt readers or halt your ongoing escalation of tension.

- **SWITCH AT BREAKS.** Switching points of view mid-scene can confuse readers. Trade narrators at chapter breaks. You can switch between scenes, but you risk readers feeling like they're watching a tennis game, with the characters hitting the microphone back and forth.
- **BE CONSISTENT ABOUT SWITCHING.** Willy-nilly switching can be disquieting to readers, who should sink into the fictional world and stay there uninterrupted. Establish a switching rhythm, such as alternating girl-boy-girl-boy, only breaking from that pattern for a dramatic deviation.
- **SWITCH TO INCREASE TENSION.** Create a cliff-hanger effect by breaking away from one narrator at a pivotal moment and moving to the other. Yes, this can halt the momentum as effectively as throwing an anchor out your car window, but it can be an awesome tactic if well deployed once or twice in a story.

Whichever pattern you establish, make the switch clear so readers know what's happening without having to interrupt their reading to work it out. Ways to do that include writing one narrative in present tense, the other in past; using first person (*I, me*) for one narrative and third person (*he, she, they*) for the other; using the narrator's names as the chapter titles; and giving them vastly different voices and outlooks on life.

Choosing Your Tense

"Should I write this story in past tense or present tense?" That's a common question for writers, and you'll almost certainly wonder about it at some time in your writing career. There's no rule about which is better in New Adult fiction. It's usually a matter of your comfort. Some writers, readers, editors, and agents feel that past tense is more traditional and thus familiar to readers, therefore you should stick with it so as not to distract readers in any way. Flow of reading is indeed a good thing. Others feel that present tense feels more immediate, as opposed to those who find it too self-conscious since the narrator can seem to be doing a play-by-play of every move she makes. If you try to write present tense but you find it a bit awkward to do, chances are good that your readers will feel your awkwardness. Readers themselves may have a personal preference for tense, which is something you can't control. The point is, tense is usually a comfort decision.

Sometimes when your story just isn't working, shifting the tense will give the manuscript the jolt it needs to "feel right," so be open to writing in either past or present depending on what's right for a particular story. Some stories will just make more sense in one tense versus the other. As with point of view, experiment until you find the approach that works.

About the only rule with tense is that internal dialogue—those moments when the narrative includes phrases that are really just dialogue one lip shy of being spoken—is almost always presented in present tense, even if you're not in favor of italicizing internal dialogue.

> Waves crashed on the sand. Seagulls called. Little kids frolicked in the receding surf, plastic shovels in one hand and dripping pails in the other. *This is the life.*

Many people don't italicize internal thoughts in adult fiction, preferring to leave it roman and then tag on "he thought" when clarity calls for it. In teen fiction, using italics is pretty much the standard. Again, NA is in between. Regardless of type treatment, dialogue is present tense since it is uttered in the literary present, even if it is confined within a character's head.

Choosing Your Words

The words you pick and the way you craft them into sentences, passages, paragraphs, and all the other parts of the page gives your narrative a tone (think: attitude) and mood (think: emotion, also influenced by setting and plot events). Tone and mood combine with your point-of-view and tense choices above and your narrator's sensibility or outlook to give your narrative a distinct voice. Some people like to think of that as a narrative's *personality*, which helps clarify why every narrator can "sound different"—each narrator brings a different perspective to the table, and then you deliberately sculpt the way he puts together his words, phrases, and sentences to express that perspective. This section offers strategies for crafting language itself to create a voice for your narrative.

- **ASSIGN A WORD PALETTE.** Deliberately use a *palette* of words across your manuscript in order to create a desired tone, much like a painter might choose one palette of dark, somber colors to paint a night scene and a different palette of bright, energetic colors to paint a day scene. The meaning of words matters for this palette, but so do the letters themselves. If you fill a page with angry words—ones that are hard in your mouth with *k*s and *p*s, for example, and that evoke violence and unpleasant associations—you're creating a feeling—a *tone*—that is harsh, unpleasant, unforgiving, and emotionally aggressive. If you fill your page with words that evoke skin sensations and corporeal elements like arms and legs and goose bumps and sweat, you can create a tone suitable for a scene that focuses on a character's physical strength, weakness, or attraction. You can do this with passages, with scenes, with chapters, and with the whole book. Some authors create *word banks* to assist in this, such as the one I used for my teen novel *Honk If You Hate Me,* in which fire was a symbol and then an active player in the plot. I created a page of fire- and heat-related verbs, adjectives, and nouns that I could work into the book, being careful to sprinkle them in so as not to sound repetitive or heavy-handed. Using this technique, each of your books can have truly distinct tones that make them feel different from your other books and that reflect a specific character journey and plot.

- **CHOOSE DYNAMIC VERBS.** If you fill your scene with bland action words like *walk, sit,* and *look,* you'll end up with a bland scene that accounts for the action but lacks energy and personality. Instead, choose verbs like *stumble, lounge,* and *scour* that suggest moods and manners of movement. These will help you avoid adverbs (generally *-ly* words) that tell you *how* something was done, such as *walking clumsily* or *sitting casually* or *looking carefully.* The result is fewer words, to richer effect.

- **REPLACE CLICHÉ LANGUAGE WITH EVOCATIVE LANGUAGE, ACTION, OR SPECIFICITY.** Readers eyes breeze right over cliché words and phrases, like *he couldn't believe she said that* or *he worked our knuckles to the bones,* which have become nearly meaningless in their overuse and can make some readers feel like you're a lazy or shallow writer. Include all the cliché phrases you want in your rough draft so that you can vomit your story onto the page, but when you go back to revise, replace them with rich words and phrases that evoke specific emotions, senses, visuals, mannerisms, and mood. Perhaps you'll even replace the phrase with an action that demonstrates the sentiment in "Show, don't tell" fashion. And where you can, be specific, such as talking about a character's mini troll key chain instead of her keys. It's all part of creating a voice with personality rather than just filling a page with words. You can judge if you have a tendency toward clichés or bland language with the Stop Looking Test, which I've included in Chapter 12's self-editing advice.

- **CHOOSE ACTIVE OVER PASSIVE VOICE.** *Passive voice* happens when you structure a sentence so that the subject is receiving the action instead of executing it. In a larger sense, a passive storytelling voice leads with too many clauses (often starting with the word *as*), incorporates more minutiae than we need, and has a vague, distant quality to it. For example: *The keys were forgotten.* There's nothing distinguishing or revealing about that sentence; it merely does its job of telling us what's happening. When you do this a lot, the overall effect is a less immediate voice, a feeling that the story holds the readers at arm's length. The voice tends to lack dynamism and personality.

Instead, use more active language, letting the character commit the actions instead of receiving them: *Ted forgot his keys.*

- **STYLE SENTENCES FOR THE VOICE YOU WANT.** The way you string your sentences together contributes to the formal, casual, or regional flavor of a narrative.

  - **FORMAL.** This may be just right for a narrative that is serious or in a story taking on heavy issues, such as rape or sexual harassment. Still use contractions with formal phrasing, since omitting those can make writing feel stilted. For example,

    > I had an interview scheduled for this afternoon. It would be tough, certainly, but I'd rehearsed probable answers all night.

    The sentences have everything in its place, with expected punctuation and a clear, logical train of thought from beginning to end and through the entire passage.

  - **CASUAL (OR COLLOQUIAL).** Want it to feel as if the reader is kickin' back, listening to a buddy fill them in on the situation? This is "real life" kind of sentencing, where grammar rules aren't so important, casual turns of phrase feel right, and roundabout sentences give us repetition that emphasizes important points:

    > I couldn't be getting all worried about that stuff today, not with luck kicking my ass so much lately. I had that interview to go to. To *survive*, truth be told.

    These sentences might send your middle school grammar teacher into a bit of a huff since they don't conform to proper styling, with subject and predicate blatantly present and accounted for. Yet there's nothing technically wrong with them—they simply play loosey-goosey with grammar and subjects. The logic and progression is absolutely clear even as the passage has a very casual quality, so this style is great for a first-person narrative.

  - **REGIONAL.** To evoke the flavor of a region or culture, use phrases that suggest the region, like, "He knew not to let his mouth overload his tail." Or use the area's jargon, like calling soda "pop" if your story is set in the Midwest. I recommend against writing regional accents like *writin'*, which is where many writers default when they want regional flavor. Written accents get distracting, with the reader focused on trying to pronounce the accent rather than on the content of the words.

- **USE SENTENCE VARIETY TO GIVE THE NARRATIVE A NATURAL FLOW.** Lack of sentence variety is a surprisingly common pitfall for novelists, particularly in early drafts when they're focused on fitting the story together. What you don't want is narrative that smothers readers in pages of long, complex sentences, or that reads choppy due to a string of straightforward statements of action stacked on top of each other, like this:

> Shelly walked out on Ted without even leaving a note. It wasn't his fault. He didn't mean to hurt her feelings. He always tried to do the right thing. She just got mad all the time.

A more natural, flowing version of that example would have a mix of long and short sentences, and a mix of statements of action and bits of exposition. It might also draw out the important part using a sequence of comma-separated items:

> She was gone. No note, no phone call, no text. Nothing. Not that it was his fault. He always tried to do the right thing, opening the door for her, carrying her bags, taking the sunny seat so she could have the shade. His heart was in the right place. Too bad that place wasn't *her* right place.

A text with variety is one with personality.

Also consider how sentence variety affects pacing, which reflects a character's state of mind and emotions as it changes through the story. A calm first-person narrative might gain tension and faster pacing by switching to abrupt statements later in the story, deliberately taking on that choppiness to reflect stress or anger. More on this in Chapter 9, "Cranking Up the Conflict, Tension, and Pacing in Your NA Fiction."

- **CHOOSE WORDS, PHRASES, AND PUNCTUATION THAT SEEM TO EMBODY THE EMOTION YOU'RE TRYING TO CONVEY.** You can quicken a heart with periods and harsh-sounding letters like *k* and *t*. If you need to slow a character's spinning world, choose words that force people to read slowly, to breath in many slow beats using commas that feel like slow exhales rather than blurting short sentences with hard period endings.

Let's look at a heated moment, where we want hard action and strong negative emotions. I'll employ a palette of violent words that make harsh sounds that readers will subconsciously vocalize, and I'll use abrupt sentences and declarations and few narrative beats. You'll of course have led up to this moment in the story with your pacing and by building up tension as I discuss in Chapter 9, making the emotion even more powerful when read as part of a whole chapter or book. Here's a straightforward passage in which a girl comes home after a trying day:

> She walked through the front door, tossed her keys on the counter, then dropped down onto the couch. What an exhausting day.

There's little emotion here, even with the dynamic words *dropped* and *exhausting*. It's taking care of business but not much more, which could be fine if this is an inconsequential moment. But if you've got bigger plans for this scene, you can take it to a whole new emotional level by choosing evocative verbs, slowing pace with letter sounds that require slow breaths like "s" and "oo", and inserting commas that carry on a thought even as they force you to pause and breathe. Here's that passage at an incredibly stressed moment in the girl's life:

> She slammed the door then leaned on it, nearly gasping with fury. *Enough!* She sagged to the floor. The cool wood was soothing. Silence muted the echoes of his searing words, her breathing slowed, her eyes settled on the icicles sliding down the windowpane next to her. Down they slid. Down … down … down … disappearing at the bottom ledge. "Enough," she whispered.

In this example, there's almost no fast way to read lines like "cool wood was soothing" because of the "oo" sounds and the "s" that requires you to breathe the letter out slowly. She doesn't fall to the floor, she "sags," which must be executed slowly. Finally, repetition makes us stop in that moment, making the passage feel like it circles back on itself, injecting a sense of rhythm into the passage even as the repeated phrase feels entirely different now, completing the emotional progression of the scene.

Finding YOUR Voice Is a Matter of Finding YOUR Blend

I've thrown a lot at you in this chapter, and I've acted as though it makes sense to pull the threads out and still call it a rug. Ultimately, you'll consider all these things when you're writing without necessarily considering them individually. Some of it will be done when you do prework while creating your characters (next chapter). Know that it will become second nature to you, if much of it hasn't already. And know that it's all malleable, experimental, and discardable, just like the explorations and experimentations of new adulthood itself. If you don't like something you try, delete it and try another language styling. Don't be hard on yourself; be open.

Above all, be true to yourself and your creative vision. Be inspired by your idols, yes, and be conscious regarding what about their voice and narrative stylings resonates with you. But then let your own preferences and your own story take the lead. That's one reason why readers get hooked on certain authors—they like the author's individual style. If you try to sound like someone you're not, it just sounds awkward. You're funny? Then be funny. If you relish atmosphere, indulge in sensory elements and metaphors, and make use of the many tips I'll give you in Chapter 11. It's your story, your characters, your book. Allow it to be just that.

AUTHOR INSIGHT: GIVING CHASE A VOICE

BY MOLLY MCADAMS, AUTHOR

There are times when you write and you only hear one character's voice—and others where you hear two or more ... but no matter how many voices are talking to you, you have to write for them all. While writing *Taking Chances*, it was Harper in my head, and Harper only. When I decided to write *Stealing Harper*, I was faced with not only having to mirror *and* change a story I'd already written, but now I needed to get Chase to start talking when he never had before. I'd thought that would've been incredibly difficult. I was *so* wrong.

The times when I was mirroring *Taking Chances*, he was difficult—he'd hide in the background, and I could just picture him smirking at me, saying, "This isn't *my* story." But the second I'd veer away into the parts we *hadn't* seen before, the parts that made *Stealing Harper* so different, it was as if I'd been holding him back while he'd been screaming at me to tell his story, and now that I'd started, there was no stopping until it was all out. He finally had a voice, and he was using it.

Music is a big part of my life—I relate everything to music. I also can't write unless it's the only thing I'm hearing. But I've never had a story more connected to music than *Stealing Harper*. I've never understood why. All I know is every time I sat down, before I began writing, I'd put on the playlist for this story. As I listened to the songs, every emotion and everything that just made Chase *Chase* would fill my world and pour from my fingertips, and I would fall in love with him all over again as he told me his side of things.

Molly McAdams is the author of the New Adult contemporary romance series Taking Chances and Forgiving Lies. (www.mollysmcadams.com)

CHAPTER 4

Filling Your Fiction With Characters Who Act Their Age

*I*t's not enough to set the age of your character between eighteen and twenty-five and then stamp the words *New Adult fiction* on the manuscript. Convincing NA protagonists act in ways that exhibit the mind-set of new adulthood and struggle with the battles of that stage of life. This doesn't mean NA authors are all writing the same character any more than it means every character in YA fiction is some angst-ridden teen fighting tooth and nail for popularity and a cute boyfriend. New adults are dealing with a vast range of issues, and they have an infinite kaleidoscope of personalities and life histories that you can bring to bear in your story. This is one of the reasons NA fiction is so exciting in its infancy and so enticing in its long-term potential: There's a bottomless well of experiences and human nature to dip into.

This chapter gives you strategies for piecing together NA characters who feel fresh and distinct, who are intriguing and strong enough to shoulder a full novel, and who reflect the perspective of real new adults—their dreams and fears, their decision-making and coping skills, their intense relationship experiences with family, friends, and lovers. I'll talk about techniques you can use to reveal your character's strengths, flaws, personality, and moods. I'll cover strategies for cultivating satisfying character growth and empowering your protagonist with the resolution to her own problems. And I'll arm you with techniques to breathe life into your characters. We'll do all of this without falling prey to pit-falls, such as stereotypes and predictability. In fact, I'll provide Character Dis-covery Exercises throughout the chapter to help you avoid stock characters and explore whole new facets of the ones who passed muster.

We'll put the supporting cast under our microscope, too. We'll craft friend and family characters that contribute to your main character's journey, and we'll develop antagonists who are rich and even sympathetic in their own right. No cardboard villains or stock best buds in your novel.

THE ROLE OF CHANGE IN AN NA PROTAGONIST

Change rocks our world. Good or bad, change means that things are different, and "different" puts us on alert for things lurking around the corner. That state of being alert is experienced as *stress*, and stress is home turf for new adults because new adulthood is a veritable tornado of change. These young people aren't kids anymore; they're exchanging the baggage of childhood and teen-hood for the responsibilities of adulthood and learning what it means to be self-actualized. Suddenly they are responsible for the overall trajectory of their lives as well as the minutiae of it. Suddenly they are … *free*. Whoa. That's a mental and emotional trip, for sure. Excitement. Hope. Uncertainty. Fear. It's all there, roiling and percolating, with you poised to throw fistfuls of conflict into the brew. That right there is some juicy fiction about to happen.

COMPELLING CHARACTERS UNDERGO CHANGE

Your protagonist is your book. Every element in your story exists to push that character from a place of need to a place of triumph and greater maturity or enlightenment, all on the tracks of a plot that moves unwaveringly, relentlessly, even viciously toward that conclusion. A strong protagonist sticks with that journey no matter how tough the ride, and readers care about her evolution.

The thread of your character's growth through the story is called the *char-acter arc*. Another way to refer to it is *internal arc*, a term that underscores the fact that this growth is about the character's inner feelings, wants, wishes, and needs. Your character thinks and feels one way at the beginning of the story, and by the end of the story she thinks and feels another way that reflects some new knowledge or maturity. Maybe she's not wholly conscious of these feelings at the beginning of the book, but she (and readers) will have a palpable sense of being in a different place by the end.

Hand in hand with the internal arc is the *external arc*, which is the character's physical movement through the plot of the book, from first problem to final solution. Chapters 6, 7, and 8 help you create a plot that will push your character through her evolution. I must talk about internal and external storylines as if they are separate elements. Really, they are part and parcel. In your final draft, your arcs will be intertwined and working toward a shared goal: palpable, satisfying character growth.

The plot and the character's inner journey are two sides of the same evolution. Here's an example of an NA protagonist's two arcs working together:

> Twenty-year-old Sam uses his buff physique to mask his lack of confidence and discomfort in crowds, the fallout from a childhood of being bullied. Yet the need to earn tuition money has Sam signing on as a bouncer at the busiest club in town with his new roommate—where they both get caught up in a drug deal gone very, very bad. Sam must throw himself deep into a world of clubs, parties, and backstage concert orgies in order to clear his name—and grow from broken boy to confident man.

Character growth is the difference between a rich and compelling character and a flat one. *Flat* ... the literary f-word. Flat characters say and do things in a wholly expected, straightforward way, and they walk away from the story only as wise as they were when they entered it. They don't surprise readers, they don't keep us guessing about their sincerity or their plans or their motives, and they don't show readers the possibilities that arise from human resilience. Their behavior and actions are equally straightforward, supporting exactly what the character says in each scene. A manuscript filled with characters saying and doing what seems like the logical thing to say and do without serving up anything intriguing or new lacks subtly, richness, pizzazz. It feels, yep, *flat*. And that's not likely to score you five stars on Goodreads or massive recommendations to friends on Facebook and Twitter. Flat leads to another f-word: *forgettable*.

One of the first things to know about your lead character is the beginning and end point of his internal arc. This doesn't mean you know how the story starts and ends plotwise, but rather that you understand how he's going to change as a person. This will help you work out the traits that a character at the beginning of that journey would have. What new awareness would you like him to reach about himself by the end of the book, and how might his personality traits influence that new awareness? After you understand the internal journey this particular protagonist will take, you can work out how the details of his personality, history, behavior, relationship, and decision-making fit into that. To help you brainstorm these things, I've included a character profile worksheet at the end of this chapter; the next section will guide you as you profile your protagonist.

BUILDING A PROTAGONIST WHO'S NA ALL THE WAY

At its barest, an NA character needs to be age eighteen to twenty-five, post-high school, and exhibiting the characteristics and mind-set of the new adult stage of life. But bare isn't the stuff of awesome lead characters and memorable novels. Your new adult must be compelling enough to intrigue readers. She must resonate emotionally and be distinct enough to be memorable. You want readers to love the characters enough to read past the first few pages of your novel and keep going, and to come back for later installments in a trilogy or series, and to shout their excitement about your book all over the Internet and in their reading clubs and to their friends. That kind of love is totally doable. Think about your own favorite characters from NA or any other category of literature. Gosh, I feel like I'm a magician telling you to pick a card so that I can tell you what that card is. Actually, that is the case: I bet I *can* tell you a few things about the beloved characters you picked:

- **YOUR BELOVED CHARACTERS AREN'T PERFECT.** They have flaws that make them feel real.
- **YOUR BELOVED CHARACTERS HAVE HERO POTENTIAL.** They have strengths that will help them prevail, even if they don't know it yet.
- **YOUR BELOVED CHARACTERS CAN SOLVE THEIR OWN PROBLEMS.** Characters who are empowered make readers feel empowered.

- **YOUR BELOVED CHARACTERS HAVE MORAL CENTERS.** Ultimately, their intentions are earnest and they will do the right thing.
- **YOUR BELOVED CHARACTERS CAN BE LOVED BY OTHER CHARACTERS.** If someone can love you, there must be good in you.
- **YOUR BELOVED CHARACTERS HAVE THE DESIRE TO CHANGE.** They are active participants in their story, rather than passive recipients of everyone else's largesse and solutions.
- **YOUR BELOVED CHARACTERS CONNECT WITH READERS.** They offer readers emotional resonance and the chance to see themselves in their books.

I know these things because they are universal qualities of strong fictional characters. Now, put that deck of character cards down, because it's time to rub our hands together with glee: We get to build a character who will become someone else's beloved.

THE FOUR-PIECE CHARACTER STARTER KIT (WITH THREE TOTALLY NA BONUSES)

Four basic elements work together in one big literary orgy to make a character whom you can believe in, root for, and fret over:

- a key flaw
- a core strength
- a defined goal, want, or need
- a seriously unpalatable fear

Of course, all of this will have an NA twist. (If you want to remind yourself of new adult qualities, take a peek back at Chapter 1.)

Now, it's possible you're an I-discover-my-character-as-I-write-the-story kind of writer. I'm not undermining that in this section. If that's the way you work, I'm all for it. I respect that approach, just as I respect the process of writers who prefer to map out as much detail as possible before writing. Creativity comes in all shapes and sizes. Wherever you stand on your process for discovering character nuances, understanding these four foundational items before you launch your character on his adventure helps you lay a strong foundation for a fully rounded character, so it's worth the time to do this prewriting work with the character even if you're not going to preplan the specific steps of his journey.

> "I either don't outline at all, or I outline loosely, usually as I go along (just ahead of what I'm writing). I definitely know my main characters before I get started, or I wouldn't care enough to write about them. I get to know them more as I begin to write, of course, especially my first-person POV characters. I know their voices and their histories, but I'm not sure how they're going to react to what I throw at them. They reveal themselves as I write them, which is the most fun part of writing for me."
> —**TAMMARA WEBBER**, *The New York Times* and *USA Today* best-selling author of *Easy* and the Between the Lines series

1. Flaws Give Characters Something to Overcome

Think of a flaw as your character's internal nemesis. This enemy within will hamper your character's efforts to overcome her problems, or it will lead to decisions or behavior that worsen the problems. The flaw will be something your character must overcome in order to complete her internal arc.

Flaws may be social, emotional, psychological, or intellectual in nature, or rooted in personality. Think impatience, a short fuse, shyness, cynicism, the tendency to blurt before thinking. It's easy to think of a physical imperfection as a flaw—a limp, perhaps, or blindness—but the problem with a physical handicap is the emotional baggage it causes. Lack of a particular skill can be a flaw if it causes the problem to worsen and conflicts to increase; the character will have to actively foster the skill, putting in the physical and emotional effort necessary to do so. There may be more than one flaw, but there should be one Big One that truly acts as an internal antagonist. Sometimes, a flaw can be turned into a strength.

You might worry that giving your character a flaw will render her unlikable, but really the opposite is true: People hate perfection. It's annoying, and it's simply not real. Readers can't identify with perfect characters. Make your

WRITING NEW ADULT FICTION

characters capable of messing up, of worsening their situations and increasing the tension through the story until things come to the point where the character faces either full ruin or satisfying salvation. Your bravery in assigning flaws may mean the difference between writing a surface-level story and writing one that delves deeper into the character's inner journey.

Lack of perfection is particularly glaring in young people, which totally works in your favor. They're all about trying and learning new things—and of course trying and learning involves flubbing things up. They lack deep experience with just about everything, so they're hardly going to be successful at everything they do. Here are three examples of universal flaws that can assail new adults in general, synced with flaws that a particular character might bring along from teenhood:

1. **A LACK OF ORGANIZATIONAL SKILLS COMBINED WITH THE INFLATED EXPECTATIONS OF NEW ADULTHOOD.** This character might see his internship as the shortcut to the corner office, but he's unable to juggle the workload and is passed up by other interns who are on top of the details in a big project.

2. **IMPATIENCE COMBINED WITH THE NEW ADULT TENDENCY TO TAKE RISKS.** This character might use a frayed rope found dangling from an old tree to swing herself to the opposite river bank while her fellow hikers look for a safer way to cross the quickly swelling river, catalyzing a story where she's alone in the wilderness with no supplies, no field survival skills, and a massive storm bearing down.

3. **UNWILLINGNESS TO SHOW VULNERABILITY COMBINED WITH THE NEW ADULT TENDENCY TO HAVE HIGH EXPECTATIONS FOR YOURSELF.** This character might be willing to lead a charge on the supposedly impenetrable prison that holds her people's rebel leader but be closed off to the input of a sensitive, bumbling, ever-so-handsome villager who tries to impress upon her that what her people really need is her inspiration, not rebellion.

Notice that there's nothing inherently unlikable in these characters. As long as they are earnest, with good core intentions despite their mistakes, they stay good people whom we can root for. Believably real, not annoyingly perfect.

2. Strengths Fortify Your Hero-to-Be

Every protagonist must have the potential to be the story's hero or problem solver of her own adventure. She may have help from a co-star who in some way complements her contribution or brings out her best, but we must believe the power to triumph is in her in the first place. This is a credibility issue. Early on, the hero-to-be must demonstrate traits that will conceivably allow her to overcome her big flaw when the climactic scene rolls around. If it's her skill that saves the day, that skill must be a basic part of the character's personality and reveal itself in various forms, degrees, and incarnations long before it comes into play in the climax.

As I talked about with flaws and handicaps above, you might be inclined to assign your character a skill and call that the "strength," but really the strength is a personality trait required to master that skill. A character with pinpoint accuracy with a crossbow may use her skill with that weapon to save the day, but the true strength that boosts this character from crack marksman to story hero is the extreme patience and poise needed to carefully aim that crossbow while battle rages around her. In her shoes, the nonheroes in the book would duck and cover. When you pick skills for your characters, be able to state what those skills demonstrate about your character's personality or mind-set. Or, you can work in reverse, where you know the personality trait and need to pick a skill that will reveal that trait to readers.

The more points of connection you create between your character and your readers, the more vested that reader will be in the character and her journey. If the reader can believe that they, too, could muster such strength if given the chance or if put in a similar situation, then you've created a point of connection. Universal new adult traits include their almost inhuman optimism, their belief that they will overcome adversity if they simply keep trying, and their feeling that they can make a positive difference in the world or in the lives of people in their immediate social circle. And since you'll be injecting universal strengths into characters with original and distinct backgrounds and emotional baggage, those strengths will look different on each character. They'll feel fresh and specific to your story.

As with flaws, strengths can be detrimental to your character at times. A ballsy risk-taker can muck up things as often as he triumphs, but ultimately he'll learn to harness that boldness and apply it with more care, allowing him to assess when it's best to take the risk and when it's wiser to stay his hand. With experience (which he'll acquire through the story), he learns to wield his strength to his own best ends. Wisdom attainment is a part of successful character arcs, just as wisdom is part of the new adult journey. Even our failures make us wiser.

Your character's strengths lead directly to your story's resolution. The strengths will blossom as each obstacle tests your character until finally he's cognizant enough of his strengths and weaknesses to deliberately apply his strength to overcome a weakness.

3. Wants and Needs Motivate Characters

Every protagonist needs a goal to strive for, chapter by chapter. The definition of *goal* gets a tad fuzzy when you consider that the character is moving through two separate, albeit intertwined, arcs. Her external arc may require her to overthrow an evil overlord—something you can easily call a *goal*. Her internal arc, though, may be about her need for unconditional love. So her external plot goal is different from her needs and wants. Sometimes, what a person wants and what she needs are two different things, which is a flavor of enlightenment in its own right. When we talk about plot in Chapters 6 through 8, I'll use the word *goal*, but when talking about constructing character psyches and emotions, I find *want* and *need* more useful.

Consider that some universal wants and needs are specific to new adults. By choosing to write about characters in this phase of life, you're automatically lobbing into play the need for all the items I covered in the first chapter of this book, such as independence, self-actualization, self-identity, and so forth. What does your character need? What does she want enough to strive for it?

For example, Markus Zusak's award-winning novel *I Am the Messenger* features a nineteen-year-old underage cab driver that feels adrift because he has no sense of purpose. (*I Am the Messenger* was published as Young Adult in 2009, shortly before New Adult fiction burst onto the scene and was recognized as a category. Zusak was already an award-winning YA novelist, so his story of NA angst and searching was naturally put out by his YA publisher at that time. It's popularly recognized, however, as an early NA.) He's got no career, no respect in the community. He's surrounded by people achieving greatness, yet he's no more than a lump behind a steering wheel at work and a lump on his couch at home. He's the poster boy for "failure to launch"—but at least he's aware of it. For him, that's step one on his path toward what he needs: a purpose. Being the seminal writer that he is, Zusak gives him a series of purposes—delivered right to his mailbox, no less!—and then threatens him (quite literally, using thugs with knobby fists and ugly guns) in order to make him act until he finally starts acting because he wants to.

4. Fear Forces Characters Through the Storm

Identifying what your character fears most in the world arms you with a powerful whip. As the Zusak example above shows, sometimes a need or want isn't enough—be sure to put teeth in the consequences of failure. You can keep your character hurdling the most unbearable obstacles if you threaten her with even more unbearable consequences.

Knowing your character's worst fear pairs nicely with knowing her key want or need. A character who wants (or needs) something enough to struggle onward and who also fears the consequences of failure enough to not give up will be a truly driven star for your novel. There's great page-turning potential there.

If you've ever had someone respond to your story with a shrug, saying that it was hard to stay in it, then fear of consequences is a great element to examine for your revision. You may not have put enough at stake, and thus the consequences of failure just aren't awful enough to make us worry for the character. Raise the stakes to raise the tension and push your readers through the story as forcefully as you'll now be pushing your character.

"It's about the storytelling first and how the writer develops the experience of the character." —**STACEY DONAGHY**, Agent, Donaghy Literary Group

---

Bonus: NA-Worthy Foundational Elements

The above four foundational elements are necessary for any protagonist in fiction, but since you're writing new adult characters, you'd do well to know three other foundational items about your character before you set about discovering his nuances in the actual drafting of the story.

1. **KNOW HIS FUTURE.** New adults may not know what they want to do "when they grow up," but they're in the process of forming a Life Plan. That plan is subject to revision on a daily basis, but the point is that they're actively working it out as they explore their interests and strengths. Even the biggest goof-offs know that decision time is lurking, so there's a palpable sense of big decisions being made or pending.

   Brainstorm the kind of career and family future that would suit your new adult character. You don't have to be specific, as in "He'll be a police officer with a wife and three children." Rather, you'd predict that the fully developed character at the end of this book would be drawn to a career that lets him help people and would want a house full of love and activity. Having a sense of the character's future puts you in a great position to understand the decisions that character makes when you start lobbing the obstacles his way, and you'll understand the internal journey he's embarking upon even if you don't know its specifics.

   If the character seems to refuse any effort you make to ponder his future, consider why he might be digging in his heels. Is his denial intentional? Why? What is he hiding or avoiding? Is he being short-sighted? Lazy? Fearful? This can affect his behavior in his daily situations.

2. **KNOW WHAT GIVES HER COMFORT.** Instability reigns in the new adult experience, causing stress. If you know what makes your character feel more secure, you'll have insight into her—and a good bead on what to deny her when you want to crank down the thumbscrews. Identify what makes her feel "stable" when things are nuts. Music? Open spaces? Long walks? A home-cooked meal with siblings bickering playfully around the table?

3. **KNOW WHAT TEMPTS HIM.** New adults are risk-takers and experimenters, and if you know what to tempt him with, you've got his number. What wild oats does he want to sow? What will get him into trouble and reveal his weaknesses and strengths to readers—and perhaps to himself? You're now in a position to put these temptations in your character's path during his journey.

Also, consider if this character is one to give in to temptation or abstain, and ask yourself why that is. For a person in this phase of life, when personal accountability is finally on his shoulders, it's important to know how equipped he is to handle that.

My character profile worksheet has all of these elements on it. With the four foundational elements and the three bonus NA ones, you'll have a great starting place for your character discovery. Now you're ready to build your character physically, mentally, and emotionally, learning to reveal that physical embodiment in ways that are artful, fun, and rich, pushing your craft far beyond simple description.

CHARACTER DISCOVERY EXERCISE #1: SHOW ME THE MONEY

Goal: To determine what's important to your protagonist and if that importance changes by the end of the novel.

Grab your pen and promise that you won't think, you'll just write. Consider it blurting with a pen. Ready ...

Your protagonist just won the lottery in the first chapter of your book. Write her list of ten things she is going to do with that money. Make sure it is the protagonist's list, not your list for the protagonist. Only spend thirty seconds.

Go!

Now let's do this again, but with a twist: Your protagonist just won the lottery *on the last page of your novel.* I'll give you three minutes to make her list this time. This second exercise gives you a chance to think and prioritize, much as your character (who should be wiser or more mature by the end of the novel) would do. The order of the items on the list matters—although *how* it matters is up to you. Importance? Size of the expense? Obligations first (if they even make it onto the list) and then fun stuff second?

Go!

WRITING NEW ADULT FICTION

How do the lists differ? Why did your character make the changes she made?

TIP: If you find this exercise challenging, try making a list for yourself as if someone just knocked on your door and handed you that giant lottery check. What ten things would make it onto your list? Do the exercise a second time, but this time don't put any obligatory items on the list—only list those things you'd do if you didn't have to be a "responsible adult." So it's more of a wish list. How do your lists differ?

BREATHING LIFE INTO YOUR NA CHARACTERS

Here we'll focus on embodying your characters, and then we talk fun, varied techniques for revealing those bodies and personalities. I love this part! We'll move from understanding the character and your goals with him to piecing that character together physically and revealing him to the world through words, thoughts, and deeds. That's *characterization*, and it's where magic happens. A character who has existed as a concept or dream now "comes to life."

NA fiction is usually character-driven, even with stories that are high action and high concept (for more on that, check out Chapter 2). NA readers want to fall in love with characters. They've even been known to take on the characters themselves in fan fiction because they can't let them go. In the case of hotties, they have "Who is the hottest hottie?" contests online. The more "real" your characters seem as they walk and talk their way through your story, the happier your readers will be. This section is about creating and revealing characters' physical attributes.

WRITING STRONG BODIES

People are more than their hair and eye color, yet those are the go-to physical traits for novelists. What do hair and eye color actually tell you about the character? That they're easy-going, or perhaps tense? Persistent or pessimistic? Does it tell you their financial circumstances? Do you now know if the person is fit and perky or out of shape and feeling low? Readers would much rather know that this person has long, slow strides as she crosses campus or if she clippity-clops her tiny legs at Mach 10 from car to classroom. That gives us insight into the spirit dwelling within the physical shell. We can picture both of those characters in motion. Tell readers if the character is deft with her fingers or a fumbler whose fumbling could worsen under stress. Knowing details like these makes all the difference when we get to the climactic scene in which that character mustn't fumble a live grenade!

Rather than trying to describe your character so that readers can "picture him," aim to evoke a sense of the character's physical presence so that we can *feel* him as surely as if he were right there in the room with us. Focus on physical features that reveal more about him than the eye can see. Give us mannerisms and movements that will reveal moods, personalities, and current states of mind. I want to know if this is a broad-chested guy who strains his T-shirts or a reedy guy whose pants hang in that way that makes you imagine wrapping your arms completely around his waist while in his embrace.

You can certainly provide the hair and eye color—some readers feel robbed if they don't have those elements right away, considering them essential for the mental picture—but don't stop there. Talk about the quality of those eyes and the state of that brown head of hair. Readers will have a different reaction to a guy who wears his hair greasy and one who knocks you over with the smell of Prell. Physical traits that do more than give you something to picture add depth to your overall characterization.

Characters can have distinct physicality related to their age and situation, so keep in mind how being between the ages of eighteen and twenty-five can affect your NA characters' bodies. Studies show that humans attain maximum levels of finger dexterity during their early twenties, for example. Typically, new adults exhibit more energy in their movements than older people. They're likely to be more fit than older adults and more settled into their bodies than teens, who are still dealing with the effects or immediate aftereffects of puberty. Those new adults who are stressed out by changes and responsibilities will reveal that stress in their bodies. Those who are troubled may exhibit poor nutrition, jittery nerves, physical ticks, or slacking personal hygiene, while those who love their lot in life may be physically thriving and easy in their mannerisms.

EMBODIMENT IS MORE THAN BODY PARTS

When you sculpt your character's body, don't stop with the way that body looks and moves. The image a person presents to the world through clothing, hairstyle, and other physical enhancements, such as nose jobs or tattoos, expresses who she is, gives clues about where she comes from, and hints at where she wants to go. The way you alter outward affectations can give readers a feel for your character's personality, mood, and state of mind at any given moment in the story.

Style choices can reveal social or media influences, role models, comfort with personal expression, financial status, social or cultural background, even religious upbringing. They can reveal a character's preparation for or comfort with a setting, as with a guy caught wearing flip-flops in a rainstorm or wearing a short-sleeved white button-up at a posh gala event. Or how about the girl with a bulky Gucci shoulder bag on a desperate hike through the mountains? The mismatch of shoulder bag to mountainous hiking reveals a mismatch between character and environment, suggesting a crisis at hand. Even without knowing the specific story set-up, this single image gives us something intriguing to picture, to ponder, and very likely to worry about.

Clothing and hairstyles may seem obvious items to tell your readers about, but as with just about every writing element, I challenge you to be more thoughtful with those items. You're not simply dressing a mannequin in brand names or identifiable fashion stylings. Ask yourself what the character's outward appearance can reveal about her beyond being rich or poor, fashion conscious or fashion free. How can clothing and hair show where she is on her internal journey? For example, a character who has a problem letting go of things in life might be well served with cargo pants or carpenter-style jeans, with all those little pockets in which she can squirrel away goods. Later, when that character has her world turned upside down and her budding Life Plan seems shot to hell, you can have her in company-issued slacks without any pockets to tuck her stuff in, leaving her flustered about where to stash the items she believes she must keep on her person at all times. Such pants would be a tiny element in the book, but by presenting it in concert with the many other elements of your storytelling, this detail will contribute to a rich, distinct character.

MOLDING MINDS AND HEARTS

We are as much our minds as our bodies, so mull your characters' mental, psychological, and emotional traits as well as their physical presence in the story. Most members of your cast will have at least eighteen years of living under their belts, which is plenty of time to have developed strengths and weaknesses of the mind and heart.

Evidence suggests that there's significant personality change from adolescence through the new adult period. By the time they finish high school, young people are so incredibly done with what they've been doing. Done with the going-to-high-school-every-day routine. Done with dealing with their high school social status, whether it's one they've worked for or that was assigned to them by circumstances. Done with the parents telling them what to do and what their daily minutiae should look like. They are ready for change, craving *new*. As they set about figuring out what their futures will look like, they are experimenting and revising their plans and starting to take action to make it happen. In their new self-actualized phase of life, these young people become more goal-directed in their work-related efforts, which shows increases in self-control and the tendency to be more reflective, deliberate, and playful. Studies also show a decrease in negative emotions like aggressiveness and alienation in new adults. This happens at a time of life that's emotionally charged, with excitement over potential clashing with fear of the unknown and of not measuring up.

This plays right into our hands as fiction writers, whether we're talking about a contemporary realistic story where they head off to college and try to forge their identity or about a science fiction story where they have to solve some kind of task or save the world. You may not know the depth of your character's emotions or psychological state or how they'll respond in times of crisis until you put them through the wringer and see what they do, but you can have an idea of who you're sending into combat when you start your story. This is where you get emotional resonance, and you have great opportunities to connect with readers on common ground. Emotional pain is universal, for instance, as is hope for your future. When you start wrapping this in individual experiences and expressions of that hope and pain, you are developing a character who resonates with many readers and yet stands unique to your story.

CHARACTER DISCOVERY EXERCISE #2:
KNOW MY STUFF, KNOW ME

Goal: To get away from your character's physical traits, instead try defining him by what's important to him. This will also give you ideas about what props to include in settings, like the living environment, or what to deny your character when he needs to find a sense of peace or normalcy.

Make a list of ten things your character would take with her on a deserted island. Now tell your character that she must evacuate her home because of fire and has time to take just ten things. Write those items down. Did her list change? What do the two lists reveal about your character's priorities and about her wants versus needs?

AVOIDING STEREOTYPES

I talked about *flat* being the literary f-word. Well, nothing is flatter than a stereotypical character. *Stereotypes* are those stock characters whom we all know instantly. The timid virgin girl new to college; the sex-crazed, loud-mouthed roommate; the tattooed math-tutor-by-day-MMA-fighter-by-night. There was a time when these stereotypes were new and exciting for readers, but these characters have inhabited so many NA stories now that there's no surprise left in them. It's hard for readers to feel any fluttering of curiosity and intrigue when stereotypes walk on-scene, even if you plan to undermine the stereotype or push the characters beyond initial impressions. Too often, writers use them as shortcuts.

You can personalize a character by finding the personal in the universal. I've presented many characteristics of new adulthood, but they aren't simply a list of ingredients to mix and match. Rather, view new adulthood as a rich pool in which you will dunk characters who have come from distinct experiences, families, and social circles, with their own distinct hopes and goals based on those things, and then see how they'll react. Knowing the characteristics of your character's phase of life allows you to create universal points of connection with your readers, who are living through that same period of life or have done so in the past. They understand the factors at play, and will enjoy seeing how each individual character negotiates those factors. Your specific themes and your goals and plot needs distinguish your story, while universal elements help readers connect. Be conscious of fitting personal details and histories into universal experiences to create a distinct story that still resonates with a large number of readers.

You can get personal by using two words to get into your character's heart and mind: *How?* and *Why?* These words are particularly useful when a character seems to be doing all the things you'd expect her to do. Push her (and yourself) beyond the obvious by asking questions starting with those words, forcing your character to consider her particular circumstances and personality. For example, instead of asking your character, "Would you change your mind if the boyfriend you are about to dump wins the lotto?" you could ask her, "*How* would your life change if you decided not to dump your boyfriend when you heard he won the lotto?" Then probe the response: "How would *that* make you feel?" "How *else* would it make you feel?" then "How *else*?" until you have the character shouting her deepest shameful but truthful answer. Then: "How could you get rid of that feeling?" This kind of interrogation, which only has to happen in your head, is a great way to find out your character's most guarded fears and desires. And of course, knowing those things exposes them to merciless author manipulation.

TECHNIQUES FOR REVEALING YOUR CHARACTERS

It's all good and dandy to know your character—the real test is getting your readers to know your characters. Obviously, you're not going to stick your character sketches in an appendix for them. I'm being playful in saying that, but in a sense, some writers do that very thing. They describe the physical features, they describe the personality, they report the character's past and tell us when and how the character is changing. That's not telling a story, that's reporting and info-dumping. Here are seven ways to *reveal* your character. You can mix and match them throughout the story, with all of our characters, making for a lush and lively cast.

1. PROVOKE ACTION AND REACTION
Character revelation starts with you, so put on your mean girl or mean boy pants and start shoving your characters out of their comfort zones. Writ-

ers often describe themselves as receptacles of the story, reporting that "the book just seemed to write itself." The truth is, those writers set up situations that forced the characters to reveal themselves and move the story forward. So while a writer may "receive" a story, his own deliberate set-up spurs that reception. So get manipulative and pushy and set up your character for revelation. You are in a power position. Seek conflict. Push buttons and escalate. Deny and bestow. I'll talk a lot more about this pushing and shoving in the plotting chapters, but it's important to bring up now because it's your role to stir the pot. You can make your characters act and behave and respond to stimulation that reveals their personalities, backgrounds, mind-sets, and moods. Use the plot against your protagonist, use secondary characters against your protagonist, use every character in the flippin' book! Consciously reveal your characters through their reactions to other characters and to situations.

2. SHOW, DON'T TELL

Perhaps the most popular axiom in fiction writing is "Show, don't tell." I've mentioned it a few times in this book already. But let's truly focus on it now, because it's awesome. For you, this means not describing how your new adult is going through her journey, how she's changing, what she looks like, what she's feeling. Instead, evoke the feeling, suggest the vision, let her internal changes be evident in how she moves, talks, behaves. Instead of describing actions, movements, and behaviors, write a scene that gives your character the chance to reveal her mood, personality, and physical state as she moves through the scene. For example, you've got a scene wherein a guy fetches a stepstool, sets it up next to the kitchen sink, then climbs up to reach the Vodka bottle that his frat buddy just stashed in the cupboard without any stepstool at all. Do we need to be told outright that our guy is short? And determined, by the way—that was quite a production to get to the booze.

Here are four ways to "show."

- **BODY LANGUAGE.** Characters' movements can make feelings and thoughts quite clear to readers. A character who lounges conveys a different mood than a character who sits ramrod straight in a chair. A character who paces is probably not the calmest person in the book. Conversely, you can inject intentional confusion by having the character behave in ways that contradict what he is saying.

- **CONVERSATIONS AND MANNER OF SPEAKING.** "God, Tom, ever heard of showering?" It's pretty clear what kind of hygiene that roommate's got going on, eh? But don't just focus on the content of what a character says—the *way* he talks can reveal more about what he's thinking or how he's feeling than the words he utters. Speaking slowly and thoughtfully to demonstrate intelligence; using elevated vocabulary with one crowd while slang-slinging with another; blathering in run-on sentences when nervous; trailing off with ellipses when unsure; giving minimal, clipped replies when secretive; interrupting others when impatient or rude. You can reveal confidence or lack thereof with commanding and mumbling. For more on dialogue, see Chapter 5.

- **PROP MANIPULATION AND ENVIRONMENT.** A character who can't carry someone else's gym bag without a struggle may be weak, ill, or simply diminutive. A girl who hurls her alarm clock across the room is hardly excited about getting up for the early shift. You can reveal and manipulate your characters' state of mind by showing how they interact with props and by manipulating their environment. I talk in Chapter 11 about physically evicting your protagonist from the places he's comfortable when comfort is vital to his sanity. You can sprinkle mini frustrations throughout the book via props and scenery, like a character who can't cut a piece of paper because there are no lefty scissors around. If the character has that kind of minor prop interaction at the right moment in the internal journey, that moment may catapult them forward—in the plot and as a person.

- **SENSORY DETAILS.** Don't forget how powerful sound, touch, smell, and even taste can be. Writers easily employ sensory details when writing love scenes or when showing one character responding physically to a love interest in a nonromantic scene. Warm, flushed skin. The scent of cologne. The taste of cherry ChapStick during a kiss. But often they'll forget to use it for other characters at other times as well. Don't forget to describe the feel of a scratchy sweater on your character's skin when comfort is the last thing you want her to feel.

3. USE STATEMENTS AND DESCRIPTIONS

Sometimes it's okay to simply state in the narrative (regardless of point of view) that a character is pissed off. Or that someone has long, beautiful fingers. Yes, that's telling. But variety makes for dynamic storytelling, and direct statements and descriptions are legitimate storytelling tools to throw in the mix. Sometimes, a statement or description just feels right.

4. MAKE COMPARISONS

Playing one character off another can reveal much about both characters. "His hand swallowed mine when I shook it," for instance, gives insight into their respective sizes. Comparison can also reveal mood or mind-set, as in a scene where one character repeatedly jumps up to peer through the peephole while another sits at a table, slowly turning over cards, one by one by one, only to then slowly flip them facedown, one by one by one. ... Who is the freaked-out person in that scene?

5. ASSIGN HOBBIES, SKILLS, AND INTERESTS

Assign your characters passions, talents, and dreams that reveal the kind of people they are. This can be quite separate from the core want or need that drives this story's internal arc. It's about understanding how this character fills his free time, about what skills he develops just because it's fun, relaxing, or satisfying for him to do so. This is about knowing what makes him comfortable and then, if it suits your story, denying him the time to indulge in that hobby or activity.

6. ESTABLISH THEIR PRIORITIES, THEN SHOW HOW THEY CHANGE

Your character's priorities will likely change as part of his internal journey. Consider a historical fiction novel that has a protagonist with Vaudeville dreams facing the choice to leave home or to stay and act as ma or pa for younger siblings. Which would your protagonist choose at the beginning of the story? How might that change by the end of the story? The exercise earlier in this chapter called "Show Me the Money" can help you pinpoint your protagonist's priorities at the beginning of the novel and then at the end.

7. TRICKLE OUT THE BACKSTORY

The more real you want your character to feel, the more real you need to make his introduction to the reader. In real life, we meet someone and only know what we see and hear on the spot. A friend may lean in and whisper an important detail like, "She always wanted to be a vet, but her mom made her join a nunnery," but otherwise we're not handed bio sheets or résumés. We discover a person's backstory as we form friendships, have conversations, and share experiences with that person. Let readers have that fun with your characters. Mostly that knowledge is for you, anyway, as you use that history to create a character who responds organically and authentically to your stimulations. All your prewriting character discovery has done its job. Now leave it be.

CREATING A SUPPORTING CAST THAT DOES ITS JOB

Because your book is ultimately the story of your protagonist, the only reason secondary characters should be given precious screen time in your book is because they serve that protagonist in some manner. They push or challenge her, sometimes in a bad direction; they support her; they provide factual information and place and plot context; they add depth and texture to the story; and they help reveal your protagonist through their relationships with her, as with the roommate who pushes the star's buttons or the parents who try to control their daughter despite her age and abilities.

The richest supporting characters exist in their own right, with distinct personalities, strengths, flaws, and dreams. They may even have wants that form a subplot in your book, eventually dovetailing with your main storyline. Consider creating a basic character sketch for each character who gets a substantial role in your book, identifying his relationships to the protagonist, his contribution to the protagonist's journey, and his personality traits, right down to core flaws and core strengths. Just as knowing your protagonist well helps you predict what conflicts to create for her, knowing your secondary characters as more than just game pieces on a storyboard helps you write scenes in which they respond organically, deeply, and uniquely to your protagonist and to the plot events. Also, NA fiction is rife with sequels, companion books, and series that spin out secondary characters to star as protagonists in their own right. Creating deep characters from the get-go will get readers excited about the spin-offs and make your life much easier as you set about telling those stories next.

This section talks about who secondary characters are and how you can manipulate them to serve your internal and external arcs.

THE NA SOCIAL CIRCLE

New adults have mostly left the nest or are trying to, so they're in the process of forming new social circles. In many cases, the social circle they're leaving was a lifetime in the making, either with the immediate family or with friendships that began in school or in the neighborhood when they were all young and playing together. This is the first time your young person gets to start with a clean slate, and it can be intimidating, refreshing, and certainly stressful. Even those NAs on the older end of the spectrum are constantly forming new acquaintances and moving away from old—new adulthood is a time of transitory relationships, and everyone understands that. Who comprises that revolving social circle? Take a look:

- **FRIENDS AND CO-WORKERS.** These are the most important relationships next to lovers. The peer group becomes the new family, the ones with whom your protagonist spends his daily encounters and to whom he turns for advice or support. If the friends and co-workers are peers, they're going through their own NA struggles and so aren't necessarily dependent on the protagonist. There may be times when they're each going about their own business. This is different from the way a high school friendship is so constant and active. There's plenty of time to be on your own now, creating all kinds of opportunities for the fictional relationships to ebb and flow—giving characters room to grow in relationships and on their own.
- **ADULTS IN POSITIONS OF POWER.** Generally the older folks are nonexistent or in the extreme periphery, like the professor who lectures but hands you off to the hot assistant teacher. Or the detective who shows up on-scene but doesn't do much but push a few buttons before he leaves. A wizened old sorcerer in a fantasy world must be kept far away so as to keep the resolution solely in your young person's eager hands. In teen fiction, these old folks are more omnipresent even if they keep hands off, but in NA you can ban them almost completely and really should. Those new adults who haven't left the nest have unique relationships with parents—the parents are part of the setting, but they aren't integral relationships for the character.
- **PARENTS.** This gets complex in NA stories and can be mined for conflict as well as great protagonist growth. This is a period of great change as your character steps away from the structured world and into a realm where she

sets the structure, from daily life to jobs to classes to living arrangements and friends. The apron strings are severed or nearly so.

Your new adult should either want to be free of her parents, who have power over her even if she does seek advice, or she should be fighting for that freedom. The parent can represent a familiar, cozy childhood and be there when the story calls for that kind of breather, but ultimately, you have to put it all on your new adult character. There are few steadfast rules in NA, but this is one: Your new adult must weather the storm on her own and resolve it on her own or with her NA partner. Mommy and Daddy's jobs as problem solvers are done.

"Allowing characters to fend for themselves and get to know themselves appeals to the New Adult market." —**KRISTINA DEMICHELE**, Editorial Intern, Entangled Embrace

---

- **LOVERS.** These characters are so vital they get their own chapter: "Love and Sex in the Age of Experimentation" (Chapter 10). The romantic leads in your story should both be fully fleshed out so that we know what each one wants, what each one brings to the relationship (good and bad), and how they can serve each other in their respective journeys. New Adult fiction often gives equal billing to the two romantic leads, frequently alternating narrative points of view chapter by chapter. In that case, you need to treat both as protagonists, with full personalities, problems, and personal growth.
- **ANTAGONISTS.** Antagonists come in many flavors—and they can fall into any of the above categories. They can be total bad guys, intent on hurting the protagonist, such as the ex-boyfriend who stalks her. Still, they can have depth to make them believable and even as sympathetic as your protagonist. Do all the work with your antagonists that you do with your protagonist. Understand why they are doing what they're doing so that you can write the richest scenes possible.

Antagonists sometimes look like good guys … and in fact some really *are* good guys. They're just making life difficult for the protagonist—they are *antagonizing* in the truest sense of the word. Maybe it's an outright friend or a trusted loved one who is simply trying to help or do something right in the world even as they misjudge and hurt the protagonist. Maybe the antagonist is a *frenemy*. We tend to think of this term as the way to talk about those high schoolers who act like your friends but stab you in the back. The frenemy relationship plays out that way in new adulthood, too, as everyone jockeys for opportunities. And to a certain degree, many of them in the early stages of new adulthood may not have worked out how the relationship games have changed yet and still do the friend-to-your-face-knife-in-your-back thing. Plenty of people keep this up into adulthood, after all.

CHARACTER DISCOVERY EXERCISE #3: TAKE OFF YOUR BLINDERS

Goal: This exercise will force you to think beyond the bad in your antagonist and consider the good in him, as well as the hurt that contributed to his antagonism. If you have understanding and empathy for your antagonist, you can write an intriguingly deep person who behaves badly but who has or had decency about him at some point.

Take one minute to write ten mean things your antagonist did to other people during grade school/childhood. This is very much a brainstorming exercise, forcing you to blurt what you know down deep rather than run things through an editorial filter.

Now take one minute to write ten nice things your antagonist did for other people during grade school/childhood.

Now spend one minute writing ten ways other people hurt your antagonist during grade school/childhood.

GIVE YOUR CAST THE TOOLS TO DO THEIR JOBS

Give your secondary characters—including your antagonists—their own lives. This will make your story stronger because a character with a deep history is a character with deep emotions who can behave in complex and story-enriching ways. Introduce secondary characters only when necessary, and then only with the amount of detail necessary. Just as you don't overwhelm your readers with backstory, don't throw too many characters at them at once. Bring each character into the story as they are needed. And when you do bring them on-scene, don't stop the story to plunk down a bio for them. The secondary cast will demonstrate their relationship to the character in "Show, don't tell" fashion; no need for you to tell us that they've been best friends all their lives and that the main character needs the best friend as her ballast. We'll see that play out in the relationship and feel it in our guts, even if we don't consciously say, "That's her ballast." There's a subtext there, and subtext is about a visceral knowledge, not necessary explicit knowledge.

I'll end this chapter with eight ways to make sure the rest of the cast is doing its job.

1. FLESH THEM OUT

Avoid stereotypical social relationships by fleshing out the secondary characters. Do thumbnail sketches and even full character sketches if the character will have more than a brief appearance. This will be important if you plan to have this character take over the POV in the next book, as often happens with love interests. And it will help you from falling back on a stock character, especially when you've got characters who have jobs to do, like the BFF or the Roommate or the Hottie. Characters who are distinct and layered with things to discover throughout the story get our attention. We notice. We wonder. We let them into our brain and hearts. We find points of connection and then we're hooked. How do you avoid turning to familiar stereotypes?

- **SET A RULE.** Any person who walks into your novel has to ante-up with one physical trait, one mental/psychological trait, and one history element that isn't expected in a person with that role in the story.
- **HAVE BLANK CHARACTER PROFILES AT THE READY.** When a character shows up suddenly in the story, finish the scene but then grab your character profile worksheet and write down the four foundational elements for that character.

- **DO THE OPPOSITE.** Set up expectations with the stereotype, then defy those expectations as soon as possible. Need a sidekick for the guardian who just showed up to save the city from a zombie takeover? Give the sidekick a lame leg that slows his progress but makes his hands quicker than anybody's.

2. DON'T LET THEM STEAL THE SHOW

Don't give the best parts to the secondary characters because you're not worried about their likability. If the secondary character is stealing the scene, that's your red flag that you're playing it too safe with your lead character. Rather than focusing on minimizing the secondary character, heighten the main character: highlight her flaws and push her harder to force her out of her comfort zone and into taking action.

3. ALLOW THEM TO CHANGE, TOO

Secondary characters may change for the better or for the worse as they work on their own journeys. Thus, their relationship with the protagonist may change, and if it does, it's for a distinct purpose that somehow serves the protagonist.

4. LET THEM MESS UP

Secondary characters may be involved in important subplots. They do have their own lives going on, after all, so use those separate lives deliberately. If they're messing up in their own lives, the damage can spill over into your protagonist's life, perhaps forcing your lead character to prioritize, maybe giving a nice breather for your main storyline as she deals with the others' problems. Or maybe your protagonist will decide not to be there for a friend and then suffer guilt from that. The secondary character's troubles could serve as mirrors for your protagonist's struggles.

5. ALLOW FOR FRENEMIES OR MISMATCHES

We don't always make the best choices of friends, and sometimes we don't spot the error for a long time. And even though new adults are on their own, they aren't always at liberty to choose, as with assigned roommates or co-workers or partners in crime who are pushed together by circumstances.

6. SEND THEM AWAY AT CRUCIAL MOMENTS

Send prime secondary characters off to do their own thing at vital moments, denying your lead character the succor she needs on the shoulder of her good friend when things get bad. This also creates holes in your story that will prove useful should you revisit this story from another character's point of view in your next novel. The follow-up book could tell us what that best friend was off doing when she should've been back in her dorm room comforting her brokenhearted roomie.

7. BRING THEM ON-SCENE AT INOPPORTUNE MOMENTS

Sometimes we want or need to be alone, or to be with a certain person, and the appearance of other characters mucks things up. The roommate who shows up at the wrong moment can prevent the consummation of love, frustrating the lovers and escalating the sexual tension. In a thriller, a co-worker can show up at work after hours, foiling the protagonist's plan to break into her boss's office. If that co-worker has been carefully drawn, his appearance there will feel right instead of like an event you brought about simply because you needed the disruption.

8. HAVE THEM PUSH BUTTONS

Some people don't know when to keep their opinions or nosey noses to themselves. Parents, for instance. Or well-intentioned friends or co-workers. Or maybe the intentions aren't so well. People after the same job or promotion can be great obstacles. Shopkeepers who push products and call attention to protagonists who've ducked into the store to hide from a pursuer can force the protagonist to do something she doesn't want to do. Use your secondary characters to push your primary characters.

CHARACTER DISCOVERY EXERCISE #4:
WHAT KIND OF FRIEND ARE YOU?

Goal: To help you focus on two friends' differences and their roles in the friendship and then to focus on the reason they're best friends in the first place. It is not about

WRITING NEW ADULT FICTION

writing pretty prose, so just hack it out on the keyboard. I've developed a second
version of this for girlfriends/boyfriends in Chapter 10.

Your protagonist and his best friend are going to have a fight. Each character must make an accusation, and each character must concede something—that way we get the full breadth of an argument, from accusation to resolution. The fight is about roommate issues. The two characters have just moved in together as roomies, and now the best friend has had it with the protagonist. It's come to a head, and, as most fights are, it's about more than dirty dishes or someone leaving their chainmail in front of the hearth again. Use these three phrases somewhere in that argument: "You always ...", "You don't understand ...", and "I didn't know that." You can set this "scene" in your story era or in a totally different one just to have fun with it.

To test if you've revealed things, read the finished argument to a partner. Ask the partner to write down one thing the characters learned about each other through the fight and why he thinks they have a useful friendship for the story.

CHARACTER PROFILE

Use this worksheet to sketch a character profile of your protagonist and key secondary characters. If this is for your protagonist, you may find it useful to write your hook at the top of this page to help you stay focused when tangents tease (see Chapter 2).

THUMBNAIL

Name and age: _____

Need/want/goal: _____

Driving fear: _____

Key strength(s): _____

Key flaw(s): _____

FOR SECONDARY CHARACTERS

Relationship to protagonist: _____

Contribution to the protagonist's internal arc: _____

_____

_____

_____

EXPANDED CHARACTER SKETCH

Race/Ethnicity: _____

Faith: _____

Attitude/outlook at beginning _____

_____

Attitude/outlook at end: _____

_____

Future family/career: _____

_____

_____

Role models: _____

_____

Comforts: _____

_____

Temptations: _____

_____

Hobbies/activities/special talents: _____

_____

_____

Physical attributes: _____

_____

Manner of movement: _____

Mannerisms at ease: _____

_____

Mannerisms in times of stress: _____

_____

Fashion sensibility: _____

_____

Social status: _____

How would he/she describe his/her childhood? _____

_____

_____

How would he/she describe his/her adolescence? _____

_____

_____

How would he/she describe his/her family? _____

_____

_____

What is his/her relationship with parents? _____

_____

_____

CHAPTER 5

How to Talk Like a New Adult

*D*ialogue is more than characters gabbing at one another. It's a powerful tool for exposing characters in ways they aren't aware of, for stimulating them into action they wouldn't otherwise take, and for revealing vital plot information in a way that intrigues readers rather than info-dumps them into a dead-eyed stupor. Above all, it creates a sense of immediacy and intimacy essential for readers yearning to connect with your character. And boy, do NA readers clamor for that connection.

Your job is to make all that rich story-building stuff happen while sounding convincingly like a real person—in your case, like real new adults, even if you're well out of new adulthood yourself. That's what this chapter is about. The techniques and strategies below tap into multiple storytelling elements to influence and support the words you put in your characters' mouths, even as you wield technical between-the-quotation-marks mechanics. The result will be flavorful, convincing conversations that'll enrich the entire reading experience.

"The NAs rising to the top are good with dialogue." —**AMANDA BERGERON**, Editor for William Morrow and Avon, imprints of HarperCollins

---

STRONG DIALOGUE IS AN AMALGAM OF STRONG CRAFTWORK

Dialogue is a team event. Plot, characterization, setting, sensibility … they all play roles in what a character says, when she says it, and how she says it. Sometimes, those elements even do the talking in place of spoken words, as in the case of actions that reveal what that character is thinking without her uttering a sound. Those actions and anything else you can stuff into the *narrative beats*—the narrative material between lines of dialogue during a conversation—contribute to the effectiveness of the words you position within the quotations marks. For example, the unremarkable words, "Honey, I'm home," can be drenched with a tidal wave of sinister irony when you couple those peppy spoken words with action in the narrative beat:

> "Honey," he crashed his boot through the center of the door, then put his sneering face to the hole, "I'm home."

If you leave it to the words within the quotation marks to do all the talking, you miss out on depth like this. You end up instead with flat dialogue that, when you really need some emotional pow, swings into overwrought melodrama. Let's look at that same scenario of the booted dude trying to gain entry again, only this time I won't support or contribute to the dialogue with other elements. The spoken words between the quotations marks must shoulder the whole load:

> "Let me in! Now!"

> "This is *not* the day to be locking me out. … I don't have the patience for this. … Open the door!"

> "I'll bust down this door if you don't let me into my own home!"

Those examples show how fussy punctuation can get when the dialogue is overburdened, with exclamation points and ellipses trying to convey the emotion. Dialogue tags like "he shouted" or "she hissed" often accompany this heavy-handed treatment of dialogue as the writer does her utmost to wring emotion out of the spoken words alone. Dialogue like this earns the critique, "The dialogue feels forced instead of natural." Authors aware of the need to give a conversation rhythm may toss in some generic action so that it's not just a page of dialogue, but although their hearts are in the right place (they are trying to write an emotional scene), they aren't making full use of their writer's toolbox.

"Let me in! Now!" he shouted, pounding on the door.

In that example, the pounding shows us an excited guy in action, and the verb *shouted* lets us know his voice is raised in case we didn't figure that out from the twin exclamation points. Of course, my offering this snippet out of context leaves room for you to argue that other things in the scene would clarify whether he's *happy* excited or *angry* excited or *desperate* excited, but isolating this line shows us that the elements in this sentence certainly aren't conveying specific emotion themselves. They could easily do so, and should, and that's what this section is about.

I'm going to arm you with five ways to unburden your dialogue by teaming it up with other core elements of storytelling, including your setting, your sensibility, and your characterization tools like body language and prop interaction. Use the strategies in this section to relax your dialogue so that it feels more natural and it works with the other elements to contribute to the scene rather than depending on the rest of the scene for full meaning. Successful conversations require all the elements to work in concert for balance, for effectiveness, and for a lovely emotional wallop.

1. SYNC THEIR DIALOGUE WITH THEIR SENSIBILITY

It may be tempting to put advanced vocabulary in the mouths of new adults as a way to make them sound older than teens, but we need to keep in mind that handing a kid his high school diploma doesn't kick his vocab growth into hyperdrive. Rather, what does change are the thoughts these newly independent kids express as they finally get to venture into the wild on their own and start gaining experience and worldliness. With that experience comes a greater tendency to take other people into account, an increased sophistication in the way they frame their thoughts, and a new focus on issues that all young people encounter as they duck and dodge and press forward through new adulthood. What these young people talk about and the way they talk about it should reflect the way they now think.

New adults still have some of the self-focus of adolescents, but their perspective is turning outward year by year, experience by experience. You can evidence each new adult character's degree of self-focus when they talk. And you can consciously adjust that at certain times in the story, such as in times of distress, when you can have them backslide into talking about how the situation affects them first and foremost. So on a calm day, when all things are good, your young guy might say, "The commander has a lot going on. He'll want this done fast." But with that stressed-out commander on his case threatening severe reprisal if the job isn't completed *right here and now, buddy,* the dialogue can be worded with more self-focus: "I gotta get this thing done or I'm screwed." Younger new adults may do this more often. Teens, of course, do it a whole darn lot. It's part of our maturation process to expand our focus outward as we get older, like ripples in a pond, moving from our immediate social circles outward, from grade school through middle school and high school and then into the big, round world.

Your new adults can also talk in ways that reveal their growing self-awareness, or ability to be cognizant of why they're doing what they're doing. They're still well short of being psychoanalysts, of course, so let them mess up when they try to self-analyze or analyze other characters. Let them talk to others as though they understand the other's motives, perhaps even sounding condescending or judgmental in how they word that analysis, and in the end saying the absolute wrong thing and worsening their problems. After all, when you try to tell other people why they're doing what they're doing without having a fully developed tact filter, the things that tumble out of your mouth can land you in deep doo-doo. With life experience will come increased tactfulness.

All this is not to say that you can't work in more advanced vocabulary than a teen might use; just be measured about it. Your character can sound too old or just plain unnatural if she's spouting fifty-cent words all the time. Even adults don't normally speak with extreme erudition in real life, not during informal conversations, at least. Consider the circumstances of each scene while you're writing it. Your leading lady's vocabulary is likely to improve when her boss is in the room. Her vocabulary will also reveal her energy and mood. I'll talk more about word choice later in this chapter when I get into nitty-gritty sentence crafting techniques. For an extensive look at the new adult mind-set and sculpting your characters' priorities, see Chapter 3, "Crafting a Youthful Yet Sophisticated Voice and Sensibility."

2. COMBINE CHARACTERIZATION
AND CONVERSATION

Who your characters are influences what they say and when they say it. Highly educated, underprivileged, sarcastic, conservative, devil-may-care ... their personalities and their lives before Page 1 of your novel inform the thoughts they think and the words they use to utter them in your book. That's why basic character prewriting work is useful even when you're not an outliner, and why I preceded this dialogue chapter with a chapter on characterization. You should have at least a vague sense of who your character is before you start writing her dialogue. Eventually, it will seem like she's talking on her own, but it's you who sets her mouth in motion.

Hearing directly from characters creates a sense of intimacy, of connection, for readers. In speaking for themselves, the characters reveal things about themselves—often beyond the information they articulate. For instance, they can reveal "facts" about their background, their values, their priorities, their IQ. I'm not talking about delivering facts as info-dumping statements, such as "I went to Miles McKearney High School, which was the poorest school in the whole state." Rather, I'm talking about having your character make comments about things he envies or admires or perhaps finds ridiculous:

> "That guy over there in the preppy vest, we would have eaten him alive at my high school. I'm so done here. C'mon, I need a Bud."

When a character talks about his impressions and reactions, we *feel* his past influencing him as a person rather than hearing it as a biographical fact. This is more of the *showing* instead of *telling* approach that's so crucial to fleshing out a character. Thus, dialogue contributes to characterization even as your characterization influences what your character says.

Your character's personality will play into her way of speaking, too, as will her mood in each scene. A confident character can make statements such as, "Put it in the cauldron," whereas a character lacking self-confidence may frame things as questions: "Put it in the cauldron?" If your character is at the beginning of her book's journey and totally clueless or unwilling to venture a guess at the next action, she might just blurt, "What do I do with this?" You don't have to say a word about her feeling clueless in the narrative now—in fact, doing so and then following with this dialogue will feel like beating your reader over the head with characterization.

Relationships are revealed in dialogue, too. What your characters choose to discuss with each other shows the depth and nature of their relationship. Dialogue that has characters not answering direct questions—practicing "artful dodging"—may indicate a relationship lacking in trust or perhaps clue us in that one person isn't that into the other. If you want to show long-time close friends, you can have them completing each other's sentences or uttering incomplete thoughts that the other character totally understands. Remember to think about every secondary character's relationship to your protagonist when you introduce that character to the story.

Dialogue helps readers get to know the character, but it also helps you get to know them, too. Many authors will "interview" their characters before or during a book as they look for insights. The authors listen to the answers and to the way the character talks back to them, picking up clues just as readers do. Character interviews can also be helpful if you need to work yourself through a rough spot in the story.

3. LINK THEIR DIALOGUE TO THEIR SETTING

Your characters' physical location influences what they say and when they say it, so manipulate your settings with an ear for adding zip and depth to dialogue. When you're choosing a setting for a scene, consider ways you can use that setting to stimulate the gab. For example, you can tell a lot about a person by the words that pass his lips—and nothing gets those words flowing better than a setting that challenges him. Imagine the words of someone you send trudging through brackish swamps in sandals or stumbling through a screen door he didn't see.

The props in your location can provide vital touch points for conversations between characters. Imagine two characters sitting at a café discussing a plan. Since sitting and talking is ho-hum action, you're likely to try to make the spoken words more emphatic or emotional, which burdens the dialogue. That's not fair. Move those characters out of that setting or do something to that environment to give your characters something to do besides look at each other, frown, nod, and laugh while they're there. In the example below, I've moved that discussion out of the café and assigned a prop to the narrative character to give the guy something to focus on besides the emotion I'm trying to convey and the facts he must discuss:

> "So then he told me they come out at sundown and to not be outside after the sun sets," she said. "Jim?"
>
> He jiggled the key. Stupid lock was stuck again.
>
> "Jim."
>
> Goddamn stupid lock, how many times did he have to call the super to get the thing fixed? How had Vinny not been fired yet? He twisted the key, jerking and shoving, then pulling and yanking as the key stuck fast. It popped out abruptly, causing him to fumble it to the floor. What a lazy waste of flesh—
>
> "Jim!"
>
> "Wha—ow." He rubbed his head where he'd banged it on the doorknob picking up the key. "What?"
>
> She held up a new key, its pristine silver glinting next to her pink nail polish.
>
> "Where'd you get that?" he asked.
>
> "I just told you, Vinny was at the meeting. He gave it to me and said don't leave after sunset unless you like being wolf bait. That's not how I plan to go, thank you very much. I plan on getting old and grey and hobbling around with a walker and fifteen grandkids running around my ankles."
>
> The new key turned smoothly in the lock. "I'm not cowering inside all night. The flintlume powder will do its job."
>
> "It didn't for Wexler."
>
> "Wexler didn't add felium. I did. I told you, we're safe."

We get the facts, but more than that, we get a juicy glimpse into this couple's dynamic. I chose to give the male character clipped, impatient dialogue as he tunes out the long-winded girl and gets worked up by that key prop. We'll get into the wonderful power of setting props more fully in Chapter 11.

Social context is part of a story's setting, and it can be as vocally inspiring as location, with your character reacting to changes in the dynamics of her social group or simply talking in jargon that reveals the community or era she grew up in:

- "I suspect the Emperor has other plans for your highness. Severe plans, I dare say."
- "JD's gonna shove that crown you think yer wearing right up yer ass, *princess,* and I'ma help him."
- "Your inciting of the public is not acceptable. There will be an investigation, but I assure you it's merely a formality. You would be wise to prepare for a lengthy imprisonment."
- "Ooh, uh, maybe not the best idea, you know? You might want to, like, take it down a notch?"

If you're receiving critique feedback that your dialogue feels forced or unbelievable, don't automatically start hacking at and repunctuating the words within your quotation marks. Instead, take a gander at the setting and see if tweaking things there can lighten the burden on your dialogue and strengthen the whole conversation in the process.

4. STRIKE A BALANCE BETWEEN THE DIALOGUE AND THE PLOT

Dialogue is an important tool for revealing plot as well as for pushing it forward, but you can't be too literal about those tasks. When you have characters talk about story facts, readers can feel like they're being fed information. As I touched on in No. 3 above, full conversation about plot facts can become a dry, task-oriented lump of an info dump. So what do you do when characters need to talk about the events in their lives and their plans for dealing with them, particularly when you've got a complicated plot? Teach yourself to think of authentic dialogue as reactive rather than as a delivery tool. Have your characters' conversations focus on their reactions to the situation, on their hopes for what they'll be feeling about it after they take action. This way, the characters aren't delivering plot info but rather reacting to that information. To do this, turn the facts into a back-and-forth. For example:

VERSION 1, INFO-LADEN

"We need to put a wagon under that window. I'll fill it with straw so you can jump out of the window into it, and then I'll drive off. Trust me, we'll be gone before they realize you're even out of the room."

VERSION 2, REACTIVE

"See that window?"

"Oh no. Uh-uh. I know what you're thinking."

"It's just a few feet."

"Feet is what I'm thinking of—as in I don't want mine broken."

"I'll fill it with straw. It'll be soft as a pillow."

"That won't—"

"Yes, it will. Trust me, will you? You'll land like a marshmallow on a pillow, and then we'll be gone before they even know you're out of the room. Come on, you know you've always wanted to fly. And I've been looking for a chance to drive me a wagon. Bonnie and Clyde, right here. Me and you. Boom-chaka, baby."

As we see in the example above, dialogue is a powerful way for one character to manipulate another, and for you to manipulate your readers and force them to make judgments, too. Imagine what that wagon example could be after you've added setting and character-revealing action to the narrative beats. What's their body language like? What props are they manipulating? What could those things reveal about the situation and the relationship of these two people?

As the back-and-forth about the wagon demonstrates, being patient with revelations allows those revelations to suffuse the story rather than to smack readers upside the head. The fact that new adults are more patient listeners than they might have been as teens can tempt you to sit two characters down for a backstory discussion, but don't succumb to that temptation. It's just not fun to read scenes like that. Be patient, and reveal in pieces across the scene, the chapter, and the story. Focus on the characters' dynamics, their reactions, their hopes and fears. Those are what drive the plot forward, not simple facts.

Another deliciously patient tactic of revelation is to have a character intentionally withhold information. Your characters may lie, they may dodge questions, they may say one thing while meaning another or thinking another or while they're really talking about something else entirely. There are plenty of reasons a character will refuse direct answers: lack of confidence, having something to hide, playing their cards close to their chest, distrust, uncertainty, avoiding trouble, avoiding commitment, and stalling for time, to name a few. The point is, conversations don't always have to be so direct, with straight answers and head-to-head confrontation. Add interactivity to the scene by making readers figure out what is *not* being said or when what *is* being said is deliberately misleading. When you set up a dynamic where characters are less than forthright with each other, readers have to fill in holes and parse out motives, which is excellent interactive reading.

A fabulous technique for making conversations feel layered and land-mined is subtext. *Subtext* plays a character's words against what he's really thinking, using his behavior to alert readers when his talk contradicts his thoughts or feelings. Subtext is the reality behind the words. We're probably most familiar with it in the context of a villain who talks charmingly as he presses the button that blows up the planet. The villain wants to appear as civil as any refined Good Guy, but his innards are the height of incivility and what he wants can only be accomplished via inhumane behavior. But this clash between saying things to make others believe the opposite of what's in a character's heart, mind, and spirit isn't just for villains. Good guys deliberately say one thing when they think the opposite. From little white lies to active manipulation of other characters for their own ends to protecting themselves from judgment or reprisal, every character can mislead. This makes for fun scenes where characters (and readers) have to parse and guess and eyeball each detail to work out what's what. It's a useful tool for thrillers and mysteries, obviously, but any story can use subtext to stoke tensions between characters and to patiently reveal things to readers about what the character really, super deep down inside, wants and thinks.

5. BRING IT ALL TOGETHER FOR EMOTIONAL RESONANCE

Step-by-step, I've encouraged you to think more about dialogue beyond the obvious words within quotations marks. Tapping into a character's mind-set and sensibility will affect what she chooses to talk about, working in sophistication that reflects her age and stage in life will affect her spoken words, and manipulating the setting and the plot will enrich her dialogue. All of that contributes to one final whiz-bang aspect of dialogue: emotional resonance.

Your characters' emotions influence what they say and when they say it, and those emotions then affect readers' emotions. Emotional resonance is vital to a positive reading experience. Readers want to connect with their characters, and dialogue is a powerful bridge for that connection. Remember that the new adult phase is marked by high sensitivities and emotions. New adults are stressed, and you get to poke at that stress with the pointiest stick you can find. Emotions will be crackling in your story; with their lack of experience, these young people can't brush things off as easily as they might just a few years later in their lives.

I've spoken several times about overburdened dialogue that emotes the hell out of itself. We call that melodramatic dialogue. *Melodrama* is exaggerated emotion, to the point of hokiness, and it makes readers think, *Oh, gimme a break. No one would say that in real life.* Check out this bit of melodrama:

> "I *hate* you! You're a lying, cheating jerk, and I want nothing to do with you *ever*. You deserve to rot in hell!"

Ouch, right? No, not the sentiment—although being wished an eternity in Hades does pack some sting. I mean ouch about the visual assault of italics and exclamation points and the feeling of overwrought writing. That sample line gets the emotion across, sure, but powerful storytelling is more than bludgeoning readers with your message. I'm encouraging you to be a merciless manipulator, not a reader beater.

Instead of resorting to melodramatic dialogue, score emotional resonance by turning all the storytelling elements into a happy team. You're a conductor, really, directing a symphony of storytelling elements for one beautiful composition. The following example incorporates all the things I've talked about, all to score a single, powerful emotional connection with readers:

> "Aren't you thoughtful?" She took the rose he'd handed her and walked to the sink where she kept her vase. Two other roses rested in it, one from the week before, wilting slightly. Both were peach, matching the tight bud in her hand. He loved to give her flowers but dismissed red roses as cliché.
>
> "I stopped by Sue's apartment today," she said, turning on the water, her back to him. "She had a rose on her kitchen table." She reached forward, past the running water, past the vase, to the switch on the wall. Resting her finger on it, she turned and smiled sweetly at him. He'd stopped in the doorway, one glove off, the other dangling from his fingers. He wasn't tugging on it anymore. "A peach rose in a tall vase," she said, "right there next to her violin." She poked the bud's stem into the garbage disposal then flicked the button. The grinder roared as it sucked the flower down, flecks of peach petal flicking free, but he heard her clearly: "You told me you hate musicians."

This woman's pain has penetrated into her soul, settled deep down where it could seethe, finally coming out of her mouth not in a screaming tirade of accusation and condemnation but in quiet statements, the final one making you cringe from the intensity of its delivery. Everything leading up to that final delicate statement, all the action and the facts about the rose color, helps build up the tension for that final statement, which says nothing about the rose but is all about that rose. In fact, this passage focuses on the roses but is about something entirely different: his fidelity. This patient, richer emoting can be sustained for an entire book, whereas a book full of screaming, dish-throwing outbursts gets overwhelming.

TECHNIQUES FOR CRAFTING AUTHENTIC DIALOGUE

Even as you intertwine spoken words and core storytelling elements, you've got glorious mechanical techniques you can apply to the words between the quotations marks to make the dialogue feel realistic, youthful, and emotional. For example, freaked-out, worried, tense characters can use sentence fragments and incomplete thoughts. Impatient characters can interrupt others. Nervous characters may let their dialogue trail off using ellipses, or they may ramble, or they may express their thoughts as questions, as in, "I have to go there? Myself?" High emotions often involve exaggeration, as in, "This always happens" (even if it doesn't really *always* happen). We get to focus on those nitty-gritty techniques now, aiming for dialogue that hits readers' ears as rhythmic and wholly natural. We want readers forgetting that they're *reading* dialogue and instead simply hearing the characters talk. We want them praising your dialogue as "real."

Real. A misleading word when it comes to dialogue, but a popular way for readers to describe dialogue that works. Here's a very important thing to keep in mind as you make your decisions with dialogue: Strong dialogue is not real, it's realistic. Real everyday speech is meandering and sometimes boring and often flat-out incoherent when typed onto a page. Real speech is full of *um*s and *uh*s and *you know*s, and *like*s. It contains run-on sentences that change topic midway, sometimes even multiple times. *Realistic* dialogue strips out the babble and civilities of everyday exchanges. None of the "Hey, what's up?" "Oh, not much. What are you doing?" business, and none of the babbling we do as we think and talk on the fly. Here's real talk, unfiltered:

"He was like—I don't know, I never saw him that way before, you know? All strung out, and, well, just strung out and looking like he couldn't take another thing, you know? It's all just, so, jeez, I don't know, stupid is what it is. Stupid. We gotta get out of this, okay? I mean, like, right this very second, you know? Before he just collapses and then it's all on us because no way do we want this thing on our heads. Let's just take off. Right now. Seriously, just run and be done with it."

Here's the realistic version, streamlined for pacing, clarity, and personality:

"He was totally strung out. There's no way he can handle another thing. We were stupid to get involved in this. Idiots. Let's get out, now, before he collapses and it's all on us. Let's just go."

I've left in repetition for emphasis and to convey desperation and a casual speaking style, but the passage isn't bogged down with verbal ticks that readers would have to filter through. In real-life conversation, your ears may not pick up those things coming from a live person sitting across the table, but on a page, verbal ticks and filler words are distracting. Worse, they bury the heart of what's being said.

Here's the other doozy advice you need to keep in mind as you strategize and craft your realistic dialogue: *Strong dialogue is inseparable from the narrative that surrounds it.* That's been the theme of this chapter, and if I could I'd string it with flashing neon lights right here on the page. I'll have to settle for italicizing the sentence, leaving the neon to your imagination. I'll lead this technical section with a big spotlight on the narrative surrounding your character's spoken words and the tags (the *he said, she said* stuff) that tell us who says what. I'll follow that up with a host of specific techniques to build emotion and tension and create the natural cadence of authentic conversation.

MAKING THE MOST OF NARRATIVE BEATS

I touched on narrative beats earlier in this chapter. They're like the mayo in a ham sandwich—you've got a sandwich without it, but it's a dry one. Narrative beats are essential in a conversation, adding pauses that let the readers breathe and soak in what was just said, even as you set them up for the next line of dialogue. Authors seem to instinctively get this rhythmic use of narrative beats, perhaps because authors tend to be avid readers themselves and so have inter-

WRITING NEW ADULT FICTION

nalized rhythm over their reading lifetime. But too often they fail to realize that these beats are more than rhythmic pauses—they are opportunities to deepen the emotion in the conversation, to reveal things about the character, and to deliver information in interesting ways. Those authors will fill the beat with some generic action like pushing bangs out of eyes or smiling or looking. Readers' eyes slide right over that—opportunity wasted.

Make the action count by inserting revealing action that supports or contributes to the dialogue's meaning or emotion, or that illuminates characters' mood or psyche. In Chapter 3 I talked about the value of using revealing physical actions to embody our characters. Narrative beats are fabulous places to reveal physical details. Don't waste them on blah items like:

> "Reporting for duty, sir," Maven said, pushing his blonde bangs out of his eyes.

Sure, readers love help in picturing the character, but this generic bang-pushing isn't boosting our understanding of Maven's attitude here. That beat could reveal something about Maven's eagerness for duty, making the entire exchange an insight into the dynamic between a hardened warrior leader and his eager (or not) plebe:

> "Reporting for duty, sir," Maven said, blowing his blonde bangs out of his eyes. He should have gotten a haircut before reporting to the commander.

Or:

> "Reporting for duty." Maven's blonde bangs hung in his eyes, and his uniform lay crumpled on the cot. The commander didn't blink. *I'll get Tex back for this.* Maven sighed, straightened his back, slid his feet together, then raised his hand to forehead. "Reporting for duty. Sir."

We know a lot more about that Maven guy now, don't we?

I went further with my second, longer revision of Maven's narrative beat in order to show you how you can use multiple elements within a beat. I included internal dialogue, setting props, and exposition that lays out what's happening with the commander. Don't do this with every beat, because it can get to be too much, and because you can easily interrupt the flow of a conversation.

Instead, vary the length and depth of your beats throughout a conversation to keep it from sounding staccato or choppy. Again, it's about establishing balance through variety.

Sometimes a narrative beat will be simply the dialogue tag that identifies the speaker or just provides the basic rhythmic breather, like "... he said." Note that you don't need dialogue tags as often as you might think. Overuse can make a conversation sound choppy. Sometimes you don't need tags at all. Use them for clarity and rhythm, not automatically.

I want to caution you against filling your narrative beats with adverbs (usually —*ly* words) and clauses that describe how the line of dialogue was delivered, as in:

> "... he said eagerly."
> "... he said, saluting crisply."
> "... he said as he saluted."

If you do the rest of the dialogue work I've outlined in this chapter, you won't need to tell readers that the action was done eagerly because they'll know that from all the other clues. Adverbs can be a sign that you're telling instead of showing, and they can make a piece of writing sound like it's trying too hard to makes its point.

I recommend sticking with the most basic tags to avoid calling attention to them: *said, asked,* and *replied.* Readers register those and thus know who is talking, then move on to the important stuff. Also, don't use tags that are physically impossible. *Hissing* can let us know there's a heavy whisper going on, but if there's no *s* in the words being hissed, you can't hiss them. *Laugh* isn't a speaking verb, and neither is *smiled.* If you want your character to laugh, you can do so once in a while (using that verb often sucks the power out of it, reducing it to unrevealing filler action), but stick it in the narrative beat as an action instead:

> She laughed. "Stop it."

CHOOSING YOUR WORDS AND CONSTRUCTING YOUR SENTENCES

New adults don't construct their sentences so differently than older teens, nor is their vocabulary necessarily much more advanced. It's more that what new adults say shows a more experienced, sophisticated sensibility, making the dialogue sound older. In most circumstances, there's a casual quality to new adult speech, even if that new adult is living in a more formal time or culture. The following techniques inject youthful casualness, many utilizing the underlying strategy of relaxing the grammar.

1. Embrace Run-ons

Constructing complete and proper sentences is hardly at the top of our list when we're chatting with people, so using run-on sentences in your dialogue helps the realistic quality. However, real-life run-ons can be more like run-aways, with people addressing one point at the beginning of the sentence but wandering off to something new mid-sentence, and ending up who knows where by the end. In your dialogue, harness that run-on quality to emphasize your character's point, to rush the pace, and to tweak the rhythm of the conversation, but always keep clarity in mind. Play these run-offs against shorter sentences to give them added oomph:

> "I ran, but he just kept chasing me and so I hid and he still kept coming and, oh my God, Tory, I totally thought I was going to die."

> "It was my first concert, what did I know? I thought, you go to a concert and you listen to music and dance around and hang with friends and maybe get a little high and what's the big deal? Now, here I am, fired. Lovely."

2. Be Repetitive

Run-ons are well served by repetition, where a piece of dialogue circles back on itself to create emphasis. A character who repeats himself signals his priorities to the other characters and to readers:

> "All I wanted was a little help. But no, nobody would give me the time of day even though all they had to do was stop for five seconds. Five seconds was all I needed, and I would have reached her in time. My sister's dead because nobody on this goddamn planet can spare five flipping seconds for a stranger."

The character's obsession with the five seconds shows his frustration by focusing on the timing, even as we get the dramatic punch of a single mention of death—

the very thing you'd think a person would focus on. This character focuses on the five-second delay. For him, life and death is in that five seconds, and readers are aware of that because of the repetition tactic.

3. Trail off, Blurt, and Interrupt

New adults are still developing their tact and may talk without fully thinking things through first. Thus, blurting can give your dialogue a youthful quality. It can also push the story forward as the characters worsen their problems with ill-considered words. Also, they may start to speak, only to have their tact filters kick in halfway through the utterance, in which case they cut themselves short (punctuated by em-dashes: —) or trail off (indicated by ellipses: …). Ellipses also indicate hesitation, and em-dashes can indicated interruption by someone else. All of these add great variety to dialogue and help reveal what a character is thinking or feeling at that moment. Interruptions and cut-offs are also super ways to speed up your pacing. I just caution you not to get too generous with ellipses and em-dashes, as a page filled with dots and horizontal lines is visually distracting. This is yet another "make it count by being judicious" item.

4. Strip Out the Mumble-Jumble

This is about clearing out the minutiae of regular real conversations. We talked about this above when comparing real and realistic. As tempting as it is to fill the dialogue with "like" and "you know," that's distracting to readers. Never sacrifice the content of the dialogue in your quest for authenticity. The same with fillers like *um* and *uh*. Yes, those are useful for showing hesitation, so writers tend to fall back on them. But "falling back" is not powerful storytelling. This takes us back to the writer's toolbox, where you have other ways to convey hesitation that are more flavorful than:

> "You're coming with me, right?"
> "Um … yeah, I guess."

Instead, you can create a narrative pause with a simple beat—a *he said* or *she said* tag, or maybe just a quick action. Or it could be a longer beat that uses the moment to reveal the relationship or the character attitudes, as in this example:

> "You're coming with me, right?"

She glanced at the book in her lap. Her evening could be Romeo and Juliet, or smarmy frat boys looking for a buzz and a babe. Why did Sara always do this to her? She closed the book and heaved herself up. "Let me change, at least."

5. Chill on the Slang

It's tempting to use slang to make characters sound youthful. There are indeed times when a generation's slang may be useful for the overall effect of a story, like one set in the 1970s where the culture of the era is a conspicuous story element, making terms like *groovy* natural vocabulary. Most of the time, however, slang can date your story, and it's likely to sound forced. People may say, "Hey, dude, what's up, man?" or "That's rad" in real life, but in fiction it can come across as trying too hard to sound real. Instead, use phrasing that conveys the sense of super informality that you're reaching for with the slang. For example, "He was totally in my face about it," sounds hip without being heavy-handed.

6. Make Your Swearing Purposeful

You're writing books where explicit sex is fair game, so profanity is certainly allowed. In that regard, you have a lot more leeway than your YA writer counterparts, who have to deal with gatekeepers like parents, teachers, and librarians who hesitate putting books with profanity in their young people's hands. Having that freedom, however, is not reason to fill your fiction with four-letter words. Only swear if swearing is organic to your story and you believe the readers of that particular story would appreciate it. A guy hanging with his frat brothers at a tailgate party would very believably and organically say, while ogling a passing girl, "Nice tits." That said, there's no need to risk alienating readers when you can just as easily skip the cuss words. Yes, people in real life do respond to extreme situations by swearing: "Holy shit!" And yes, people in real life do use swearing as natural emphasis: "I was fucking pissed." But often, this is like using italics for emphasis—that is, you're taking the easy way out and selling your story short in the process. Instead of the "Holy shit!" response to something extreme, how about using setting and body language?

He blinked once, twice, three times. Then, his face a mask of silent fury, he spun and punched his fist through the stained glass window.

Much like carefully timed exclamation points, a carefully timed cuss word can have more dramatic impact than a page full of them. Make sure you're swearing because it's the right thing for that character, at that moment, in that particular story, not because that's the first thing that popped into your head or simply because "real people cuss in real life." Strong dialogue isn't about being real; it's about being realistic and contributing to all the other elements of the story.

CRAFT CLOSE-UP:
MAKING SENSE OF THE VOICES IN YOUR HEAD

Readers want insight into their protagonist's hearts and minds, and internal dialogue can provide that. *Internal dialogue*, also called *interior monologue* and *direct thoughts*, is really dialogue that stops on the tip of the character's tongue. It's often italicized but doesn't have to be. YA fiction tends to italicize direct thoughts, but adult fiction eschews the italics treatment, often requiring the tag "he thought" to make it clear that this is a thought and not a regular part of the narration. NA writers can use either approach, although italics are the style more often than not.

> He pushed back the curtains and peered into the darkness. Ten guards flanked the wooden gate. *It's over.* There was no way he'd get past ten guards, not without any weapons.

> He pushed back the curtains and peered into the darkness. Ten guards flanked the wooden gate. *It's over*, he thought. There was no way he'd get past ten guards, not without any weapons.

> I pulled back the curtains. It was dark, but I could make out ten guards, five on either side of the gate. *It's over.* There was no way I'd get past ten guards.

If you choose to italicize internal thought, you don't need a dialogue tag. You do need to write internal dialogue in present tense, just like regular dialogue.

Make sure your internal dialogue truly sounds like a snippet of dialogue that's bitten back just before utterance. Sometimes writers will set a first-person narrator's mental mulling in italics as a direct thought when actually those are *indirect thoughts* and should be treated just like any other piece of narrative. For example:

> I pulled back the curtains. It was dark, but I could make out ten guards, five on either side of the gate. *It's over. There's no way I can get past ten guards, not without any weapons.*

Incorporate mullings or narrative observations into the regular narrative. Save the italics for true internal dialogue so you don't bog down your pages with passages of italicized text:

> I pulled back the curtains. It was dark, but I could make out ten guards, five on either side of the gate. There was no way I could get past ten guards. It was over.

Some writers rely too much on internal thoughts to convey plot information or to pose hypothetical questions meant to force readers to ask those questions, as in, *I wonder what he's thinking? Could he be after my money? Or am I just another notch on his bedpost?* A string of italicized hypothetical questions can make an otherwise strong narration feel forced. It seems to scream, "Pay attention to me. I'm going to ask the questions I want you to be asking yourself, reader." The subtlety of making a reader wonder things gives way to you feeding the questions to readers. If you're writing in third-person point of view, you can easily work this into the regular narrative. Or just trust that the reader is already wondering those things because you've used all the techniques and strategies in your writer's toolbox to push the story to the brink of those questions.

If you've chosen first person for your story, you probably won't have a lot of internal dialogue because the whole narrative is being presented as the narrator's thoughts. Your narrative is already one big insight into the protagonist's heart and mind.

CHAPTER 6

Strategizing an NA Storyline That's Fresh and Wholly You

*N*ew Adult fiction is more than young people dealing with life and love in the dorms. Forty percent of Americans don't head to college straight from high school. Some join the work force or the military, some start families early (by choice or surprise), some live on their own for the first time ever while others shack up with roommates or stick around their parents' house, and still others take a gap year to "find themselves," with any adventure anywhere on Earth being fair game to them. Depending on genre, fictional new adults may be forced into the family horse-and-buggy business as revolution brews, or flee conscription by the interstellar bombardiers on their eighteenth birthday, or trade in their Gucci briefcase for a glass shiv and then chase zombies through nightclubs where oblivious peers twerk with daemons in disguise. There's an infinite range of circumstances through which NA writers can explore the minds and hearts of young people learning what it is to live self-responsible lives.

The common thread is the notion that these eighteen- to twenty-five-year-olds are in an in-between time, being officially adults but still finding their way, separating from parents (or notably not) and searching for love and life purpose as they overcome significant challenges on their own. For most of them, this will be the least structured phase of their lives, and with so many opportunities for big successes and big failures due to that free rein, they exist in a state of imbalance. While that makes these young people spectacularly flexible in the face of adversity and thus strong heroes for our stories, it also makes them easy to totter over. And we writers say, "Booyah for that!"

You can use your knowledge of new adult tendencies to push your tottery yet earnest protagonists into delicious mishap. This is the beginning of my focus on developing NA plots that feel like they really could happen to people of this age. The next three chapters will push you deeper into the specifics of your plot; first you'll build your story framework, and then you'll pace your conflicts for an irresistible read. Here, I point out universal new adult concerns and behaviors to help you come up with strategies for making your protagonist jump through hoops of your design. Whether those hoops are big or small, striped or on fire, is up to you—this is about creating fresh storylines from a universal phase of life.

FINDING "FRESH" IN THE UNIVERSAL

Every writer should know their audience's general expectations about the stories, characters, and themes in that category or genre. Being aware of that doesn't doom all writers in a group to writing the same basic thing about the same basic set of characters. Creativity doesn't work like that. What makes each story of, say, first love special is its unique cast, the characters' circumstances, and the light that the protagonist's emotional and psychological journeys shed on the experience of falling in love.

Tapping into universal experiences and perspectives makes stories relatable to a particular *readership*, while the specific details of each story make each novel appeal to particular *readers*. Writers are creative people, and creative people resist constraints on their creativity. Knowing your audience's traits and hot buttons means knowing what's important to them, an insight that will help you write a novel that resonates with your readers no matter what details you fill it with.

And hey, wasn't the whole New Adult fiction revolution about creating something new? The established publishing engine had said no one wanted to read stories about post-teens/pre-adults, and so no one could sell them. NA writers wrote the stories anyway. NA writers sold the stories anyway. NA writers found their readers all by themselves. What a bunch of rule-breakers! I urge you to continue defying the rules as you work to roll out your plot.

FIND THE "FRESH" IN SITUATIONS AND SPACES

It's hard to be excited about an event in a novel when you feel like you've read that event in plenty of other books. Cliché plot events are an easy pit to fall into when writers are trying to get to the next plot step with their characters. Getting to the next step is not a reason to include an event; you're not check-boxing your way to the end of your story. Do you need your fictional lovers to meet so you can get into their romance? You *could* bump them into each other in a classroom doorway since new adults commonly meet their loves on campus ... but other writers have done that well and thoroughly already. Don't just plug in any old thing so you can get to the good stuff—make *this* the good stuff. Even small events should be fresh. Look at the specifics of your characters' personalities and plights, then bring your couple together in a way that is related to their common interests—or perhaps their conflicting interests. Your new adult lovers could still meet on campus but in side-by-side empty parking spaces, for example, each flabbergasted that their car has been towed. That opens up more possibilities for unique follow-up scenes than the bump-and-meet scenario: Instead of writing about characters returning mixed-up items after a regular bump-and-meet, your parking structure characters could end up sharing a rental car that could then become a place of conflict when they have to carpool after a fight. They could wind up having their most personal talks in that car, turning it into a useful device throughout the book.

Choose uncommon settings, or present common settings in an uncommon way. How about those NA lovers who meet in the apartment complex laundry room, a believable gathering place in a big complex but also an expected one? Why not have your fella roll a bowling ball down the apartment hallway and almost crush the gal's sandaled toes when she steps out of the elevator? That gives you a very distinct and memorable meet-up. And now the coffee date that would predictably follow could be a silly-fun bowling date that ends with the girl defending herself against zombies in the back alley with a bowling pin. By introducing unique elements into your story, you create opportunities for a story subculture. Your characters could reference that bowling ball episode later in the book, perhaps injecting a moment of levity into their otherwise dark fight against sinister creatures, which is a wonderful way to keep the emotional bond going between characters in a high-action plot. Perhaps that bowling skill will factor into the climax of the book when our hero bowls a grenade into a crowd of zombies and saves the day. Putting a fresh spin on common NA situations and environments can domino your plot in invigorating ways.

FIND THE "FRESH" IN CHARACTER CHOICES

Even as we move characters around and throw different circumstances their way, we also have them make choices. They must judge, act, and react to every plot point we put in their path. The new adult mind-set comes into play with that, big time. New adults are still relatively inexperienced, so they have a handicap in the decision-making department. And their life is an unstable one with all their changes swirling about them, so they're trying to make decisions among instability and no real knowledge of what their future holds. Add in your fresh situations and settings along with the unique set of variables you chose for this story and you've got immense opportunity for a story that feels both wholly NA and wholly fresh.

TACTICS FOR MINING THE NA EXPERIENCE FOR YOUR PLOT

So let's get specific about how you can bring these juicy insights about new adults to bear on your storyline. I'm going to list some ways to actively manipulate your characters using these insights; they'll work whether you're writing a contemporary story, historical, speculative, thriller, or whatever.

TORPEDO HEIGHTENED EXPECTATIONS WITH HARSH REALITY

Teens fantasize about running their own shows; new adults get to live that fantasy. Or rather, they try to. The problem is, fantasies can lead to high expectations, and when reality falls short, the thud can be devastating. There's stress in that clash between expectations and reality, and we writers know what a stressed-out protagonist means: conflict with others. Excellent! Stress also leads to flawed decision-making. Even more excellent. Bad decisions lead to more conflict and more bad decisions and so on. Most excellent, indeed. You can wield this NA-tendency toward inflated expectations a million different ways in your plot. Your only limit is your imagination. Example: A high-achieving high school graduate expects to sail through her first college economics class but finds her class filled with high achievers from other high schools who raise the grading curve to the moon. *Stress*. Another example: A college intern who expects to zip through the internship and land a coveted opening position with the company doesn't anticipate the viciousness of competition inside that company. *Stress*.

MAKE MONEY AN ISSUE

My eight-year-old son recently asked me, "Mommy, why do people care so much about money?" Oh, child. Would that we could all stay innocent of money woes forever. But the truth is, money matters. When you've got it, it matters; when you haven't got it, it matters. Financial stress can be a whopper, especially when you're new to financial independence. That paycheck of yours takes on a whole new meaning. Your job just got way more important.

---

*"In YA the characters may be working at Starbucks for extra pocket money, whereas NA characters have to make money to survive, so the stresses on the characters are much greater. They can't just blow it off." —***STACEY DONAGHY***,* Agent, Donaghy Literary Group

---

You can crank up your character's problems and stress level by manipulating his bank account. Does the guy need to buy tools to reach his goal? Don't let him. Empty his wallet and force him to improvise. In a science fiction book, you could deny him the resources to own the technology he needs to overcome the government's oppressive Neural Net. What would he do then? Would he have to break into a facility to get the equipment and risk being caught? What about that guy who can't afford the tux he needs for his new girl's sorority Spring Ball? What's he willing to do to get the dinero? Does he admit it to his new sweetie? In Chapter 2, I wrote a sample hook about a college boy who must live homeless for six months in order to get his inheritance. Money sure matters to that guy.

Likely for the first time in their lives, new adults are having to come up with their own money. Your financial decisions for these young people matter to your storyline. In your story, consider how much Mom and Dad are capable of and willing to help out, and if your protagonist is even willing to ask them or take what they offer. It's a tricky business, this financial independence. In what fabulous ways can it impact your storyline?

MAKE YOUR PROTAGONIST QUESTION HER SELF-RELIANCE

Your new adult character craved independence, but now that she has it, can she handle it? She's got to identify her own needs and problems, devise her own workable plan of action, then set about executing that plan herself. If Mom and Dad are around to help, they're pretty much removed, emotionally or otherwise. Or perhaps your character still wants to be independent even when she can't actually see any way out. There's a fantastic push and pull as the reality of shouldering the burden for your life sets in. You can work the issue of self-reliance into your storyline to force your character into actions and situations she finds uncomfortable. *Stressful.* You may even have her give up in a scene or at least consider the option. We all have those days when we want to throw in the towel and go all fetal under our kitchen tables with our thumbs in our mouths. What will your character do to pull herself out of that tailspin so she can confront the external problem? You can exacerbate this stress by contrasting a beleaguered protagonist with peers who seem to have it all going on. See Chapter 4 for ways to use parents, pals, and adversaries to undermine the protagonist's efforts at problem solving.

DENY THEM THE "IDEAL" NA LIFE

Kit-and-caboodle with new adults' tendency toward high expectations is their idealization of life after high school. The college years are their time to party and sow their oats and find out who they are and what they want to do, everybody knows that. To some degree, most new adults think this, and studies show that most of American society is willing to indulge them. If this mind-set sounds like your character, push his buttons by forcing him into a structured position that requires accountability and no time to party hearty. He'll chafe at that. Then make him feel worse by surrounding him with characters who get to live that carefree life. How will he react? What will he do? This tactic can help you goose your character into actions he'd otherwise not take, which is always a great way to cause conflict and worsen problems in your plot. Deny him what he wants, and then revel in the actions he takes as a result.

THREATEN PARENTAL INPUT— OR YANK IT AWAY

Parents can be an important factor in new adults' lives, particularly those who are still fresh out of high school. Your protagonist can be desperate to go it alone, and keeping the parents in the picture can totally stress her out. Sylvia Day's *Bared to You*, the first book in the Crossfire series, stars a rich girl who tries to live her own life but whose mom can't let go. Mother even traces Daughter's cell phone to monitor where she goes at night. This is a serious struggle for the young woman. Carrie Vaughn's supernatural *After the Golden Age* stars a very green forensic accountant who happens to be the "normal" daughter of the world's most super superheroes—which makes her a repeated target for kidnappers. The bad guys nab her to strike at her parents. She struggles to live a life out of her parents' shadow, without their help at all and without the label of being their daughter. In this process, she consciously rejects the sarcastic, rebellious impulses she'd felt during her teen years and now strives to rise above rebellion and instead focus on embracing her life. This is a phase of NA identity establishment. For your storyline, you can threaten your character with parental input to push your story along.

Conversely, young characters who "fail to launch" need a little kick in the tush in order to recognize their strengths and then engage them. Give 'em that kick by having the parents refuse to step in. Send the parents on vacation to Tahiti if you have to, or have your aliens blow up Mom and Dad's house with the parental units inside. Summer Lane's *State of Chaos* separates her protagonist from her father with a man-made apocalyptic event, forcing the young woman to do what she thinks her father would do if he were there. Heroine-in-the-making that she is, the protagonist strives to muster survival skills her father had taught her even as she deals with the emotional uncertainties of her new reality.

You can use parental issues in your storyline, woven with whatever details work for your character's situation and goals.

ROCK THEIR STABILITY

I swear, new adult characters are just asking for this: Just when your young protagonist thinks she's mastered or solved something, muck it up. Do not let her ever get on solid ground. This is a tactic for all fiction writers, regardless of the age of the protagonists, but it's especially suited to your NA fiction because these characters are in such a hypersensitive, unstable state.

"With New Adult, I can explore adult situations with adult responsibilities yet still capture the heightened emotions and experience that you still have when you're nineteen, twenty, twenty-one."—**JENNIFER L. ARMENTROUT**, writing as J. Lynn, author of the Wait for You series

---

FORCE THEM TO REJECT OR ACCEPT CHILDHOOD

For the first eighteenish years of our lives, we're defined by our family situation and the fallout from our parents' decisions. The high school years have us chafing against such imposition, spawning all that teen rebellion we know and love. New adults get to leave those definitions behind and start with a totally blank slate. At least, that's how their slate looks to the new people they meet. Inside, the new adult still lugs baggage. You can put your characters in situations that force them to confront what they're lugging around and then actively reject or accept it. This is a great opportunity for personal revelations that are fresh and totally unique to your character.

WORK THEM THROUGH THE SCARS OF A TOUGH TEEN EXPERIENCE

Some of that post-high school graduation "baggage" may have to do with traumas survived but not resolved. The new adult phase is marked by the beginnings of wisdom attainment, which is knowledge and maturity gained through experience. You can harness this NA quality in your story by having your character start to understand that survival is more than just living through something—it goes deeper as you mentally, psychologically, and emotionally deal with and overcome that trauma. In Jennifer L. Armentrout's novel *Wait for You* (written under the name J. Lynn), a nineteen-year-old girl thinks that by moving away to college in a new state she has removed herself from the traumatic high school bullying she'd suffered after she'd spoken out about a sexual attack. But moving to college is only a physical action; she needs to heal emotionally and psychologically. Living through the experience and moving away were about survival, while finally dealing with it is about healing and moving on. That's a mature journey, and it's perfect for NA fiction.

INFLUENCE THEM WITH RISK-TAKING BEHAVIOR AND (YES, STILL) PEER PRESSURE

Remember what I said in Chapter 3 about the prefrontal cortex not being fully developed until age twenty-five? That's the part of the brain that helps us inhibit impulses, that helps us plan and organize our behavior to reach a goal, and that's in charge of our reward system. This means teens and emerging adults are hyper-interested in risk-taking situations, with their bold selves hoping there's something to be gained from those situations. Yup, that'll sure affect what they do in your plot.

But wait, that beautiful blooming brain keeps on giving! One of the side effects of that wonked-out reward system is that these young people are still highly sensitive to peer pressure, certainly more so than they will be as adults. So that peer pressure stuff we love in our YA lit is *still* sloshing around in the NA brain. My dear fiction writer, can you spell G-I-F-T H-O-R-S-E?

This is all exacerbated by our culture's willingness to accept the college years as the time to indulge oneself and experiment. This is the peak phase for indulging in many "bad" behaviors like binge drinking, drug use, and risky sexual behavior. You can tap into this in any number of ways for your plot. Throw in opportunities for characters to get into trouble. Determine your character's particular temptations, let him indulge, then have him suffer the consequences. Do throw some friends into the mix, too, letting them egg on your protagonist either actively or just by their presence. That prefrontal mushiness that makes peer pressure a lingering factor comes into play here: a twenty-year-old may be more likely to engage in risky behavior if a couple of friends are watching than if he were alone. Take advantage of this element of the new adult experience with your fresh situations, physical places, and character choices.

EXPLORE MENTAL ISSUES

Sadly, this is also an age range in which many mental issues are triggered or come to the forefront amid the stresses. Mental illness can be an important theme in a novel, and it contributes to conflict and impacts both the internal and external journeys of characters. With crossover readers often looking for escapism in NA fare, mental illness may not top their list of desirable problems for protagonists, but as NA fiction expands, the number of darker, issue-driven stories may rise. YA fiction has embraced mental and social issues as a solid part of its rich literary landscape; perhaps you will choose that direction with your NA fiction. It's an option, if not for your protagonist, then for the people in her life who she may have to support with her newfound strengths and wisdom.

USE THEIR HEIGHTENED EMOTIONS AGAINST THEM

Teens are known for their exaggerated reactions to things—their "teen melodrama." New adults still have a lot of that all-or-nothing in them, the difference being that they're starting to wizen to it and temper it. The words *starting to* in that last sentence are your open door: Set up circumstances in your story that will stress them out, and then let them have that meltdown that they are trying so maturely to avoid. If you build up the tension through events over a period of time, this meltdown will be earned and thus not feel overwrought but rather inevitable. This is a great tool to employ with your climactic event, when you bring outside events and internal emotions to a head at the same time and force your character's epiphany, which will lead to one final push and the resolution of their problem. (More on *climax, epiphany, final push*, and *resolution* in the next chapter.)

EMBRACE THE COMPLICATIONS OF FORGING A NEW SOCIAL CIRCLE

Another aspect of NA instability and stress comes from the need to establish new social circles. Most new adults move out of the social circles that defined and structured their teen years, and they've cut the apron strings (or are in the process of doing so), so there's major room for you to manipulate your character by manipulating her social circle and all the relationships, activities, and self-discovery that goes with socialization. Embrace that and make it yours.

GO BIG ON LOVE

Love is a big part of NA storylines; your task is to make it feel fresh in your book. New adult romantic relationships aren't like those of high school, and they're not like adult relationships. New adults aren't ready to look for Mr. or Miss Right, but they are very interested in being in a loving relationship, and part of that is learning what they want and need in a relationship in the first place. Chapter 10 explores ways to keep this universal NA item fresh in your story.

BRING ON THE SEX

Sex is a common part of new adults' identity explorations. Who are they as sexual beings? What are they looking for in a partner? Where do they fit into the cultural spectrum of sexual practices? You have lots of room to explore this with NA characters. Chapter 10 focuses on love and sex in New Adult fiction—the tools of it, the graphics of it, and the plot versus subplot of it. Besides the issue of how explicit to get with your sex scenes, there are situational opportunities here: betrayal, one night stands versus committed relationships, matching the experimentalism of your partner, pregnancy scares, the risk of AIDS. (Note that other sexually transmitted diseases seem to be reader turn-offs.) Sexuality and acts of sex are universal NA elements that you can incorporate into your storyline, with the particular circumstances of your couple's sexual relationship being wholly yours.

PLAY MUSICAL CAREERS AND HOMES

It's common for new adults to change living situations frequently, from dorms to apartments to houses to moving in with boyfriends and out again. That contributes to the instability of this phase. It also gets into their independence issues as they have the freedom to just up and leave. As they become able to afford better living conditions, their financial independence comes into play, too. You can use this nomadic quality in your storyline to great and varied affect. It's physical movement, but it taps into emotional and psychological journeys as well.

Similarly, there's a lot of job-hopping in the new adult phase as young people work short-term jobs to pay the bills, enroll in internships with their eyes on future careers, and then embark on the early years of a new career after college. Best-selling author Alice Clayton's *Wallbanger* features a young woman moving into a new apartment and working in a new career. The main character's besties are also new to their careers; one is a professional organizer who'd driven her friends crazy during college with her "OCD tendencies" and so they suggested she go pro with her organizing. This reflects another aspect of the identity exploration that marks the new adult phase: young people exploring their interests and discovering things about themselves that they believe they can channel into a satisfying career. Whether that belief is a high expectation to be torpedoed by reality in your book is up to you.

EMPOWER YOUR NEW ADULT

Because conflict and problems drive a plot forward, we tend to concentrate on how these young people can get overwhelmed or wrong-headed. Ultimately, though, we need them to triumph. Go ahead and give your protagonist some victories, or give victories to your secondary characters so that readers can see that young people (with whom they relate) are strong and capable and resilient.

As with teen fiction, you need to keep the older adults—even the meddlesome ones—out of the final resolution. Work your plot so that your lead character gets to solve the problem herself. Along the way, build a foundation for her salvation by incorporating scenes that reveal her strengths in action. We don't want to feel like the ability to win has come out of left field just when she needs it. The specific details of her strengths and victories are totally up to you. Strive to keep them unexpected.

CHAPTER 7

Structuring a Satisfying Storyline

*Y*our primary task as a novelist for this passionate audience is to serve up a satisfying read about characters living and struggling during the new adult phase of life. *Satisfying.* I want to slather that word in glue, sprinkle it with glitter, then climb onto a stepstool and hang it above your writing desk with fishing line and a thumbtack. Satisfied readers are happy, loyal, vocal, returning readers, and that's a darned satisfying goal for any storyteller.

Reader satisfaction comes when a story reaches into the reader and engages her emotions, getting her *feeling* and *worrying* and just overall *needing*. Needing to know. Needing to cry for victims. Needing to scream at bad guys. Needing the hero to triumph. You as the storyteller *need* to structure a storyline that'll engage those emotions and swell them—deliberately and with vicious relentlessness—until the need is so strong that when it's finally met, the reader sighs in satisfaction. You're orchestrating an emotional reaction with your fiction.

This chapter helps you structure a purposeful, logical, escalating string of events—a *plot*, also called the *storyline*—that'll push your character through the personal journey you so desperately want her to have. The next chapter will get into crafting the individual pieces of the plot, like riveting openings and effective flashbacks; for now, let's wrap our heads around your fiction's overall structure.

WHAT PANTS AND PROMISES HAVE TO DO WITH PLOTTING

I purposely left out all reference to the word *outlining* in my introduction to this chapter. I advocate neither for nor against outlining your story before you write it. Every writer—and in fact, every story—has a unique creative process, and I respect that. I do, though, see great value in formulating a clear vision for your novel's overall progression through the character's two arcs, the internal and the external, no matter your creative process. Remember, the *internal journey* is the character's emotional or psychological progression from a place of need to a place of attainment. So if your protagonist started the story needing a sense of family, he'd end the story with a sense of belonging in a social circle that functions as family to him, such as a fraternity or a coven of warlocks. The *external journey* is the progression from a problem to the resolution of that problem, but with the caveat that what happens in that external journey helps the character attain his internal need.

A satisfying story has a sense of rhythm and escalation, and being aware of your place in that escalation as you write allows you to make decisions about what to include and when to include it. For example, sometimes you need to give the reader a breath, a sort of rhythmic pause in the action that doesn't bring your momentum to a screeching halt. Understanding your story's overall structure helps you time those breathers. Whether you're an outliner or a fly-by-the-seat-of-your-pants-er, you've got to make decisions about events in your story, and that's where knowing your overall structure comes in.

As we move into working out your story's structure, do so with two promises tucked firmly into your pocket:

1. You will strive to provoke with your plot.
2. You will strive to create fear with your plot.

PROVOKED CHARACTERS *DO* STUFF

The sequence of events you unleash on your character, whether due to your advance design or your in-the-trenches discovery, should present serious challenges for your character, forcing her into action. A calm, easy life with Leading Lady passively cruising through her new relationship is hardly a riveting read.

Promise yourself that your story events will always provoke your protagonist into action or reaction. Make her so uncomfortable that she starts doing things without fully thinking through their consequences—action should worsen fictional situations before it improves them. Chapter 9 is all about increasing the conflict and tension in your story so that your readers feel a tangible sense of escalation. At this point, deciding on a series of provocative plot moments gives both pantsers and outliners something to aim for.

FEARFUL CHARACTERS DO ILL-CONSIDERED STUFF

As you envision a series of provocative moments in your storyline, don't just think about events that'll add conflict—think about events that'll endanger things your protagonist holds dear. Fear is a stunning motivator. Put big things at stake and make failure truly untenable. *Hey new adult character, you don't think failing Astronomy 101 is bad? Okay ... but if you flunk this class, you flunk out and lose your inheritance and your parents will disown you and you'll be living on the streets using twigs to scrape Panda Express noodles off trashed Red Cups.* Or, *Can't keep up life on the run with mobsters and Tommy guns around every corner? Fine, stop and take that bullet through the temple already.* Scare the daylights out of your protagonist and your readers; mirror new adults' high expectations for success with overly dramatic fears when failure seems imminent. Truly make them feel that failure is not an option even as they don't see a way out. Risk affects character connection and tension. Risk makes students who fear *F*s hire hot-but-arrogant tutors. Risk makes the hunted run until they can devise ways to end the hunt without a bullet to the brain, impressing readers with their bravery and ingeniousness. Raise the stakes in your NA fiction. Force your characters to act, to reveal, and to discover by letting them know you'll make them suffer if they don't deal with what you throw at them.

STORY STRUCTURE: SEVEN STEPS OF ESCALATION

Every event in your plot should contribute to pushing your character further along on her journey from a place of need to a place of attainment. I'm going to lay out a seven-part structure for accomplishing that in your fiction. Basically, you will write a list of key story moments you need to hit and then let the rest of the story reveal itself as you write it or outline it in full with the storytelling pieces I'll cover in the next chapter.

This isn't some cookie-cutter Formula for a Novel. Rather, these steps are a guide for shaping and pacing your plot. By moving through each step, you can roll out a plot that gains a palpable sense of escalation with each new incident until, finally, things come to a head. Tangents can be avoided, as can those scenes that kill the momentum because, as swell as they might seem in isolation, they don't contribute to the relentless pushing, pushing, pushing you'll be doing with that protagonist of yours.

The common thread with most story structuring methods is that the beginning of the novel presents the conflict and goal, the middle is where the story plays out to a climax with the stakes and tension rising along the way, and the end is where the conflict is resolved, the problem overcome, and the goal attained in some form or another. You can realize both arcs this way, at a strong pace. I lay out the steps in worksheet fashion at the end of the chapter; you can use that to work through this process with your story.

1. UNVEIL INTERNAL AND EXTERNAL GOALS WORTH STRIVING FOR

This first step is about orienting yourself and your reader. Your hook-writing work (see Chapter 2) is going to pay off now as you reveal to your readers what your character wants more than anything else and hang it dangling out there like a big ol' carrot. This is your goal as much as your protagonist's, as everything you include in the plot exists to move this character along toward that big Want. If what he really needs is different from what he consciously wants, you can hint at that juicy disjunction, too.

If you haven't already spent time crawling inside the head and heart of your new adult protagonist, pop back to Chapter 4 and start poking around. You need to know what your Good Guy wants the most (and what he *needs* the most, if that differs from what he consciously wants), and what strengths and weaknesses he will bring to bear in his struggle to attain his Want. You need to know what will motivate him to jump through the hoops you're about to hold up for him.

2. REVEAL THE PRIMARY PROBLEM

This is when you let readers know what's going to happen in the external story arc—in the plot events—that your character will concentrate on as he undergoes his internal transformation. This usually happens concurrently with Step 1, although it'll likely be more overt.

Regardless of formal ordering, this is the moment in the story where you present the chief obstacle, or *conflict*, that will stand in the way of your character's attainment of his want. He's got to battle something. A complicated plot may throw lots of little conflicts at the protagonist, but there will be one primary conflict that must be confronted in some kind of a final showdown.

Aim to reveal your big problem in the first or second chapters. The sooner, the better, so that readers can get caught up in the need to overcome that problem right away. You can withhold details about it, but we must know the general problem that'll be plaguing your protagonist up front.

3. UNLEASH AN EFFECTIVE CATALYST

The *catalyst* is the event that sets the main story in motion, and it's best if you get to it in the first chapter, certainly by the second. This may be when Leading Lady finds out that Hot Guy is her new advertising agency's biggest client and he just requested that she be added to his account team, as happens with the handsome Gideon Cross in Sylvia Day's *Bared to You*. Or it may be when Leading Lady ejects from the spaceship just hours before she's to be forcibly married, as in the first pages of Aubrie Dionne's science fiction novel *Paradise 21: A New Dawn*. In Markus Zusak's *I Am the Messenger*, the catalyst is the appearance of a letter in the protagonist's mailbox instructing him to accomplish a mission. Hot Guy strikes, the escape pod is launched, the mission is assigned, the catalysts are delivered. Game on!

4. PUMMEL YOUR PROTAGONIST

Now that the catalyst has set your character in motion, you'll keep throwing new problems at your character until he gets to his breaking point. This is the bulk of your book. Prolific, award-winning YA novelist Jean Ferris articulated this process to me years ago as throwing rocks at her protagonist. She'd use the catalyst to chase her lead character up a tree, and then she'd throw a succession of rocks, one bigger than the next, at that character. Would the character dodge the rocks? Would the rocks hit her? Knock her off? Would she finally catch one and throw it back? Would she climb back down that tree, bruised but triumphant?

Traditional storytelling calls for three obstacles, including the catalyst, before the character finally makes a final push to overcome the biggest hurdle yet (in the *climax*). New Adult fiction seems to stick to this convention—although this upstart category exhibits a willingness to dispense with "convention" when its writers and readers see appeal in doing so, so you have room to experiment with that number. Each problem that you throw at your character will force her to take action, even if that action is to run away. If you feel like she's running too often, you need to raise the stakes on her. Remember your promises to provoke and stoke fear? Make it clear to her that she'll really suffer if she doesn't react strongly enough to what you're serving up. You may need to come up with a bigger conflict or put more in jeopardy, at which time things should really get rockin'. Characters pushed to places of discomfort and fear reveal things about themselves, discover things about themselves, and decide things about themselves. Push for that emotional escalation with each of your obstacles.

This is when you'll start maneuvering your subplot, if you've got one. You'll find more on managing subplots later in this chapter.

You can (and in most cases should) work in some *brief* pauses between the obstacles. Tension is good, but stories have rhythms, and it's nice for readers to catch their breath now and then. You'll be letting your character try to collect herself now, too. Of course, she *won't* collect herself, not totally. You'll make sure of that by slamming her with some new and worse problem. Imagine a quiet moment in the countryside where she feels like she's gathering her strength, or maybe she's having a comforting cry on a roommate's shoulder in their cozy city loft. Perhaps you'll give your character a lovely date with her cute guy in the middle of a tumultuous relationship, where she thinks, *Okay, this relationship is doable and we really can be happy.* She gets a wee victory. But then you rip that rug out from under the gal with another big problem that truly batters the hope she was starting to feel. Each fall will be that much more painful thanks to that little bit of hope you allowed her. Escalation!

At the end of the third obstacle, things should look hopeless for your protagonist. This is a big moment with lots of tension since the problem still exists and, in fact, is almost unbearable. We don't see how things can possibly work out well. Will the character finally break?

5. DELIVER THE INEVITABLE EPIPHANY

Alright, we've been abusing the protagonist long enough. It's now time to let her either realize what her flaw is or have it exposed to her. Either way, she realizes her big weakness and realizes that she has a strength and that she has it in her to give this whole thing one last big *go*. This is the end of the Middle.

I use *epiphany* because that's what this plot moment is traditionally called, but the word is a bit misleading because it implies some *sudden* awareness or insight. Your epiphany should not come out of the blue. That's not fair. That's the author pulling a rabbit out of her hat at just the right moment when the reader didn't even know there was a hat around. The epiphany must be an organic step in the story, something you've been building up to as you showed readers that this character has some key strengths inside her. She may not have been aware of this strength, and you may not have explicitly revealed it, but you'll have *shown* it to us in many scenes throughout the book as the character moves through her life. She has always had the potential to be the heroine. That's why I call it an "inevitable" epiphany. You'll have built up to it and thus earned it.

The new awareness usually happens when a character thinks something through to the point that she has a new vision of the possibilities, of her abilities, of what's important. Maybe she realizes she was going about this problem the wrong way, that she should follow the example of someone she respects. Or maybe she finally questions whether she's been striving for the right thing all this time. Maybe what she wanted is very different from what she *needed*—and she now realizes she wants what it is she needed from the beginning. Regardless of the approach you use, this awareness will come after you've put your character through the wringer and she just can't keep going on the path she was headed. She needs to change, and change is the ultimate goal of all character arcs.

6. MAKE A FINAL PUSH THAT EMPOWERS

The Final Showdown can come in any number of forms that all share something very important: The protagonist is empowered with the action. She may have some help, as in a faerie's quest with a team of travelers, but she's the leading spirit of the effort and the one who will strike the fatal blow. The character figures out how to overcome her flaw (or harness it and turn it into a strength) and how to employ her strength to make one final effort that overcomes the biggest obstacle. The conflict is most intense here, as is the scary potential for loss, and the protagonist is at her most empowered. It's do or die time. By now the story may even feel out of your hands as the protagonist digs in to control her own fate.

This is where *internal logic* matters, big time. You need to set up the epiphany and final push with a strong foundation. You can't be pulling that bunny out of your hat. This is the culmination of your character's internal arc as well as your external plot arc, so we have to have seen this strength in the character throughout the novel even if she didn't see it herself. Heck, she might've viewed it as a flaw! What we saw as confidence in her, she may have seen as unattractive pushiness. But by now she's learned how to be smart about this trait, how to be tactful, how to allow others to shine even as she runs the show—and you've used the "Show, don't tell" tactics we've talked about in Chapter 4 and throughout this book to show this. Her growth will show in this final push and will be what overcomes the Biggest Obstacle.

7. TRIUMPH!

The character resolves the problem. This is when she gets the Want, when her internal and external arcs dovetail, as do any subplots. The *denouement*—the winding down of events, where you tie up all the loose threads—is in here, too. This may be just a single chapter; it's not likely to be much more because at this point the reader is done. Close up shop and move away with a satisfying final scene. *Satisfying.* Our glittery goal for our readers.

Of course, if this novel is a volume in a series, then you're going to leave at least one major thread hanging in this step. That thread will *not* be the main external arc of this book, but rather the series arc. Every series has an arc that won't be finished until the last book, while each volume in the story has its own self-contained adventure or episode in that series that needs to feel complete. (I break down series strategies in Chapter 2.)

STITCHING SUBPLOTS INTO YOUR STRUCTURE

How do subplots figure into all this? In a nutshell, you include subplots to illuminate, or in some way serve, your main storyline. You do not include subplots because there's this extra little thing you think would be fun to explore between side characters, or because that little thing could show up in a later book that moves these secondary characters to the forefront and you want to set the stage for it. Readers will start wondering why it's there, and they'll surely notice at the end of the story that it didn't really have anything to do with the main plot. At best, this strategy distracts readers from your story. At worst, it kills the pacing and derails the flow of the main plot.

You need to make that subplot feel like it belongs—by making sure it *does* belong. Give it a job serving the main storyline, just as you give your secondary characters a job serving the protagonist. Your subplot can reveal things about your characters that end up playing into the main plot later. Or it can be a way for you to work in information or plot twists. It's a way of showing that a character does have other things going on in her life besides the main story— but that there's a link between all the things in that life that flows through this single character.

The subplot should contain a logic of its own, with a beginning, middle, and end sequence that makes sense and that builds toward something that complements the main plot or themes. Otherwise, you're just throwing some random episodes in there. For example, roommates who don't get along can provide funny anecdotal scenes throughout a novel, but that's a random collection of encounters, not a subplot. To develop that into a subplot, you would give those roommates some kind of problem to solve—perhaps a conflict between themselves, or maybe something they team up for, such as an upstairs neighbor who plagues them with late-night music whom they finally need to take a stand against. You'd play out this mini-storyline over the course of several chapters or perhaps the bulk of the book, then swoop in with a climax and resolution for it that helps the main story. Maybe it would embody a theme that runs through the protagonist's main story arc. Maybe Protagonist Polly needs to stop viewing anyone interested in knowing more about her as an enemy, and forming an unlikely alliance with Roomie Rachel would get her to reveal something of herself to Rachel and they'd connect in the beginnings of a friendship. This in turn would help push Protagonist Polly into her epiphany for the main storyline: The only way to connect with people is to let down your guard. She'll let her guard down with her Main Dude and finally find love thanks in part to Rachel and the obnoxious upstairs neighbor.

If you want to set up that sequel book with your subplot, that's excellent— just be sure that this mini storyline in some way affects the main plot of *this* book so it doesn't feel conspicuously tacked on. In most cases, the subplot will be bumping up against the main plot throughout the story as it does its job of distracting the main character or feeding her information at opportune moments, etc. In all cases, that subplot will converge with the main plot by the end of the story. Maybe not by the end of the first book in a series, but by the end of the series arc for sure. This brings closure, giving readers that satisfaction you're striving so hard for with your story structure.

Avoid overcomplicating your novel with complex subplots or with too many of them. Your main storyline must remain prominent, since that's what readers bought your book for. If you find yourself wanting to add more subplots or to beef up the ones you've got to the point that you're worrying about spending too much time away from the main story, then stop and ask yourself if you're trying to make up for something in your main plot. Have you put enough at stake in that main plot, keeping its tension high? Have you pushed your protagonist hard so that she has to act and react and continually make things worse? Or is she sitting back on the couch with her feet up as everyone else does the work, a passive protagonist who won't earn her hero badge in her own plot? Check out the next chapter about using conflict to increase tension and push characters (and readers) through the story. You've got plenty of other tools at the ready. Heck, it may turn out you don't need a subplot at all, and that's okay—no one says you *have* to have a subplot to have a satisfying story.

SEE YOUR STORY'S STRUCTURE IN SEVEN STEPS

Working title: _____

Hook statement: _____

_____

_____

Want: _____

Problem: _____

_____

Catalyst: _____

_____

Obstacle 1: _____

_____

Obstacle 2: _____

_____

Obstacle 3: _____

_____

Epiphany: _____

_____

Final Push: _____

_____

Triumph: _____

_____

_____

CHAPTER 8

Writing a Seamless Story From Beginning to End

*O*ne of the best compliments you can get as a novelist is when a reader says of your novel, "I forgot I was even reading!" She sank into your fictional world and lived it alongside your character. Why? Because you stitched together a story that flows naturally from event to event and seamlessly employs a variety of storytelling elements. You made that reader lose all awareness that an author existed. Bam!

Seamless is the key word here. I want to help you cast an invisibility spell on yourself by showing you tools and strategies for writing a manuscript that renders its craft unseeable. I'll focus first on beginnings that eschew welcoming handshakes in favor of grabbing a curious reader's outstretched hand and pulling her right into the story. I'll slide into middles that flow relentlessly forward despite the momentum-chopping potential of scene breaks, chapter breaks, locations shifts, character exits, and plot changes. Finally, I'll roll into endings that flow organically out of everything that preceded them, earning their surprises by creating a logical foundation from the very first page of the story. Our goal will be mixing and matching a host of techniques and strategies so that each element in your book is so right for the story that it calls no attention to itself. Your goal is for each transition from one paragraph, scene, or chapter to the next to be so smooth readers don't even know they were transitioned.

WRITING OPENINGS THAT INTRIGUE AND THEN ESCORT

It's no secret that readers need to be captured by your writing and the story right away. That puts a lot of pressure on you to write great firsts—first lines, first pages, first chapters, first appearances of characters, and first backstory information. Below are strategies that will help you navigate that challenge even as you then go about the next step: drawing in that reader whose attention you just captured with your great first.

MAKE *IN MEDIAS RES* YOUR FAVORITE PHRASE

We're so trained in "Once upon a time …" beginnings that we can easily fall into the trap of opening our stories with soft introductions that take a reader's hand and walk her gently into our fictional world, handing her a map, a compass, and a playbill that lists the characters and describes the situation. Don't gently hold hands—grab 'em and yank! Instead of starting quaintly at the beginning of a day or adventure, fling the front door wide for readers at a point in the story when the ball is already rolling. Start *in medias res*, or in the middle of things. This has your reader walking on-scene when notable things are already happening and protagonists are already reacting. The reader's interest is piqued even as they ask, "What's going on?" You'll fill them in on the goings-on easily enough—the more important task at this moment is the piquing.

Starting your story in the middle of things will help you avoid cliché introductory openings, such as the character waking up on her first day and going through the action of getting ready for class or work. We watch her brush her hair and get dressed, get to know her style and her hopes for the day as she goes about her tasks … but so what? We can get to know those things in a far more dynamic and intriguing opening. How about opening that same story with that character already at her new job but lost in the unfamiliar halls, pulling open one door on an employee stealing office supplies, then another on a boss cussing out a subordinate—who later turns out to be your protagonist's boss? Now that's an awesomely awkward first morning.

When you sit down to write your opening scene, forget that you're "introducing" or "welcoming" readers to your story and set about revealing your character by showing her reacting to something in those opening lines. In her reaction she'll evidence her skills, goals, needs, personality, mood, and hopes for the day or the adventure. With those things on the tip of your pen, place her in an event in a provocative setting that she'll have to react to.

There's certainly plenty of opportunity for "provocative" in the fact that new adults are often starting new things—a new living place, a new school, a new job, a new social circle. Your character is already in a place of stress even if that new thing is a good thing—all change carries a degree of stress wadded up in a snarled mass of hopefulness, ambition, fear, and uncertainty. Throwing someone feeling those emotions into a setting that's unfamiliar to him, probably with people who are equally new, forces him to explore or to work through discomfort. Unfamiliar settings give you reason to start worldbuilding right away since your character will be noting details of his new surroundings. You could skip the first day and instead start out later in the first week or the first month of a new thing, allowing your character to note how things are becoming familiar even as the conflicts or challenges of that situation have emerged.

Perhaps you'll decide to go whole hog with the opening action, leading with the big catalytic moment. Now that's *in medias res*! Carrie Vaughn's *After the Golden Age* opens with the protagonist being kidnapped (catalyst) by the end of the page, with the reason for the kidnapping unveiled in Chapter 2 (problem). Melanie Card's *Ward Against Death* leads with her protagonist trying to raise from the dead the woman who will be his love interest. We don't walk up to the dead girl's mansion with our protagonist, shaking hands with her family and getting directions to the room where her body lays in state. We start in the middle of relevant, revealing action.

OPEN WITH ACTION THAT'S MORE REACTION

I'm not suggesting you need to press the detonation button on a nuclear device when you fling your story's door open for readers. Bold, explosive opening action may fit some NA stories—as with the bank robbery that kicks off *I Am the Messenger*—but probably not most of them, considering the dominance of contemporary romance in NA fiction. Instead of explosive action, think revealing *reaction*. Who intrigues you more, a guy walking across the room with a drink in his hand or a guy running from the bartender? The first is action, the second is *reaction*.

In starting your story with someone reacting, you create for your readers the sense that there's a life already being lived and that, although the reader may be new to it, the character isn't. Joe Character is going on with a life that started eighteen or more years before we rolled on-scene. Thus, you're tapping into a flowing story rather than trying to get the ball rolling yourself. For example, Chapter 1 could start with your protagonist halfway up a tree in her front yard because her elm-climbing cat took her car keys *again* and she needs them to get to her shift or her class. Or maybe she's shoving her way out of a subway car because she's got a sorority sister begging her on the phone to come rescue her from some guy's house *now*—and anyway she's no pansy girlie girl who waits politely for a crowd to give way. Or maybe she's being interrogated by a detective who places both hands on the table and leans toward her to say, "So when did you decide to kill him—before or after the shrimp scampi was served?" All of these openings force the character to react to something in a way that reveals important personality traits and plot details.

Do make sure the action you choose to open the story with has meaning for the entire book, otherwise it can feel randomly tacked onto the front of the manuscript. It's all well and good to write a funny first chapter set in a ski lodge, but if that ski trip or the act of skiing is never mentioned again, you've started your book with an element that doesn't jive with the rest of the story. That sabotages overall story cohesiveness from the outset.

OPEN WITH A FIRST LINE THAT PULLS READERS IN

Open your story with a first line that says not "Welcome" but "Look at me." Or rather, "Look at *the rest of* me." You want your reader to feel compelled to read on because she's curious or so struck by the insight, cleverness, surprise, or contradiction of that first line—or perhaps the first two or three lines—that she has to move further into the book for a closer look. You've chosen to start your story at a place where it already feels in motion, and now you're writing a first line that pulls the readers into that flow.

You could start the book with a line of *exposition* (the internal opinion or commentary of the point-of-view character or narrator) or a narrative statement, as long as it offers the reader something interesting to chew on—a bit of something unexpected, perhaps, or a bit of contradiction, a bit of personality. For example:

> My new least favorite thing ever: telling your girlfriend that the dude who busted you up was really a blind girl.

The unusual story detail of a blind gal with a fierce upper cut would give a reader cause to read on. Or you could start with narrative that invokes an intriguing situation, sending the reader's eyebrows upward and her eyes searching onward for elaboration:

> Sue Ellen crouched at the edge of the crumbling porch, holding the farmer's rusty shovel over her shoulder like an ax poised to chop.

I wonder what Sue Ellen is ready to whack and what kind of threat it poses? I'd read on to know more about that situation. Or perhaps you could lead with something that kickstarts the process of worldbuilding. Worldbuilding is vital in the first chapter of every story, whether the book is set in a fantastical realm or a familiar contemporary one. Readers want help picturing these happenings, and arming your characters with setting props or having them react against environmental factors, like weather or crowds, gives you opportunities to reveal the fictional world and the character's mood and mind-set from the get-go:

> Duke huddled at the mouth of the darkened corridor, his shoulder against the splintered basement doorframe for support, his soaked sneaker crushing a Gators pennant—once vibrant orange, now soiled to near black in a puddle of bloodied mud and debris.

If you decide to open your book with an encounter between your protagonist and other characters, you might be tempted to write an opening line that's dialogue. That can be a fun way to start a chapter, but I suggest you do that with an internal chapter, not with the very first line of the story. Readers don't know any characters when they start your book, they don't have any sense of your world or atmosphere, and they don't know to whom they should assign that speaking voice or how to interpret the speaker's mood or sincerity. They don't have any context yet. So while readers will "hear" the spoken words, they can picture nothing and likely feel nothing. There are plenty of other fantastic first-sentence options available to you that don't come with those inherent hurdles.

ACTIVATE YOUR CATALYST QUICKLY

Perhaps at one time readers relished a leisurely entry into a book, but nowadays readers expect to be launched into the main adventure very early on. That doesn't leave you much time to showcase your character's world before it goes to pot. Depending on your story, you may deliver your catalytic event by the end of the first chapter, by the end of the second chapter, or even by the end of the first scene. If you wait until Chapter 2, just be sure Chapter 1 really warrants its existence as a separate episode—the opening one, no less. If the first chapter exists solely to describe the character and explain what leads us to the fun stuff you've got planned for Chapter 2, you're probably front-loading your book with story set-up instead of beginning where the story really pushes off. Take out your rusty shovel and whack that chapter right off! You have plenty of time to deliver the backstory details as the necessary events unfold, if indeed it turns out you really do need that backstory information anyway. And you likely have plenty of time to set up the catalytic event in the opening pages of the first chapter. Don't make your readers wait too long before they see the problem at hand and decide if that problem intrigues them enough to commit to a whole book.

In Zusak's *I Am the Messenger*, readers don't get the catalyst for the story until Chapter 2, with the sudden arrival of an anonymous note that sends the cabbie protagonist out on missions. This delay works because the opening chapter is dramatic in its own right (a bank robbery) and reveals the dynamic of the main character's social circle and their poor financial straits. The robbery scene transitions smoothly into the next chapter and will figure into a major plot point later in the book, so it earns its place as the opening chapter not only for its unusual drama but also for its strategic contribution to the story as a whole. It is related, not some random event that's fun but really bears no connection to the rest of the story beyond introducing the cast.

TEASING OUT THE BACKSTORY AS THE MAIN STORY MOVES FORWARD

Story set-up, backstory ... both of these phrases refer to the delivery of background information about the character we're about to meet or the events that have led to this moment in time. Readers do want to know background stuff if it's truly important for them to know. If it's not essential information, keep that information to yourself. It'll help you write a full character and adventure, but it's not required knowledge for your audience. If they do need the information, hold back as much as you can until such time as the reader really does need to know it. Providing it all in the first pages for the sake of orienting the reader in your world is front-loading your story unnecessarily. We call that an *info dump*, which can be as unpleasant and clogging as it sounds.

Even when readers want and need info, a big, boring lump of it is hardly palatable, so be patient, sprinkling only necessary information into the action and exposition of the first few chapters and holding back the rest for later if you can. Just as you wouldn't plop a whole bouquet of roses onto the bottom stair step and yell, "Okay, come up now!" to your lover, you need to lead your readers up the stairway, scattering petals of backstory information with light fingers, building anticipation while readers discover additional revealing and enticing tidbits with each step. Tease them through your story whenever possible.

Patient sprinkling of biographical facts has a true-to-life quality to it. Imagine walking into a party and meeting someone. An "About this Person" bubble doesn't appear over her head with her hobbies and life history. It's a party, not a social media dating site. You engage her in conversation, going out onto the patio to talk or perhaps going for a stroll, asking questions and sharing anecdotes as you get to know that person fact by fact while the action and dialogue flows. Mirror that process with the characters in your book. *You* should know your characters' pasts well enough to start writing them, and maybe you'll even know them intensely well depending on how much prewriting you did in your profiling (see Chapter 4), but be stingy about sharing what you know. Some of it you'll keep to yourself entirely, or you'll save it for later books in the series or for bonus material on your website. Or maybe you'll just let the information be made evident to readers in "Show, don't tell" manner, with the audience seeing that your character is fluent in Latin when she rips out the *Veni, vidi, vici* at her bar exam. Let the sharing of backstory information be about the fun of getting to know someone, not about the facts themselves.

Aubrie Dionne's science fiction story *Paradise 21: A New Dawn* opens with the protagonist zipping through space desperately in her escape pod just hours before she's to be forcibly married (the catalytic event) on the ship that the remainder of her race calls home. Even as she knows capture will likely mean

death, and even as she knows that crash-landing on a desolate planet is her near **future**—minutes away, in fact—the thought of freedom has her literally scream-**ing with** excitement. In this desperate, joyful screaming, we learn a lot about **her per**sonality. This is all laid out on the first page of the novel, in a scene that **shows** her struggling with her pod.

CRAFTING SEAMLESS MIDDLES

When writers talk about their saggy middles, they're not usually referring to **their** own anatomy—they're troubleshooting the middles of their stories and **wonder**ing how they can keep up the high interest they sparked in the first **chapters.** If a story slows or meanders or just plain stalls, your pacing is shot. I'll cover all kinds of ways to maintain pacing and build tension in Chapter 9. Here, I focus on a specific pacing threat: choppy transitions between scenes and chapters. How do you deal with numerous beginnings and pauses without choppiness? You've got several tools and strategies to keep the sagginess at bay and the forward momentum going.

- **ESCALATE PROBLEMS RATHER THAN INTRODUCE PROBLEMS.** After you open that initial door of the story on a character life already being lived, your story should feel like it's rolling out before readers like a red carpet rather than stretching out before them as a corridor with a series of doors they need to open and close. If you are continually introducing new prob-lems, you'll get the door feeling, not the rollout. Each new scene and chap-ter should be a reaction to the events that preceded it, with the character being more invested in dealing with the problem each step of the way. If he gets locked out, it should start raining so he has to run for cover. If he's running in the rain with his hood up, he can't see that car coming and gets hit. If he gets hit, he goes to the hospital and the woman who locked him outside three steps back is now at his bedside, forced to finish the fight—er, *discussion* she wouldn't have at home. You've escalated the problem in a clear scene-sequencing process that has raised the tension and inevitability of their confrontation coming to fruition. Readers should never go, "Hey, where did *that* come from?" Each scene and chapter lays the foundation for later scenes and chapters, even as it plays out its own issues.

- **EMPOWER YOUR PROTAGONIST.** Passive protagonists receive actions. That gets boring. You want a protagonist who takes action, even if that action is incredibly wrong and only makes things worse. *Especially* when that action is incredibly wrong and only makes things worse. *Wrong* and *worse* push a character to tap into emotional reserves until he finally digs up whatever idea or strength he needs to make his final push and triumph. Characters who take action on their own are more likely to keep pushing forward, thus your story is one of continual action and reaction. No waiting around for you to toss in some outside force to goose him along, which can create a choppy feeling.
- **USE CLIFF-HANGERS.** Cliff-hangers naturally connect one scene or chapter to another, so they are useful for smooth transitioning. They make for riveting reading, too, since it's pretty darned hard to walk away from a character who is dangling from his fingers, literally or figuratively. Your cliff-hanger could be a romantic one, with your lovebirds on the edge of breakup or makeup at the end of a chapter, or it could be psychological, with character and reader fretting some terrible loss or outcome if something very important isn't addressed here and now. Cliff-hangers are essentially about creating story tension that cannot be denied. They keep readers turning pages and looking for more of your books when they're done. Use this technique judiciously, though, as readers can get overwhelmed by a book that contains one cliff-hanger after another.
- **START AT A NEW TIME OR PLACE.** It'll probably be rare for you to start a new scene at the same place, time, and situation that ended the previous scene. I find that when writers are doing that, they've usually thrown in that scene break for a dramatic pause similar to the kind created when a soap opera character stares in shock at another character, the camera does a close-up, they cut to the commercial, and then they return from commercial back in that close-up and the character finally finds the words to respond. The effect is a heavy-handed one. You ended a scene to make it feel complete, only to open it up again. That's pointless. Instead, for the next scene jump ahead or away in some manner, even if you're just a few minutes ahead in the future with your character now fleeing down the street instead of still standing there with a shocked expression. That jump allows you to start your character at a fresh, higher level of emotion and send him

through a new sequence of problem solving, so that you're building on top of the previous emotional peak instead of stretching out that peak interminably. Just employ the tactics I talked about above, where you create echoes from one chapter to another or mirror physical motion to bridge the break. You can carry over emotions, too, ending on anger in one scene and then opening up the new scene, in its new place and time, with a focus on the emotion of anger.

- **USE FLASHBACKS WITH CARE.** By definition, flashbacks stop the forward momentum in order to make readers (and probably characters) look backward. Thus, flashbacks are serious threats to strong pacing. They can be effective when you time them well, such as when you've built up tension and curiosity about some event in the past to the point that readers are chomping at the bit to know what happened way back when. In that case, the flashback feels like the culmination of anticipation rather than a halt in the main action while we look backward for information or explanation. Flashbacks for the sake of information are just info dumps in fancy dress; there are much less risky ways to convey information.

You can use flashbacks when your gut tells you it's time to slow the story for a breather after a good stretch of major forward movement or when you've built up to a pivotal revelation that is then delivered in full, rich, emotional scene that just happens to take place in the past. That could be the case with an NA story that deals with a past trauma, something survived but not yet emotionally overcome. When you simply need backstory delivery, I recommend foregoing the flashback and instead sprinkling it into the narrative, or having characters reveal it in dialogue, or just flat-out telling readers in the character's internal monologue.

Make sure that your flashback transitions in and out well so that it feels organic to the story, preserving the sense of ebb and flow rather than feeling like a disruption. Don't just drop it in there. Try signaling an upcoming flashback with a sensory trigger, like a sound or a smell or a symbolic item. Deliver the flashback with a tense shift to make it very clear to the reader that this is an out-of-time element, or provide the flashback in its own chapter. When you come out of the flashback, the transition can be smoothed by opening the next scene or chapter with some element that feels reminiscent of the flashback, such as ending a flashback with the character stepping onto a train and then opening the next scene or chapter in the story's present time with the character stepping onto a stage or something else that requires a "step onto" motion. This will work even when the next chapter is in the point of view of an entirely different character. The idea is to create some kind of thematic or tonal link between the flashback and the regular narrative. Switching back to the main narrative tense will underscore the transition.

DESIGNING ENDINGS THAT ARE INEVITABLE YET UNPREDICTABLE

A seamless story relentlessly plots and provokes and scares your character until it reaches its final climax and resolution with a sense of inevitability. Notice I don't say *predictability*. Inevitability is about a logical progression, with every step feeling like it *had to be there* once we take it because the logic for it—the foundation—is so solid. We are satisfied by that ending because we felt it coming, even if we didn't have any idea what the specifics of the resolution would be. The main story problem gets solved in a way that's consistent with the character arc and the information, tools, and cast support you provided in the story.

This all means putting your protagonist in the driver's seat for the final act. No white knights riding in, no parents saving your heroine's butt, no buddies stepping up. Any of those folks can have your Good Guy's back, but his front is up to him—he leads the charge, he strikes the fatal blow or spikes the game-winning ball. It's his show, baby, and he needs to own that grand finale. Your readers will feel that—they've been cheering for his victory long enough, and in the best-case scenario they've connected enough with your character to feel like it's their own victory being had. They see themselves in the character and want that sense of victory for themselves.

- **END WITH A SIGH.** No matter your ending, it should be one that leaves your readers feeling satisfied. This means delivering what you promised by completing your arcs, as I just laid out above. It also means delivering things true to a new adult's ability, needs, and experience. Often new adults aren't so much striving to *survive* things—although physical and emotional survival are usually an element of their triumph. Many new adults are striving for a sense of *finishing* or finally fixing something they'd only survived in high school. As teens, they hadn't dealt with it to a point that they could accept it, feel vindicated about it, feel at peace with it, or just overall feel finished enough with it to truly move on. For that group, there's a sense that they are now adults who can put this puppy to bed. They're no longer in survival mode, waiting for their chance to grow up. This story is their process of feeling grown up for the first time and squashing their demons with their newfound maturity or power.

Bittersweet endings are valid and satisfying endings for NA stories. As long as there is resolution and the arcs are completed, readers feel as if they've had their full journeys and reached another state of wisdom or insight. A bittersweet ending might be one where the characters get what they needed rather than what they wanted. The ability to recognize when that's happened is a true sign of wisdom. That's about gaining experience in life, about attaining wisdom, which is a hallmark of the NA experience.

- **END WITH "HAPPILY EVER AFTER," NA-STYLE.** An important aspect of the NA experience is the notion of feeling in a state of *temporary*. Temporary living spaces. Temporary social circles. Temporary jobs and education status. New adults don't generally have a strong need for "happily ever after" yet. Rather, there's a sense of conquering and moving on. This is an especially important mind-set to understand when considering romantic storylines. In traditional romances, the "H.E.A." ending is required—the girl must find Mr. Right, her true soul mate, and live happily ever after. She needs him in order to feel complete. In an NA romance, the "ever after" part ain't so much the goal. This is probably their first meaningful romance, and while they want that amazing soul connection and fantastic happiness, the ever after part isn't vital to the equation. They're not looking to settle down and start a family right now. Those things may end up a part of the equation, but they're not usually the goal. It's about the characters feeling fulfilled by their firm, loving relationship, not permanently committed. The NA "happily ever after" is more like "happily ready to tackle the world together as new and stronger people who are more confident in their identities and their mutual love for each other." Dang, that's a mouthful. But that's new adults for you: They do it their way.

- **END WITH A TWIST.** Readers know the protagonist will win out in the end. But don't let them guess *how* they'll win out. Instead, twist things so that they get the win they expected in a way they did not. There must be logic in the twist, of course (remember, no rabbits out of hats). The reader must be able to trace the roots of this ending through the book and believe that this character has grown into the kind of person who can and would pull off this ending. Challenge yourself to look at the person your character has become and brainstorm multiple actions that accomplish the resolution you need. Pick the one you think readers would least expect but that is fully believable.

  If the ending is a surprise to you because you've pantsed yourself to it without specifically building up to it, in the next draft go back and add in elements that foreshadow it, and make sure that the character's internal arc jives with it. The values involved in the character's final decision, in the climactic realization of his strengths and triumph over his weaknesses, must be a part of his growth throughout the book.

- **END WITH A MIRROR.** Some writers, myself included, like to end with a scene that mirrors the first scene of the book. This time, though, the protagonist acts in a totally different—and fully capable—way that shows their growth. That creates a feeling of the story having come full circle, adding to the overall cohesiveness of the story. Plus, it lets you show off your character's growth in a tangible way. Perhaps your character was attacked by a guy in the first scene and victimized. In the final scene, she'd triumph in a showdown with a guy. The scenes could very closely mirror each other, or they could be more symbolic in their mirroring.

- **END WITH AN OPEN DOOR FOR SERIES AND COMPANION BOOKS.** If you're writing a series, readers expect you to leave some kind of plot point dangling at the end of each book, or some psychological or emotional need unsatiated. In the case of emotions or psychological needs, there should be a sense that the internal arc has at least made strides, that the character is at a point where she's steady enough to feel that this episode is somehow resolved and she can move on to the next challenge in her life. That gives you something to pick up in the next book, much as you would pick up dangling strings from one chapter to the next. Because you'll be carrying those characters into the next book, you'll have that important sense of continuity transitioning readers from one book to the next.

You may choose to tie all the ends together in this book and instead return for the next book with the character facing a new attack on that same wound, or perhaps facing something new altogether. In that case, you're probably looking more at a *companion* story, even though it's technically still a series. The books star the same characters, but we get to return to their lives because they're not done growing and, in the case of a romance, we're not done testing their relationship.

If you do feel done with a protagonist, you can still continue with her world and keep the interest of readers who loved it by writing a companion book about a secondary character, moving him up to protagonist status. Make it clear at the end of the first book that this secondary character has some business he needs to tend to or some demons of his own that need battling. His involvement in early books in the series provides the continuity that helps make a series seamless.

- **END WITH AN EPILOGUE ONLY WHEN ONE IS ESSENTIAL.** Epilogues aren't big in NA fiction. NA readers don't seem to need a "this is what happens to your characters after the story ends," perhaps because NA fiction is more about this moment in the young person's life than accounting for his long-term happiness. Some readers complain that epilogues feel like second endings. If you believe an epilogue is absolutely vital to your story, use the techniques I discussed in the "Crafting Seamless Middles" section of this chapter to create a bridge from the final chapter so that the epilogue doesn't feel tacked on. If you're including an epilogue because you feel the need to explain a "twist" ending, reconsider that twist to make sure it is truly an inevitable, logical ending and not just you reaching into your hat for that rabbit.

CHAPTER 9

Cranking Up the Conflict, Tension, and Pacing in Your NA Fiction

*I*n storytelling, the notion of *conflict* goes beyond the everyday definition of people, things, or philosophies being at odds. Literary conflict is an almost tangible crowbar-like device we writers apply to our tale to provoke character growth. With it we prod, wedge, and beat our protagonist and her supporting cast forward through unpleasant plot events for her all-important character arc. And we don't stop when the initial unpleasantness worsens—we apply the crowbar with more force, escalating our character's stresses until the poor fictional people just can't bear it any longer and finally plant their feet and stare us and our weapon of steel down. *Go on, I dare you. ...*

This chapter is about escalating conflict—that feeling of the story becoming tenser and tenser until something finally gives. I'll give you techniques for stoking conflict, along with ways to manipulate the pacing so that you know just the right moment to back off, daring to allow the character and readers a breather before laying back into them with more force than ever. I'll talk about this all in the context of the new adult experience, making your novel something your NA audience can relate to. I'll throw a little subtext in there, too, giving you some extra elbow grease as you wedge that crowbar in deeper for a story that pushes character and reader relentlessly forward.

CONFLICT AND TENSION IN THE STRUGGLES OF THE NEW ADULT

Many new adults experience their first grapple-and-toss with philosophy in college, so let me get into the Philosophy 101 spirit and throw down some Nietzsche: That which does not kill us makes us stronger. Freddie, old buddy, you could've been talking about literary conflict in the NA novel. Conflict oozes through the NA experience, so it oozes deliciously and naturally through our fiction. With all the shifting ground in a new adult's life, uncertainties seep into worry cracks, hope builds up expectations that stretch the limits of reality, the stress percolates, people break. Oh, do they break. But what makes stories great is that the break is but the fall before the rise. Triumph awaits our heroes and heroines, and your hard work with conflict and tension will have your readers clamoring for that victory.

Your conflict crowbar comes in several colors. *Inner conflict* is the war within oneself, among one's ideas and values and beliefs and concepts of what's possible. It's emotional, it's intellectual, it's spiritual. *Outer conflict* deals with institutions, nature, and other people, both individual and in a grander "society" sense. All conflict in your novel somehow adds to your protagonist's struggle to attain her goal, usually in the form of you cranking up the outer conflict in order to roil up the inner. After these techniques, we'll look at how pacing keeps readers moving through the plot.

KICK IT OFF WITH CONFLICT

To stoke the conflict in your story, set internal and external conflict a'rubbing against each other right away. In the last chapter we talked about the power in opening the book with action that's really *reaction*. That means your character was already responding to some kind of conflict even as the first word appeared on the page. Readers learn right away what presses the main character's buttons, how worked up she is going into this adventure, and what it is she thinks is worth getting so worked up about before we lob the Big Doozy Catalyst at her to really rock her world. If your protagonist's journey will involve opening up to other people in some way, consider making your opening conflict an outer conflict with another person. Right away, we'll learn that people skills are an issue for her in some way. If her journey involves a battle against authority or a philosophy, show her reacting to some manifestation of those bugaboos.

KEEP THE SOURCE OF CONFLICT CLOSE

That old adage "Keep your loved ones close, and your enemies closer" can be an inspiration for your handling of conflict, because a fabulous way to keep the conflict escalating between two characters is to force those characters to be a team. Make them dorm mates. Partner them up on a project at work. Make them seek the Ring of Power together, each with a skill, knowledge, or tool that the other can't do without. If it's an addiction or similar kind of weakness that causes your character internal conflict, continually put that temptation or a similar one in her path. The party boy who needs to get serious about his studies can find the only available campus housing is next to this old frat house. The former drug addict trying to stay clean must go undercover as a dealer to save his brother from a dealer-related crisis. Wear them down.

SET HIGH STAKES ... THEN RAISE THEM

You're putting your character through a lot; make it count. Put something big at stake so readers can believe the protagonist would stay in this fight. Make the characters so worried about the consequences that they *have* to act. In *Ward Against Death*, a dead assassin is revived by a kindhearted, bumbling necromancer. Author Melanie Card puts high stakes into play right away when she has the temporarily revived assassin flee from the people who killed her in the first place, with the necromancer in tow. If they stop running, the necromancer will be killed (unacceptable to him and to readers) and the assassin will relapse into death without him to keep reviving her (unacceptable to him). When the two fall in love and the female assassin starts revealing her good side, we add the assassin's relapse into death to the "Unacceptable to Readers, Too" list. High stakes, introduced early and then escalated.

You needn't have people dying to have high stakes. Broken hearts, broken dreams, and broken promises work because we can all relate to those when the dreams and promises are truly important. Put others' health or well-being at stake. Figure out what your characters truly do not want, will not stand for, cannot bear to lose, or will fight tooth and nail to avoid.

TAKE THINGS AWAY, DENY SOLACE OR RESPITE

As you roll out your story, be looking for those breather moments, the little victories that fool the characters into thinking things will work out just fine. You're not going to *let* things work out, not yet anyway, but they don't know that. If the characters manage to reach a point in the story where a tool they've been developing can save them, break their tool. If they've devised a great plan to sneak onto campus in the dead of night to retrieve a report from a professor's office, make it rain that night. Returning to *Ward Against Death*: Card offers her fleeing characters relief by letting them discover a grate leading up out of the horrible sewer they'd escaped through. But when the assassin sticks her head up into the city, she sees that they're in the only place worse than where they'd left: the Collegiate of the Quayestri, the highest institution of law in the lands. Worse yet, inside the Collegiate's walls are Inquisitors who can read minds. Any of them, with one wandering thought, might sense her mind over there at that sewer grate, read it, then project all her sins up into the sky like a drive-in movie. Every officer of the land would know the crimes she'd committed and every Tracker in the area would be after her, ready to deliver her to a beheading—something no necromancer could fix. Relief denied! Tension amped right up into the sky!

BUILD SUSPENSE BY WITHHOLDING INFORMATION

I talk throughout this book about the power of sprinkling information into the story for your readers instead of dumping it onto the page. Sprinkle it for the characters, too, teasing them all along with intentional gaps, forcing them (and readers) to guess, to act on their guesses, and to discover that their actions made things worse because their guesses were wrong. By manipulating the flow of the information—just like life does to new adults—you can make the character's life worse, increasing conflict and tension in yet another way.

MANIPULATING THE PACING

Pacing calls for a sense of rhythm in your conflict application and tension-building. We want readers to hold their breath in anticipation, but once in a while they do need to breathe or they'll pass out. Your character is growing—give her moments where she can realize her growth, where she can process a small victory, where she can dare to hope and think her growing pains are over. They aren't, of course. You know that. Your task is to keep that character moving forward even as you slow the pace now and then for that strategic breather. In that pacing breather, you'll slip a moment that deepens the story, perhaps by revealing something new (perhaps your character gets to pause to note another character's strength), perhaps advancing a relationship (a romantic encounter on the beach that is, for once, without arguments or interruptions), or perhaps contributing new information (such as a training session on the archery range where two characters talk about their plan as they pierce hay bales at a hundred yards). Slowing doesn't mean doing nothing. You'll be deepening, revealing, advancing, and ultimately setting up the characters for something really onerous on the next page.

The rhythmic rolling-out of a story is more than the unveiling of plot events and moments of conflict. You can do technical things to manipulate the pacing of specific scenes. Here are some ways to speed it up and slow it down that involve your word and sentence mechanics.

If you want to slow pacing, you can point your reader's brain at things that don't matter, bogging them down purposely in little details or stringing out a sequence of actions. Imagine a scene where you need to slow down a male character so that, in a parallel scene, a lady character can put the final frantic touches on a surprise romantic dinner for him. You can rush your guy to the subway car, only to have him step in gum, forcing him to stop, cringe, lift his shoe, see the pink wad stretching, pulling, glistening in its wetness, between his shoe and the concrete. He'll look around, seeing nothing to help him on his left, slowly scanning across the platform, noting that there's an odd cleanliness about the subway today, finally spotting a newsstand on his right, then hobbling his way— flat foot, toe tip, flat foot, toe tip—to the newsstand, where he pulls a napkin from the napkin holder, only to have the whole wad pull out. Sighing, he sets about stuffing the napkins back into the holder as the train leaves without him. Meanwhile, in another scene, girlfriend jams roses in a vase, girlfriend shoves shoes under the couch, girlfriend fills two wine glasses, girlfriend sits in the now dark room. And girlfriend waits. In the guy's scene I focused readers on the gum and its gunkiness and aftermath for a good long time, going almost myopic on that wad of pink. For the girl's scene, we accomplished twenty different tasks in twenty different places in the apartment in two sentences. Two totally different paces thanks to extreme focus on a single prop. This is a fun strategy, but do use it sparingly so that it exists as a great dramatic moment in the story rather than a frequent pace-killing habit.

Similarly, you can speed up or slow down the pacing in a scene by manipulating the sentence structure. Short, declarative sentences quicken the pace. A page full of short paragraphs will seem to fly by. In your mind, picture that page. Now, turn that page and see a single block of text filling the new page, one long paragraph reaching from top to bottom, margin to margin, minimal white space in sight. You *know* that's going to be a slow read, don't you? You can really get dramatic with this manipulative paragraphing by tossing in, at the perfect moment, perhaps when a phase of tension-building is reaching a peak that calls for some kind of breather, a chapter that's just one paragraph long. Or even one sentence.

CHAPTER 7
I left Brody.

Boom! Impact.

SUBTEXT—CONFLICT AND TENSION'S BFF

When the action and situation in your story directly undermines or in some way contradicts what your characters say, the reality behind the words is the subtext. I love subtext. It gives your story layers and interactive reading as your readers work to interpret the contradiction. Interactive reading is good. You want readers actively engaging with the text. When readers clue in to the contradictions you build into your story, they start questioning things, which means they're really chewing over the elements of your story, and that's good. And they start realizing things, which means they're probably feeling pretty darn clever, and that's great. And they start anticipating things, which means they're acting on that extra knowledge to guess at the next plot development, and that's super. All of this makes for a deeper, richer reading experience. Plus, because of the contradiction, the characters aren't dealing with something that they probably should be dealing with. They're leaving it to fester, and festering is not good. Well, for the characters. For us it's great because it leads to more conflict! I've got two ways that you can create subtext using contradiction, both of which contribute to the overall sense of escalating conflict.

First, you can play a more obvious meaning off a second less obvious—and wholly different—meaning. Imagine two characters who seem to be talking about one thing while really they're talking about another thing entirely. Picture a scene with an older college brother and his teenage sister who just moved in with him. The argument seems to be about a TV show, but the reader would know from earlier in the book that the younger sister got the sweet, indulgent mom in the divorce while the older brother got the strict dad, and the siblings haven't cleared the air over that yet:

> Tucker rushed into the living room with his bag of chips and his Bud. He pulled up when he spotted his kid sister sitting in his recliner, holding the remote and laughing at a rerun of *South Park*. She was licking her fingers. "Oh no you didn't," Tucker said. "Did you just eat my sub?"
> "It was just sitting there."
> "On a plate right next to my seat. I was gonna eat it while I watched the game. You changed the game. You can't just change the game. This is my house. I had the game on."
> "Yes I can. I'm the little sister."
> "What?"
> "The little sisters always get the remote. It's the law."
> "That's the dumbest thing I ever heard."
> "Hey, I don't make the laws, I just follow them. Call Mom, she'll tell you."

Second, you can contradict a character's perception of something with the realities of it. Here's an example featuring two twenty-year-old guys who've just pawned an old neighbor's valuable painting. They thought it was just some cheap garage sale painting, though, and only got five bucks for it. Now the neighbor is onto them.

> "Why are we stopping? You know she'll call the cops."
> "We can go back if we just buy back the painting."
> "We're eight thousand dollars short, Einstein. Drive."
> "Ten minutes, that's all I need." He pointed to the flashing Golden Nugget Casino sign. "I'll run up some cash, and we'll buy it back."

"Are you nuts? They'll only need ten seconds to look at your ID and kick your butt out for being too young."

"Casinos don't check IDs. They just want the money. Ten minutes. C'mon, trust me. I'm feeling lucky today."

A desperate character who claims to "feel lucky" after a string of bad choices is just asking to lose his shirt. The character's confidence in that scene is at odds with the reality of gambling: The odds are very much against him. Readers know that and can then fret about it. That's subtext, and there's great tension in it.

But here's a twist: You, the clever author, may just be setting up readers for a surprise by playing on their expectations. What would happen if you let that desperate gambler hit it big? Or what if he gets to strike it rich in another way—like, say, meeting someone at the table who's going to change the guy's life? Maybe the door opens to his playing a part in the biggest heist of the century. Or he gets to be the world's next champion poker player. You can manipulate readers with subtext, too. That's really getting into story layering and twisting the tension screws.

CHAPTER 10

Love and Sex in the Age of Experimentation

*N*ew adults fall in and out of love plenty of times, getting a feel for what they want and don't want in a partner and in themselves along the way. With the college love story comes the college sex, something 80 percent of college students say they've engaged in. But the issue isn't just higher education hubba-hubba. Sexual exploration is an extension of love and identity exploration, and premarital sex is more acceptable than ever before, so sex is a significant element in the new adult experience. Of course NA writers are going to include it in their stories. Whether the stories are about new adults on campus or new adults struggling in their first career attempts or new adults building huts for the Peace Corps in Zambia or hunting specters in graveyards or investigating how many shooters were on that grassy knoll when the president was gunned down, we get the love stories and the sex that often goes with it.

This chapter guides you in crafting romantic relationships that take into account the unique sensibility of new adults and the challenge of writing emotion that resonates with readers. I'm going to throw down some strategies to help you achieve that resonance, from stuff you can do with your characters to ways to amp up the sexual tension to writing love scenes that tap into the emotional core of the characters and relationship and often get seriously physical along the way.

Above all, I'm going to harp on freshness. Predictability and familiarity are major buzzkills for the heart and the libido. And we're talking new adults here, for whom everything is laced with a sense of newness. Love is big stuff, with the training wheels just off. Let's see them wobble even as we see the unbridled optimism that makes new adults so awesome and so susceptible to authorial sabotaging. Force them to earn their happiness, to earn that love, to earn that wisdom. No one ever said love was easy.

NA'S LOVE AFFAIR WITH AFFAIRS OF THE HEART

Love stories permeate NA fiction, and with good reason: Love is one of new adulthood's three main areas of identity exploration. Next to career investigation and developing a worldview (one's personal philosophy regarding politics, faith, and general well-being), the late teens and early twenties are prime time for people to explore romantic options. Their hormones are all primed up for that exploration, and suddenly they have the freedom and opportunity to do so. No parents to report to, equally intrigued partners at every turn, roommates game for the "sock on the door" arrangement. … Cowabunga! It's an exciting, empowering, emotional time of high hopes and deep passions. And, sometimes, of crushing pain. Remember the new adult mind-set: instability, new social circles and transitory relationships, exploration and experimentation as a means of establishing identity, optimism that defies reality. Change is a constant, and thus instability is a way of life.

This of course opens up plenty of opportunities for you to explore love and how it affects new adults in your fiction, even if romance isn't your main plotline and even if you don't include sex in your book. You're on a journey with your new adult protagonist, and that journey will likely include some kind of romantic interest. The newness and hopefulness is intoxicating, and crossover readers who miss that newness in their own happy but now settled lives enjoy re-experiencing it with your protagonist. Many NA characters will have experienced love before graduating high school, as is the case for real-life teens, 71 percent of whom have given sex a go at least once by the time they're twenty, according to an American Academy of Pediatrics' journal study. But this is love on a new level, with a lot more at stake as new adults discover themselves in terms of their wants, needs, and identities in love. With the average marrying age clocking in at twenty-seven for men and twenty-five for women, new adults aren't racing from the high school graduation podium to the wedding chapel with their high school sweethearts *en masse*. People in their late teens and early twenties are exploring options, gaining sexual experience as they figure out who they are as sexual beings.

Sex matters to NA readers and storytellers as much as to new adults themselves. New Adult fiction emerged as a category in the wake of the *Fifty Shades of Grey* phenomenon. *Fifty Shades* awakened mainstream readers' awareness of erotica, and when fans went looking for more of the same, they found some NA stories that included explicit sex scenes. Readers began to read more deeply into the NA category even as more books were published in it, discovering that they enjoy reading about young people stumbling through the new adult phase of life and that they can do so with varying degrees of sexual activity and detail. Books like Tammara Webber's *Easy*, in which Webber says she kept "to the sexuality guidelines of the books written for the mature end of the YA spectrum," sit easily alongside books like Sylvia Day's more explicit Crossfire series.

But here's the thing all this sex talk can make people forget: Romance isn't all about what the bodies are doing. Romance is a mental thing, too—maybe even *first*, before the bod kicks in. Your awareness of that, your refusal to let the physical part of intimacy supersede the mental part for your protagonist and your readers, is what will turn this tool and your insight into the new adult mind-set into storytelling gold. In your book, no matter how explicit you choose to get with your characters' physical lovemaking, your romance will matter to your character's psychological and emotional journey and readers will feel vested in it as a result.

MAKING YOUR ROMANCE MATTER

Because of its ability to engage readers' emotions, a romantic storyline is a powerful storytelling tool. Put it to work for you. Don't just stick love and sex into your fiction because you know a story about young people is supposed to have love and sex—that's a surefire way to end up with a forced, flat storyline. Instead, use romance to drive your character through a gamut of emotion and self-discovery that'll result in a happier or wiser character by the closing curtain. Opening oneself up to intimacy requires letting someone past the emotional barriers we've so carefully constructed, exposing fallacies we've labored under, revealing traumas and secrets and desires and fears so deep we may not even consciously know they're festering. A romance can expose even the toughest character's soft underbelly.

A satisfying romance affects both of the lovers. The relationship teaches them something, awakens them to things within themselves, and builds growth through that knowledge, leaving them feeling that this relationship is good for them. They learn that they can be there for another person and find fulfillment in that. This is an important maturation process for new adults and perfect for any story about the new adult experience regardless of era, circumstances, or genre. So keep both lovers in your headlights for full development and growth, even if ultimately this is just one character's tale. Upping the romance in your characters' lives may even reveal things that *you* didn't know about them yet.

"HAPPILY FOR NOW" INSTEAD OF "HAPPILY EVER AFTER"

As we've discussed, the notion that a fictional romance must have the fairy tale "and they lived happily ever after" ending is a requirement for adult category romance, but not for NA fiction. Eighteen- to twenty-five-year-olds typically are still getting to know themselves and aren't keen on passing up their chance to experience the independence and spontaneity of the new adult years. Don't get me wrong, young people aren't down on the marriage and family thing. One study says 90 percent of new adults plan on getting hitched and pumping out the pups—just not yet. They've got exploring, experimenting, and maturing to do.

An NA romance is about working through meeting and getting to know each other and falling in love and the first big tests of the romance, with the two young people all the while figuring out how all of that plays into each one's understanding of him- or herself. The general goal in a romance is existing in a state of happiness with each other. Even in a series, where readers delight in getting more page time with their favorite couples book after book, the focus is on testing what the relationship is now, not about getting to the "put a ring on it" moment.

THE "MARRIED WITH CHILDREN" HURDLE

You're unlikely to find many NAs starring protagonists who are married with children. Marriage is one of the most-cited benchmarks for determining whether someone is an adult or not, and many crossover readers don't want to read about characters negotiating life within a marriage—that's their real life, and they're reading to escape to a younger, freer time. And certainly one of the tenets of new adulthood is the notion that the young person is finally free to be totally responsible for herself and not yet responsible for others.

Does that mean you can't have a protagonist who *is* married with children? No. You're the writer, this is your story, and real life has plenty of young people starting families early. You'll certainly find wonderful fiction fodder in the emotional ramifications for a new adult who makes that choice to have a baby while her peers are out beer-bonging at the local uni. Someone who marries young must still work through their identity exploration, and having a spouse or family to consider adds interesting wrinkles to that.

While some NA readers feel that becoming a parent changes the tone of life too dramatically for this fiction, there seems to be leeway for the accidental pregnancy, which allows the protagonist to count the baby as but one of her many struggles in the overall theme of NA identity exploration. In those cases, the story is not *about the baby*; the conflict is about the protagonist and how she gets to her final happiness or wisdom. When a baby is planned, the young parent is deliberately taking on a crucial adult responsibility, choosing to settle on a "Life Plan," and that's where readers might object.

In fact, one of the first and most successful NA novels features a protagonist who decides to marry one of the men in her love triangle after she becomes pregnant with his baby. I won't spoil the surprise by revealing the title in case you haven't read this seminal NA. What's important to this discussion is that the marriage and baby come at the end of the novel; the story isn't about negotiating life within a marriage and planning for a life together. That protagonist's journey is about finding a new maturity, and the baby and marriage twist at the end underscore that she has in fact matured, which is very NA.

Also very NA? Making your own rules. If you want marriage and baby in your novel, put 'em in there. Bestsellerdom comes when fans embrace your story, not when you tick off rules on a checklist.

STRATEGIES FOR WRITING ROMANTIC CHARACTERS

You're creating a novel, not a Chippendales poster—your characters deserve depth, as do your readers. In Chapter 4 I helped you identify your protagonist's hopes and fears. Once you've figured out what journey you want to put your protagonist through, give some thought to the childhood and teenhood baggage she might lug on that journey. What did she observe in the adult relationships in her life? What was her dynamic with each of her parents? How about with her high school boyfriends, if she had any at all? What kind of dynamic would she try to mimic, and what would she seek to change? Character sketches that explore character backgrounds can help you understand the presumptions they're bringing into this relationship. Things you might want to know before you start, and certainly look for once you get into the fun of messing with your character's life:

- What is her self-image?
- How is her self-esteem?
- What does she fear from social interactions? How will she react if she encounters those fears?
- What does she like about social interactions? How will she react if she doesn't get that?
- What does she *need* from social interactions? What will she do if she doesn't get that?
- Does she need to feel in control? What will she do if that is threatened?

The answers will likely become more clear to you as you write the story, as the character reacts to all your prodding and reveals what lies within. That's the whole point with striving for *depth*. The following strategies will help you achieve that depth, with the notion of "newness" and new adult inexperience in the forefront of each. You want to make the characters feel real, respond realistically, create connection points, lace their beauty with modesty to keep them approachable, and build the romance from the foundation up instead of just slamming these two people together and calling them Lover 1 and Lover 2.

MAKE THE CHARACTERS FEEL REAL

A successful romance requires characters we can believe in, care about, and find attractive. Cliché characters who walk around ringing the same old bell at all the expected moments won't get such commitment from readers. Your romantic storyline requires you to create characters with depth—flaws, strengths, qualities, and reactions that are distinct and personal and feel wholly rooted in that character's past, dreams, fears, and personality. Deep, unique, vulnerable characters pique our interest, priming our hearts.

Being an NA fiction writer, you have a leg up. At their age, your characters have enough life under their belts to develop distinct personalities and acquire unique baggage, but not enough life to have acquired a deep well of wisdom. This pairing of inexperience and past mistakes makes for beautifully flawed, compulsively readable romance. Their inexperience sets them up to react to relationship crises in unpredictable, ill-advised ways, making us smack our hands to our foreheads in a gesture of "No you didn't. How the heck will you get out of *this* mess?" All of this contributes to unique characters with great depth—who are capable of deep, adult relationships. Above all, these new adults are earnest enough to push onward in the belief that things will, eventually, work out for them if they just try hard enough. Their earnestness is endearing. These are characters you can care about. Even as we smack our foreheads over their fumbling decisions, we will pat their hands after a boo-boo and say reassuringly, "Don't be so hard on yourself, my friend. Nobody's perfect."

Female leads in a romantic NA relationship need to be strong, even if fear and inexperience make them do stupid, harmful, even hurtful things. NA readers want to identify with strong women. They can't stand whiny girls, as comments in online retailer book reviews will attest. Their girls can need love, but they can't feel needy; they are survivors even if survival itself is going to be pretty damn painful. She must have a core inner strength that assures us she'll get up after every punch until that final, climactic moment when she will finally triumph over what needs triumphing over. Strong females are active ones. You cannot let them receive the events of the stories. They can't be sitting around waiting for the guy to show up; they can't be wondering all the time; they can't be waiting for the guy to make the move or fix the fight or arrive on that steed, suit of armor polished to the point of blinding. Even if the actions they take are wrong, the women must take the actions. Eventually they will figure out what's what and do something. Passive chicks can suck the life out of a story. Also, active characters force things to happen, which again serves to move the story forward.

All this active, vulnerable, earnest stuff goes for the male leads in the romance, too. We want them to be awesome and strong enough to be with a strong woman while letting her be the woman she needs to be, but the adage "nobody's perfect" applies here. If he wants to save her, let him blunder the salvation even as you show his intentions are in the right place. If his inner core is about good intentions and morality, then he'll remain lovable even as his efforts may not be ideal Knight in Shining Armor. He can don that suit of armor, but the polish just isn't there yet. Your leading man needs to demonstrate personality attributes we can respect, because that's important to a woman. Women want the man who is sincere and loving and who needs us for his inner completeness, even as he's physically yummy and able to stand up to outside threats. The particulars of his vulnerability are up to your wild imagination, your understanding of his past, your interest in his current needs and hopes for the future. He has to be willing to commit his emotions, even if the leading lady has to draw him to that point through the story. He has to be able to go there.

Spend time in Chapter 4, which is all about creating realistic characters, be they heroes, heroines, or secondary cast. Work to layer the characters in your romantic relationships, since one-dimensional, stereotypical characters aren't attractive. They are posters for lust, perhaps, and you can move them through a plot, but they don't touch readers' hearts.

MAKE YOUR CHARACTERS RESPOND REALISTICALLY

A romantic storyline feels satisfying and convincing when the characters respond to each other and their relationship's ups and downs in believable ways. That is, their reaction remains proportional to the trigger and fits in logically with the personality, circumstances, and baggage you have assigned that character.

Avoid overwrought emotional reactions by setting up circumstances that warrant extreme reactions. If you try to force a huge reaction from a phone call unreturned after the couple's first night together, for example, the emotion can feel unearned, and the protagonist can seem paranoid or needy. Instead, you could set up a pursuit over many scenes, where the protagonist resists for some believable reason until finally she gives in to what she really does want—which is Mr. Hottie. Then you can insert that phone silence after a night when the lover finally lets her guard down, or when she's had a huge upset in some other area of her life and needs to turn to someone but cannot, and the strong reaction feels real.

As you avoid predictable or illogical reactions, or unearned emotion, also remember that misunderstandings and disagreements are very real. Mistakes are real. These young people are inexperienced and flub up. As long as they have good hearts, they will remain sympathetic and we will root for them to overcome that bump in their relationship.

SET UP THE CHARACTERS FOR GOOD LOVIN' FROM THE GET-GO

In Chapter 8 we talked about opening with the right scene, in the right moment. That may mean opening with your lovers-to-be meeting, but it just as well might not. Eventually, though, your lovers will meet, and when they do, that meeting should be memorable.

If you're writing a story with a romantic subplot rather than featuring the romance as your main plot, your characters may not meet in the opening pages, but do get to that meeting soon thereafter, and in circumstances that force them to notice each other and that are related to your distinct plot. As I said above, make the romance matter to other elements of your plot, tying it in so that you couldn't extract it if you wanted to.

Introduce each character as lovable right away, even if they're troubled and at odds with the other lover, by revealing sincerity or earnestness about something. The macho fighter who does something that demonstrates his good manners reveals a deeply held sense of respect. The assassin who will abandon his escape route for a riskier path because a mother pushes a stroller down his preferred street and he doesn't want to risk pursuers mowing her down reveals that he treats innocent people differently than bad people.

As I demonstrated in Chapter 6's examples of the hunk whose bowling ball rolls into the sandaled toes of his soon-to-be girlfriend and the college students who meet when their cars get towed away, get your lovers together in a way that's fresh, specific to your plot, and that could factor into the plot later. Let the characters make a meaningful connection right away—even if you don't exploit that connection until a later scene, and even if that connection is an antagonistic one. Love at first sight isn't a requirement, although some appreciation of physical goodness lays the foundation for their later lust. They should get under the other's skin quickly so that the sexual tension can begin to build. Offer hints about what'll cause them tension; maybe put them at odds in some way. Maybe one or both of them think hooking up is a bad idea. A professor's aide and a student, for example, aren't supposed to date even if both want to.

LIMIT BEAUTY TO THE BEHOLDER'S EYES

As the adage goes, beauty is in the eye of the beholder. You'd be wise to leave it there. When Beauty knows she's beautiful, Beauty is likely to be called a bitch. Women are quite conscious of their own flaws, so they will relate to a female character who demonstrates that she's conscious of hers even as everyone else tells her she's hot stuff. Perhaps she can worry that the outfit she must wear will accentuate the wrong things, or you could send her into a scene on what she'd call a bad hair day and have her totally turn on Mr. Hot Stuff anyway. Readers can relate to a hot guy who misbuttons his shirt or worries about getting home to shower and shave before a date because he cares about his presentation, not because he's narcissistic. Let the people respond to the character as good-looking, but don't let the character be more than passingly aware of it, because the saying "She thinks she's all that" is never meant as a compliment. Don't give your readers any reason to make that observation about the lovers in your romance.

That male lover does need to look mighty fine. Perhaps he's not a model, but he's got the general features we can agree on as appealing: nice hair; a healthy, strong physique; strength and gentle touches as the situation calls for. The details beyond that are up to you. Chapter 4 covers looking beyond color and size to embody your characters. Do your darndest to make the character dress, move, behave, and think compellingly. Sexy is as sexy does.

ESCALATING ROMANTIC TENSION

In a romance storyline, you should be mindful of two kinds of tension—emotional and sexual—and fill your fiction with events, relationships, and exchanges that heighten both.

You get *emotional tension* when you jeopardize characters' hopes and trigger their fears. New adults lack the life experience of more seasoned adults and as fictional characters can be especially vulnerable to this kind of manipulation. Their reactions during this emotionally charged and unsettled phase of life can be quicker, more extreme, and less considered than the reactions of full grown-ups with more experience in relationships. Once you identify your characters' most passionate hopes and deepest fears, use the strategies below to keep gouging at those pressure points.

Sexual tension comes from sexual longing. It can be a purely chemical thing, with every look and touch loaded with sexual want, or it can involve emotional intimacy. Even if your story opens with pure chemistry sparking between your future lovers, eventually those characters will let down their walls and expose the supple emotional stuff. Employing the strategies in this chapter will force the walls to drop and stoke the character conflict and growth, even as you escalate the sexual tension to keep characters and readers riveted by this romance.

ATTACK THE RELATIONSHIP

For taut romantic tension, keep the emotional intimacy on the rocks, even if you do indulge the physical intimacy. Use the plot against them, use the lovers' own emotional issues against them. Don't be afraid to trip them up with misunderstandings. When you're trying to feel out a new lover's wants and needs and match them with your own wants and needs, all while dealing with external pressures, like law school interviews or werewolves or serial killers or parents who just won't let go ... well, you're likely to have a misunderstanding or two. Or twenty. Plus new adults tend to self-analyze and analyze others—often erroneously thanks to their inexperience with considering other's motives and with life in general. Make the most of misunderstandings, working them not just into the relationship's ups and downs but into external plot events, too.

Just as you undercut them with misunderstandings, grant them their disagreements. No one gets along perfectly all the time, not when life is throwing curveballs at them. In fact, sometimes a disagreement is a full-on fight, complete with yelling and accusations and smashing things made of glass with things made of steel. As long as your lovers are fighting fist-free and acting out of their own pain rather than clear-cut meanness, they'll stay sympathetic even if they do treat the other unfairly. They should realize and acknowledge their unfairness at some point, showing that they can mature and exist in an adult relationship as adults.

You can attack the relationship by sticking wedges in it. Love denied is love stoked, so design circumstances, plot events, and settings that keep our lovers apart when they want to be together. Or let them be together but stop them before they can get down and dirty. You can tease the relationship along wonderfully this way, with a stolen kiss or touch, a passionate moment interrupted, promises made. Force their yearning to go unsatisfied until the sexual tension is unbearable, and then, just when readers can't stand the tension any more than the characters can, go ahead and give the lovers their moment. Readers will revel in the togetherness, and you can revel in the fact that you're probably going to jam another wedge between then again in a few short pages.

You can whomp your romantic duo with external plot events. When we're in happy times, we usually can't see the bad times coming. Throw bad times at your unsuspecting lovers like rocks from behind trees they didn't even see. Have an old boyfriend show up just when it seems the stars are finally favoring them. Or let one of them be captured by the mobster's henchmen when we thought all the henchmen were laying in a pool of blood, riddled with bullet holes. Just be sure the justification for a plot twist is already in the storyline so you can't be accused of pulling a rascally rabbit out of your hat.

You can use secondary characters to hinder the romance. Remember how I said in Chapter 4 that your secondary characters must have a job to do in this story beyond just stand as the crowd? Here's a job!

PIT THE LOVERS AGAINST EACH OTHER— AND THEMSELVES

Some relationship issues can be traced to the lovers' personal histories. An orphan may find it hard to let anyone into her heart and so sabotages her own relationships before she can get hurt. A person with a loving, nuclear family and seemingly perfect childhood may be unduly harsh on a less-than-perfect sweetie, pushing him away even as he longs for her. Someone who has always had to prove her love to Daddy may steamroll potential boyfriends, be subservient to her own detriment, or inject any number of other problematic behaviors into her adult love relationships. Use what you know about the character's backgrounds against the lovers, pushing them away from each other in ebb-and-flow fashion in order to raise the tension in their storyline. These young people are relatively inexperienced in matters of the heart as well as life in general, and they haven't had a lot of opportunity to face their faults—or scars—and work through them. Now's the time to face those things, and the poor lovers are going to take some hits while doing it.

USE SETTING TO CREATE OR EXACERBATE CONFLICT

You can build romantic tension with a whole host of setting-related techniques and strategies, which I delve into in Chapter 11. You can choose settings that make them uncomfortable, that keep them apart, that prevent them from revealing their intimacy. You can fill the location with props that cause conflict, like photos of former girlfriends discovered in drawers during innocent digging for a sleepover T-shirt. Make full use of the opportunities that setting offers, with its enormously influential physical and social elements.

TIME YOUR "I LOVE YOU"

You build romantic tension when you don't let lovers realize or express the full extent of their feelings too early. Hold that card close to your chest. Of course readers know the characters will end up together; they're reading to see how the characters will accomplish that. They want to anticipate the protagonist's revelation that this is the person for her. They want to hear that "I love you," and they get nervous for the emotional risk their heroine is taking in saying it. This is prime ground for tension building, as you time that "I love you" for the moment when it feels inevitable for at least one of the characters. Whether you let the lover respond in kind is up to you and the story's needs. And because you are faithful to the notion of ebb and flow, consider ripping the rug from under the characters' feet as soon as they get brave enough to expose their hearts *en toto*.

If the romance is your main storyline, consider timing the "I love you" moment for the climax of the book, with everything leading up to that. The lovers will likely have had sex by then, with you constantly ebb-and-flowing the sexual tension even as you hold out on the emotional commitment. Separating lovemaking from love will let you play the two kinds of tensions against each other and show that these young people may be able to recognize and act on sexual longing, but their emotions still need some work.

If the romance is a secondary storyline, let the romance storyline collide with the other storyline at strategic points. For instance, if you have a character who's built high emotional walls thanks to an abusive childhood, then you can time news of the abusive parent's visit for the very moment that your protagonist lets down her guard with her hunky love interest and leans in for that brave first kiss. The dropping of her shields for love opens her up to an emotional strike from an outside story element. Look for moments like this to collide your romance storyline into your nonromance storyline, and vice versa. In that way, you'll constantly keep your characters (and readers) on edge, even as you give them little victories.

LET THEM DO IT ... THEN FORBID IT

Through the ebb-and-flow strategy, you can let your characters hook up early in the story and still have plenty of opportunity for escalating tension. Go ahead, let them have sex then chomp at the bit to do it again. Hook 'em, then tease 'em along by refusing to let them have sex again for a while. Oh, they might get in a kiss here and there, make a promise or toss innuendos around or even get a date on the books, but you don't allow them to fully hook up again until they're ready to burst. That kind of sexual tension is electric. Every touch and conversation makes them hot, so when they finally get together again it's an explosion.

LET THEM DO IT ... THEN LET THEM BLOW IT

The flip side of keeping them separate after a hookup is to make one or both purposely avoid another hookup even when the sexual desire is there. This is about withholding emotion, and that creates powerful romantic tension. Consider letting your couple get together early in the book thinking that the hookup will resolve their emotional issues—only to awake the next morning and find that those emotional issues are all still there. Or maybe the issues are even worsened! Imagine a hero who is more confused after sex because his emotions were triggered by *this* woman in bed—as opposed to his other meaningless lovers before—and that scares him. That poor guy might throw his emotional walls up fast and high, crushing your other character in the process.

LET THEM BREAK THE RULES

Characters who do the unexpected create tension because they keep us guessing and stressing. New Adult fiction carved its own path by breaking the rules, embracing self-publishing when traditional publishers said there was no market for their stories. Think out of the box. Kelley York's *Hushed* asks readers to give their hearts to a murderer—something we know we shouldn't want to do but end up doing anyway. There's definitely tension in rooting for love when we don't expect to.

THREADING YOUR ROMANCE THROUGH A SERIES

The challenge of writing a romance that will play out across several books boils down to one thing: keeping that romance fresh and thus interesting for readers. Retreading the same issues and breakup/makeup cycles gets old quick. Luckily, you're writing about new adults, and since new adults exist in a perpetual state of change and exploration, you've got lots of room to come up with totally new and unexpected obstacles for the couple. Here are seven tactics for keeping the relationships fresh and on the rocks.

1. EXPLOIT THE THREAT OF BREAKUP

Since new adults aren't typically signing marriage certificates, the possibility of breakup remains a constant threat to the relationship. At any time, one or both lovers in the couple can decide this game is just too rough and they want out. Keep that in mind as you plan the circumstances and conflicts for each book in the series.

2. USE CHANGE TO UNDERMINE THE RELATIONSHIP

A relationship can end well in one book, only to go all to hell in the next because things changed in one or both of the characters' lives. That's the new adult experience, after all—constant change as the young people encounter new opportunities. The story can pick at those flaws that hobbled the characters the first time around, but it must test them in a new way to lead them to a new maturity. Perhaps it's the next step in their lives, with them moving on from college to new jobs that will test the characters with new challenges. The girl in your Southern Cal couple just got an internship offer in DC. That's opportunity that'll stress a relationship. New opportunities beget change beget stress, and stress is a bitch on relationships.

3. USE NEW RELATIONSHIPS AGAINST THEM

The new adult phase is marked by transient relationships as young people find new interests that they want to explore, or take on new jobs and other affiliations that bring with them a new daily social circle. Your couple may end Book 1 together, but excitement over the new social circles can spark jealousy or anxiety between the lovers. Perhaps there's real interest in a new relationship as one partner in the romantic couple really does wonder if they've made the right choice. Those new peers will certainly bring their own baggage to the story—as every good secondary character should—and that could introduce fresh conflict in an entirely new area that your readers will love to explore with your characters.

4. TEAR THEM APART FOR A CLIFF-HANGER

A relationship may be healthy within, but it's not immune to your "think big, push hard" philosophy. Consider tearing them apart in the final chapter of the first book, in cliff-hanger fashion. This works for a series that has an externally driven plot, where you can end with the couple together yet still facing an external problem. The possibilities here abound, with outside forces keeping them physically apart or some kind of emotional rift making the relationship seem unlikely even though we do, of course, know our starring couple will hook up in the end. Enemy troops can capture a lover, forcing the other character to start Book 2 alone, frantic but determined to get Lover back.

5. DIG UP ISSUES FROM THE PAST

A common romantic storyline has one person in the relationship providing the pillar that helps the other overcome some kind of emotional battle. It's not hard to imagine that stalwart lover hiding his own battles in order to be that pillar—and Book 2 is the perfect place for that sacrifice to emerge and blow things all to hell again. Now the roles are switched, allowing readers to pine for the emotional survival of that other person in the relationship. There's much possibility for messiness there as the Lover who's used to hiding his pain must finally confront it, something sure to stress even the "perfect" relationship.

6. REVISIT THE SAME STORY FROM THE OTHER'S POINT OF VIEW

There are two sides to every story, or so the adage goes. That notion sure works well for NA fiction, where sequels that revisit the adventures of the first book from the other lover's point of view are common. At the end of Chapter 3, Molly

McAdams talked about how she as the author discovered all new things about her male romantic lead by revisiting the events of *Taking Chances* from his point of view in *Stealing Harper*. "I didn't know he felt that way," Molly told me of Chase. Tammara Webber also used this approach with her bestseller *Easy*, which was conceived as a stand-alone book and published only in the female protagonist's point of view, and its sequel *Breakable*, which covered the same events of *Easy* but from the male character's point of view. Tammara told me, "Lucas didn't 'speak' to me while I was writing *Easy*. I heard Jacqueline's voice only. I got occasional glimpses into Lucas's life, his past, and his current struggles, but most of these came as a surprise to me as I wrote; I was very focused on Jacqueline. It's not been hard to get into his head—but if he hadn't begun speaking to me a few months after I'd published *Easy*, I'd have never written *Breakable*. I only write what I'm led to write, internally." Use the tips in Chapters 3 and 4 to sculpt the other character's narrative point of view, which will dig deeper into his psyche and manner of expressing his thoughts than the glimpse we got of those things in his Book 1 speaking parts.

7. SWITCH THE POINT OF VIEW FOR BOOK 2

Like number 6 above, this option will have you working up the other character's point of view and narrative voice, too, only it will pick up the events from the end of Book 1. All the adventures will be new, which may be important to you if you're concerned that revisiting will just feel too stale to energize you and thus hinder your ability to finish the manuscript or to get readers energized about the book. Here, you still get a fresh, new take on the couple by telling the story from the other character's point of view, but you can also mine new changes that come with new opportunities and social circles. This can also be a fun way to explore the different mind-sets of men and women as you adjust the narrative to reflect gender nuances. Tammara Webber gives us a glimpse into her creative process with this choice as well: "I originally wrote *Between the Lines* from Emma's POV *only*. I was more than halfway through writing the second book—which contains Reid's POV—when I realized that Reid's voice was what was missing from *BTL*, and that the entire series was actually about *him*. I hadn't published *BTL* yet, so I put my work-in-progress on hold and *rewrote* the entire first book to alternate between Reid and Emma."

WRITING SEXY SEX SCENES

Writing a sex scene that's truly sensual and emotionally satisfying for readers takes just as much attention to craft as any other writing element. I'll cover that now, as well as point you to Chapter 5's host of techniques for dialogue and revealing action in narrative beats, and Chapter 4's strategies for conveying characters' emotions and personalities and embodying them physically.

First, though, before you start writing about your characters' romp in the sheets, you should find your own G-spot. That is, ask yourself how explicit *you* want your story to be. What are *you* comfortable reading and writing? NA love scenes have the green flag to go into full detail, but they don't have to. If a PG-13 rating is more your style, there are plenty of readers for you, and there are plenty of ways for you to tell a sensuous story that satisfies those readers (and you) without making anyone uncomfortable. At least for the ladies—and that's the majority of NA readers and authors so far—sexual satisfaction depends a lot on what goes on in a gal's head. As long as you keep your romance factor high, your sensual tension taut, and your focus on the wonderful emotions of love-making, you don't have to describe the act in intimate detail. Our minds will be right there romping with the characters. Forcing yourself to write beyond your comfort zone is just asking for ham-handedness, with you dropping in stock phrases and moving on quickly rather than lingering in the scene as the lovers explore each others' bodies and emotions. Your discomfort will show.

If you're comfortable writing more explicit content, proceed boldly and enjoy the freedom that NA offers, even as you challenge yourself to think creatively about describing the action. Even explicit content needs nuance and elements particular to your characters so that it doesn't feel like you could pull the scene out of this book and drop it into another without anyone noticing the seams.

You also need to consider the story itself. Does explicit detail fit the tone of the rest of the story? Will it feel like an organic part of this storyline, or will it feel out of step with the rest of the narrative or with the characters themselves? For example, if yours is a story of a character's first time having sex, it would make sense to include a lot of physical details and sensations as the character focuses on each new touch, explicitly stating the body parts and manner of stimulation. Or if you've got characters who are bold about expressing themselves, they're going to be bold about their sex, so stronger words and descriptions would feel organic to that cast. Let your story, circumstances, and character personalities help you reach your decision regarding explicitness.

Once you have a feel for the degree of detail you want in your love scenes, use the following strategies for writing a satisfying love scene that feels like it could only be in your specific story, featuring your specific characters.

LAY THE FOUNDATION FOR GREAT SEX

Great buildup begets great sex. If you do all the work I've suggested to build up sexual tension and make a sex scene absolutely inevitable, you've already got your characters and your readers all keyed up and you won't have to get heavy-handed. Suddenly throwing in a sex scene without proper lead-in puts too much burden on the scene to rev itself up from nothing, making it feel forced and unearned and very likely schlocky. Always think, *Story first, then sex*. If you build your characters' relationship and desires, then the sex scene will come along organically.

BE SENSUAL, NOT MECHANICAL

Instead of focusing solely on actions, write about things that trigger readers' senses and make them feel like they're in that moment of passion. Write about the setting, the crackle of the fire in the hearth and the thrum of the waves on the sand. Write about the scent of the character's hair, the amorous lick of the cool breeze on her breast when he arches his warm chest away. Write about the curtained room with just that one shaft of moonlight penetrating the darkness. Sensory detail offers you opportunities to work in contraception, since many writers want to address that but don't want it breaking the mood. Write the sound of a drawer opening, the flashing of a wrapper, the nod of her head. No awkward "Did you bring protection?" dialogue needed. You have the power to suggest things by invoking sounds, scents, sensations, and textures. Mine that power. There's certainly a time and place for direct, deliberate actions like thrusting and kissing, but surround those with sensual elements that put readers in that delicious moment.

BRING THEIR ISSUES TO BED

Write about what's in the point-of-view character's head and the reaction of that person to the sex. Has your leading lady got trust issues? Write about how she can drop the wall to this man in bed. Consider how this moment of intimacy fulfills her needs at this time. Or *not*. Also, it's easy to see how issues from childhood or previous interactions with members of the opposite sex can play into one's comfort in bed—but remember that *any*thing can come to bed with us. Stress about a big decision weighing on your character? She'll bring that tenseness to bed. Distracted by problems with co-workers or in school? Jazzed about scoring a coveted internship or vanquishing some kind of mortal enemy? That'll be a part of the sexual dynamic, too. If it can stir up your character's brain or heart, it can hinder or help her libido.

TAKE YOUR TIME

Even fast and furious sex should be indulged on the page. Readers want satisfaction from the scene, not to see you tick off a box, so give the moment its full pay. If you feel an urge to rush through it, that may be your red flag that you're just hitting a plot marker, not building deep characters and working on the internal arc. Revisit the section of this chapter that talks about making the romance storyline matter even if it's not your main plot. Use the other strategies in this section to make the love scene fun for you to write and possibly even discover things about your character's relationship you never knew, sparking your excitement about the scene. Make the scene be about more than the lovemaking so that you'll invest as much importance in it as you do any scene that you know is actively pushing your protagonist through her arc.

USE YOUR WRITER'S TOOLBOX, NOT YOUR THESAURUS

Writing an interesting scene is not about switching up the lingo to avoid repeating the same word, or using words that feel vulgar or awkward to you because you want the scene to be hot. That just ends up with more awkwardness and doesn't do diddly for enriching the scene. Your love scene deserves the same careful crafting and variety that you give to any other scene. Avoid cliché phrasing and predictable similes. Respect your audience's ability to hear strong and precise words rather than getting cutesy with euphemisms. "Her secret garden" is the stuff of cliché legend—leave it there. If your character is one who would be comfortable talking dirty in bed, then by all means go there with the sexual banter and don't be namby-pamby about it. If that doesn't suit your characters, don't be afraid to leave out the strong words. Have your characters reassure the other person with gentle words and sentiments like, "It was always you," delivering an emotional wallop. You can have them talk in playful teases or try to talk but be unable in the face of their desire:

> "That blouse …" He groans as she slowly unbuttons her shirt, her fingers pausing halfway to gently push away his reaching hand.
>
> She shakes her head. "Patience." Her fingers move to the next button.

That example uses dialogue that teases. It's about a shirt rather than a body part, and it isn't likely to punch anyone's vulgarity buttons. It uses a prop to focus readers on very precise details and anatomical regions, likely leading the way to other very specific actions and regions. And it lingers, building sexual tension. I encourage you to use all the strategies I lay out in this section, mixing them up for a rich scene that evokes all the senses. Include opinions and judgments that show emotions are being engaged and baggage being dealt with or denied. Write about all kinds of things, not just the action and the dialogue.

CRAFT CLOSE-UP: WHAT KIND OF LOVER ARE YOU?

This is a variation of the "What Kind of Friend Are You?" writing exercise in Chapter 4. Since a romantic relationship is so very different from a friendship, it calls for a different mind-set on your part. This exercise will help you focus on your lovers' differences, on their distinct contributions to the relationship, and on the reason you've romantically linked them in the first place. It's about discovery, not writing pretty prose, so just hack it out on the keyboard.

Here's the scenario: Your couple is having a fight about a cancelled date or a misplaced item. Each character must make an accusation, and each character must concede something—that way we get the full breadth of an argument, from accusation to resolution. As most fights tend to be, this is about more than the cancellation or the lost object. Use these three phrases somewhere in that argument:

> "You always…"
>
> "You don't understand…"
>
> "I didn't know that."

You can set this exercise in your story's era or in a totally different one just to have fun with it.

When you're done, consider what you learned about each character's needs in this fight. Now read the finished argument to a writing partner and ask that partner to write down one thing the characters learned about each other through the fight and at least one reason why the friend thinks this relationship could be useful to your protagonist's personal goal or journey. Compare that feedback to your expectations and goals with this relationship.

CRAFT CLOSE-UP: THINKING ABOUT SEX

What makes a person sexy? Knowing what *you* think makes a person the cat's meow will help you come up with a variety of ways to convey your romantic lead's sex appeal. It's easy to say someone is gorgeous, but what takes him or her beyond easy on the eyes to someone who makes you go weak in the knees? Why *this* guy or girl and not the one standing next to him or her? Why are they sexy *this* day and not yesterday?

I've listed a series of questions to make you think beyond the go-to ripped abs and tats, as sexy as those may be. I've thrown in some ideas to jog your thinking. Turn off your mental filter and give yourself over to brainstorming a full list of things that push you past the knee-jerk to the unexpected, which can add depth, interest, individuality, and detail to your characterization. Make a list for guys and another for girls, because if you've got a romance, you've probably got both genders in that relationship. When you're done, keep your list in your writing folder to reference for all your books, not just your current WIP (work in progress).

Have some extra fun with this by asking your BFF to join you for this exercise. Meet up at the local coffee shop, maybe call in another gal pal or two, then start group brainstorming. In no time you'll be ooh-la-laing and arguing and high-fiving up a storm, making everyone else in the café go, "Um ... I'll have what they're having."

- What does sexy look like?
- What does sexy smell like?
- What does sexy sound like?
- How does sexy talk?
- How does sexy move?
- How does sexy dress?
- What does sexy do?
- What does sexy know?
- What does sexy taste like?
- What is sexy's attitude and outlook?
- What is sexy's social position?
- How does sexy flirt?
- What are sexy's turn-ons?
- What does sexy's pillow talk sound like?
- How does sexy make love?

CHAPTER 11

Building a World Around the New Adult Experience

ixty percent of America's young people bustle off to college right after high school. It stands to reason, then, that a good many NA storytellers craft tales featuring a college setting and lifestyle. A similar tendency befalls YA fiction writers, who must send their characters to high school each day or find compelling reasons for not doing so—school vacations, perhaps, or dystopian catastrophes, or street urchincy and other exceptional lifestyles that prevent school attendance or put kids beyond the purview of authorities who would enforce it. NA writers don't have to look so hard for reasons to eschew classrooms. Daily 8:00–3:00 attendance isn't the college experience, and even college kids have full lives beyond scholastic events and other students. And what about those 40 percent who don't go to college straight after high school? They're struggling through the challenges of new adulthood and having fascinating adventures, too. Some enter the work force, some join the military, some flounder without a job or daily purpose. So the new adult experience is more than just campus and dorm room, especially if your genre is science fiction, historical fiction, paranormal, or straight fantasy. Thus, NA fiction writers have a multitude of setting choices for their fictional worlds.

This chapter guides you in choosing settings that offer rich storytelling opportunities for your new adult characters. After I cover ways to enhance your NA sensibility, characterization, and themes through setting choices, I'll arm you with a host of tactics to serve up the sounds, smells, textures, temperatures, and sensations that make a setting feel real. Above all, your characters will react to or act upon your carefully selected setting to reveal their personalities and add depth to each scene. Skillful handling of the setting enhances your characterization and enriches the entire novel.

USING SETTING TO ENRICH YOUR NA FICTION

Setting choices can have a huge impact on your characters and story, enhancing your efforts with your characterization, dialogue, sensibility, and plot, so this topic has threaded its way through this book. Here, I put a spotlight on how you can use setting to goose your new adult characters through their arcs (both internal and external), and how you can make common NA settings *uncommon*—and thus interesting for the characters, your readers, and yourself as you move through this fictional world.

USE SETTING TO EXACERBATE NA ISSUES

In Chapter 7 I urged you to push your characters mercilessly. New adulthood offers up unique opportunities to push your characters with setting.

- **JUICE THEIR FRAGILE WORLDVIEW.** New adults are actively solidifying their worldview, and your choice of setting can be a factor in your new adult characters' morals and value system. Their faith, politics, ethics, and personal perspectives have all been influenced by where and when they grew up and the social circumstances of that time and place. Now, newly independent and on their way to becoming fully self-accountable, they're weighing who they are so far and deciding if they like what they see. They have total freedom to accept or reject until they're happy with what is finally, truly their own sense of self. Test their value structures by putting them in environments that oppose what they've always known. Send them to places they don't want to be because it makes them face issues they don't want to face. For example, make your character who is having a crisis of faith pick up his friend at a church.
- **TRIGGER THE ANGST INHERENT IN THEIR TRANSITORY LIFESTYLE.** New adulthood is a time of temporary living arrangements, transitory relation-

ships, and short commitments, with its internships, classes, and just-to-pay-the-bills jobs. This causes angst that you can deliberately tap into with your setting decisions. You can send your new adults from one unfamiliar setting to another, never letting them get their footing. You can deny them any places of familiarity and comfort, or deny them the ones they do have when they need them. You can give them access to those places when the story needs a breather, granting them a moment of calm, a moment of hopefulness, a moment of thinking that maybe, just maybe, they'll pull this thing off. Then throw them back out in worse circumstances and more unyielding settings.

- **USE TIME AGAINST THEM.** Setting isn't just a place to be. It's the time of that place, too. Day versus night, Monday versus Friday, beginning of the semester versus holiday break, past or present or future … characters' behaviors and mind-sets are heavily influenced by time. Often new adults are struggling with time management and self-regulation, and you can use that to your advantage. Use their wonky schedules to keep lovers apart and build sexual tension, let their sleep deprivation be your friend in creating conflict, throw conflict at your characters at the end of the day or during a winter snow storm when leaving during an argument isn't an option. Keep your eyes on your fictional clock.
- **USE THEIR EXPERIMENTATION AND EXPLORATION AGAINST THEM.** New adulthood is a time of heavy exploration and experimentation. Put your characters in places they wouldn't normally be, at times that aren't safe, and where their self-confidence is tested. Instead of that tame stroll on the beach with shy conversation, put your lovers in a rock climbing gym with ropes and pulleys, with fear clouding their judgment and trust being tested.

FIND FRESH IN THE OLD

New adults aren't interested in the same ol', same ol'—and neither should you be, in any element of your fiction. Help your story stand out from other NA fiction by putting your characters in uncommon places, at uncommon times, with uncommon people even as you deal with universal new adult issues and themes. Finding fresh spaces in common places is especially important when you have a contemporary NA story set on campus. If you absolutely need events to take place in common settings, look for an uncommon angle on that space to keep it interesting and fresh.

Making Campus Uncommon

The beer garden outside Monty's in the Quad is a knee-jerk type of setting for many. How about picking the campus bowling alley under the Quad instead? Imagine the sounds in that place! Need your college lovers to get dolled up and dance a slow number to a live band? Move the sorority formal from that familiar ballroom in the swanky hotel to a "haunted" hotel on the other side of town, with thematic *Phantom of the Opera*–style formal attire required. A whole new set of props and costuming and atmosphere!

Making Living Spaces Uncommon

New adults are forever moving from one space to the next as finances, semesters, circumstances, and relationships change. I said that you need to make your settings feel new or present them in a way that feels unfamiliar. Imagine the college apartment we're used to, with mix-and-matched furniture and dents in that coffee table they picked up at Goodwill. What would we learn about a young person whose apartment is pristine and carefully assembled instead? Or what about a crafty-looking space, showing the character's creativity, vision, resourcefulness, patience, and attention to detail? Characterization through setting! You can do further characterization work by juxtaposing your protagonist's comfort in that setting with another character's ill fit: Walk that other character into that pristine apartment with muddy shoes, and have him toss his jacket on the floor and flip his sweaty ball cap onto a Bonsai tree near the window because he's ignorant of the care that must go into creating and maintaining such a perfect pad. His brain doesn't even process it.

Even if you're not writing a contemporary college story, you still have a living space to consider. Think about all the things one's living space reveals about them, such as their priorities, their time, and their hobbies and interests. You can choose to reflect those things in their homes, or you can do the opposite by deliberately devising a living space that is intensely *not* them. The historical thriller *Nefertiti's Heart* by A.W. Exley opens with a young woman in her dead father's dusty, stuffy study, a place that holds only horrible memories for her. She knows the exact spot in that oppressive room where her blood soaked the carpet in that last beating before she ran away so many years ago. She has to live in this house while she settles her father's affairs, but she will be a victim there no longer. The very first line shows her ripping apart the room with a crowbar, losing herself in the act of tearing apart his sanctuary layer by layer. By making her live in an environment that is not her style and which holds pain, Exley forces her into a state of discomfort. She has to physically leave the home in order to feel her shoulders relax. Ironically, the town outside her father's home is itself a painful place for her, underscoring just how much angst that home causes that she should find solace in town. It's a matter of degrees, of the writing moving up and down a scale of discomfort using setting changes.

Making Workplaces Uncommon

Your new adult is probably at the bottom of the totem pole and ripe for exploitation in the workplace. Have others give her crappy assignments that put her in rooms with bad lighting and bad equipment, or set your character on the street making a fool of herself with product demonstrations, or have her staying late in a quiet, abandoned office space stocked with unexpected props, opening up opportunities for distraction or creepiness or any number of unexpected developments that might come out of her exhaustion, stress, or ambition. Consider the social context of the workspace, where others may set up your protagonist for their own mistakes in the office place, pitting your lead character against the bureaucracy and establishment. New adults are energetic and inexperienced people, so they're likely to take on or accept more than they can do—embrace their optimism and then slam them with reality. Send them to the office dinner parties, holiday parties, picnics, and happy hours instead of always showing them relating to co-workers in their workplace. And put them in industries that offer great props in their work places, like a photography agency or a radio station or a medical clinic with freaky medical tools and patients who are alternately endearing and nuts. Have fun with new adult ambition and earnestness, combining that with your protagonist's youthful energy and then letting other workers react to her attitude in good and bad ways. Use the physical setting and the people that flow through it to show your character making good and bad choices, both the immediate kind and the long-term career kind.

Making Party Places Uncommon

New adults like their parties, and a lot of NA features college kids hitting the party scene. Keep your parties fresh and interesting by changing their locations. Instead of sending your new adult characters to a nightclub, put them outdoors in a crowded music festival, with the aroma of marijuana blending with Port-A-Potty glory. Let the breeze caress their faces as the beautiful music takes them to a new plane of happiness. Or let them win tickets on the radio to the murder mystery pub crawl downtown. If they must be in the frat house, make the shindig a theme party. Casino night. Fifties hop. Or set the party of the year on a rainy night: Nobody stays away, but everybody is drippy and muddy and still having a good time.

SETTING EXERCISE #1: WHERE I GO IS WHO I AM

Goal: To define your character by the kind of environment that gives him peace. When you know that, you can deny that environment in order to deny that sense of peace as you tighten the wringer on your poor, unsuspecting character.

Write a paragraph introducing your protagonist to a critique partner or to a fictional friend. There's a catch: You can't write about the character himself, but rather you'll write about his favorite place.

You have many options here. Your place could be your character's refuge, revealing things that give him comfort or which are intensely private. It could be your character's favorite place to go with friends, revealing his sense of humor or perhaps even risk-taking level. You might choose to write about the personal objects in that space or maybe the features of the setting, like climbing trees with low branches. You might choose to write about how your character occupies that place, focusing on its conditions and sensations. This is your character's special space, so it should reveal things about him even when he's not there. Fill about a half page to a full page.

MAKING YOUR SETTINGS FEEL REAL

I've focused so far on ways to use the setting to manipulate your characters and the story. Now let's look at ways to make your setting feel real. You can do that by applying the "Show, don't tell" approach, which has you using props and environmental details to trigger readers' senses so that they feel like they're in the scene with the characters. Or you can be more direct and just describe the setting outright, doing so in a dynamic, well-timed way. I'll give you tips for both.

But first, a warning for your own creative peace of mind and productivity: Do not try to do all this setting work in the first draft. The first draft is about getting everything in place. It's the perfect time to strategize the big stuff, such as the locations, but don't fuss over the tiny details, all the sprinkling and narrative beats and such. That's revision stuff, when you're starting to add layers to your story. I talk a lot more about prioritizing revision details in Chapter 12, which I devote to revision strategy. That strategy includes assessing your use of setting and applying all the advice in this chapter to turn a good draft into a great one.

ENGAGING YOUR READER'S SENSES

Long setting description isn't the style *du jour*. That's okay—applying the "show, don't tell" approach to setting will keep you from pummeling your readers with descriptive adjectives. Showing is about action, not descriptive adjectives. Trigger the senses and look for alternate ways to express things. You don't want to describe a snowy meadow. That's like looking at a photo. Readers want to be there trudging through the boot-sucking drifts, so preoccupied with tucking and retucking their pants into their boots to keep the snow from squishing into them that they trip on a half-buried log and fall sideways into a snow drift. The violent jam of cold into their ear and their eye and down the neck of their parka where their body heat almost instantly melts it, soaking their cotton tee. There's looking at it, and then there's living it. Let your readers live it.

Here are four ways to engage the five senses:

1. **REACT TO THE ELEMENTS.** Every location has its physical characteristics, such as lighting conditions, temperature, and noise level. Have a character react to those elements in ways that convey to readers how the elements make him feel. Don't just write that it's smoky in the canyon after the fire; have your character wet a rag and hold it to his nose and mouth, his eyes tearing up from the acrid sting. You want the sensations of that place, and having your characters react to the elements is one way to convey that.

2. **ENGAGE WITH THE PROPS.** Props offer your characters opportunities for tactile interaction with the setting, which means major opportunities for sensual details. A hot cup of tea must be palmed on a cold day, perfume samples in magazines must be sniffed, bike horns must be honked, a smooth rock must be stroked. Every interaction with a prop is an opportunity to pull the reader deeper into your story by making him feel like

he's there. For added fun, use running prop gags. That is, have some long-term fun with setting details and props, like a picture that keeps falling down; a wristwatch alarm the character can't turn off, so it goes off at the same time every day; or a car that needs water put in the engine before it goes anywhere.

3. **WRITE SCENES ABOUT THE SETTING.** I talk about this in terms of writing an NA sexy scene in Chapter 10. You can get sensual with your storytelling by writing scenes that seem to be about the setting even though they're really delivering information about the characters and plot. For example, writing about the way a character packs his suitcase—a scene that seems to be about the literal items and possessions—can reveal how he feels about that trip to see his ex-girlfriend. Writing about the way ice cream drips down a girl's hand can reveal how distracted that girl is.

4. **WRITE ABOUT THE CONTRAST.** You know that pain you get in your eyes when you step from darkness to light? Write about that pain. You know that burn you get in your butt when you're climbing up a long set of stairs and you wish you'd taken the elevator? Write about why that elevator would be better than the stairs. Focusing on the feelings you get in one setting versus another gives you an excuse to tell readers about those places. They're so busy focusing on the contrast with you that they don't mind some moments of description. And you get to reveal things about your character in the process.

DESCRIBING YOUR SETTING

I've talked about ways to "show" the setting, but sometimes you just need to describe that beautiful sandy shore or that twisted metal after the fateful car accident. Sometimes just stepping back and taking in the whole scene with our eyes is absolutely perfect for a scene. It's okay to do that sometimes and can be quite natural because you're already handling setting with balanced variety. Description is just one more method.

In fact, rethink the word *describe*. Instead of setting out to tell the reader about the place you see in your head, aim to establish a state of mind for your character. For instance, have the character compare in her head how her new digs are not like her old ones, revealing what she's come to as well as what she left, but more importantly revealing *what she is used to and how things are dif-*

ferent or more of the same. Is the character comfortable with the difference or the similarity? Does it raise the angst or frustrate her?

You will have those moments where you just want to say, "The car was sleek and black and fully loaded." Go for it. Your mastery of variety makes it possible for you to use as a tool what others overuse or misuse. Descriptions are okay if you just remember that brevity is your friend. New adults and grown adults can handle longer descriptions than young adults, but it's still not the modern reader's expectation to be blanketed with a swath of sheer description. The sprinkle technique below will help you exercise brevity with description.

SPRINKLING THE SETTING

Instead of plunking down big blobs of description so as to paint the picture for the scene and then moving on to action and dialogue, aim to work in your setting here and there throughout the scene, as if flicking wet fingers at your pages instead of pouring water on them straight from a spout. Even readers who aren't intimidated by a few lines of description could skip over big splashes of it in search of the story thread. Provide your details about time and place as you go along, in the narrative beats of a conversation. Narrative beats are those snippets of narrative between lines of dialogue. (I talked about those in Chapter 5.) Beats are those moments where your gut says you need a breath or a pause in the rhythm of the conversation. Too often writers fill that pause with a generic, unrevealing action like a character pushing his bangs out of his eyes. Don't do that! Beats are great places for the characters to interact with or react to the setting. So a line about a hot guy saying, "Hi," and then pushing bangs out of his eyes would instead read like this:

> "Hi," he said, pulling a handkerchief from his vest pocket and using that to turn the filthy doorknob. "You're new here, aren't you?

A lot of sprinkles like this, involving the state of the filthy building he's entering, will help you build up a sense of place. In the process, we get to see how the characters feel about that place. This guy is willing to go in, but he's not willing to directly touch the grime. Here's an example that's more than just a passing moment:

"Check the dining compartment." I nudged the cabin drapes aside. A gleaming silver wing jutted out of the hull just a few windows behind ours, the engine at the very end. "Go get him, will you? We need to get our story straight before we give the necklace to the Countess."

"Like she would even care where it came from." She had to tug twice on the heavy cabin door to get it open.

I let the drapes fall, sending the room back into shadow. With any luck, the engine drone would settle into background noise and lull me to sleep. Smuggling ancient Mayan treasure could sure wear a guy out.

With that example, we've got the physical props, we've got interaction with those props, and we've got exposition about the smuggling, which has nothing to do with the props. There are a variety of things going on in the beats, even as we get sensory information that has engaged our sense of hearing.

You want a lot of variety in your sprinkling. You don't just want *"Blah blah," he said, turning the knob. "Blah blah," she said back, smelling a rose.* That will totally sabotage the flow of the storytelling, and it's relying on just one trick. You are not a one-trick pony. Sometimes give us the dialogue tags and sometimes skip them altogether. Sometimes give us a physical engagement with the prop, and sometimes just state that the prop is there and be done with it. Sometimes just say, "It's hot," in the narrative. And sometimes don't say anything about the setting. Not all beats need to be about setting. Sometimes they are just exposition, like my line about the Mayan treasure hunt. The variety creates a natural flow throughout the chapter.

SETTING EXERCISE #2: SENSORY AWARENESS

Goal: Notice new details about familiar spaces and find fabulous sensory elements in brand new spaces.

I'm going to walk you through some physical spaces, challenging you to turn off some senses in order to focus on others. Let's start with the space you're in right now. After you read this paragraph, close your eyes and listen. If you're playing music, turn it off to truly take in the sounds of that physical space.

What do you hear? Planes flying overhead? The house settling? Loved ones breathing deeply in bedrooms nearby? A barista calling a name above the abrupt *zshhh* of the hot water? The clunk of the door, perhaps? The squeak of the guy's shoe next to you as he bounces his knee up and down, his rubber sneaker resting on a sticky part of the linoleum?

Put on a pair of silenced headphones or insert foam ear buds, and then watch the activity around you. What is the body language of the couple talking at that table across the café? Who is dominating that conversation? What makes you think that? Are they happy? Debating? Gossiping? Quarrelling? What is their angle toward each other? Are they leaning in? Touching for emphasis? Not eating or sipping at all? At the park, what is that child's face registering on the swing set? How is the toddler reacting to the sand she's sitting on? At the library, which person is studying? What does his expression tell you about the topic in his book? Focus on the colors of the room. Are they muted? Bright? Is the lighting affecting that? How is the temperature? Do you need an extra layer of clothing? Should you undo a few buttons on your sweater? Can you sink into that chair, or does its straight back force you to perch upright? Does that suit your mood?

After reading this paragraph, close your eyes again and pick up a familiar object. What does it feel like? Rough? Smooth? How heavy is it? Do you think it would be heavier if you were to heft it again later tonight? Why, what's different about that later time? What's different about *you* at that later time? Touch the leaf on that bush. Is it furry? Slick? Rubbery? Veiny? Does it leave residue on your finger? Wipe your fingers on your pants—can you feel the weave of the cloth? Denim? Can you feel the grain of wood on your desk? Why? Is the finish worn away? Is the finish thick and smooth? Lean down and watch how the light hits that table—do you see fingerprints or marks you hadn't noticed? Do you have the urge to wipe it clean with a sponge or polish it?

Our world is full of sensory details we don't consciously notice. Use your heightened awareness to sprinkle sensory details throughout your fiction and deepen your readers' engagement with the story.

CHAPTER 12

Revising in a Speed-Driven Market

The creative process fascinates me. As both a writer and a teacher of other writers, I find interviews of creative people edifying and inspiring. Recently I was watching an old *Inside the Actors Studio* interview with Jay Leno when something he said summed up the revision process for me. He was talking about working up a comedy bit, but it holds true for writers: "Set yourself a certain amount of time to work on the act. I mean, if you were making a table or a chair, the first day you wouldn't go, 'Well here's the block of wood, it should be a chair by tomorrow.' Well, it's not going to be a chair by tomorrow. It's going to take you a bit of time." New Adult fiction writers feel the need to publish frequently and quickly. By creating books outside the notoriously slow traditional publishing process and utilizing the speedy ease of digital publishing technology, self-publishing NA authors tend to compress their book production time to a few months instead of a year or more, and readers have gotten used to that. Never mind that the writing of a story hasn't been magically sped up by that technology. The fact that you can actually hear your readers clamoring for more via social media and online reviews adds to your pressure to write and publish quickly.

Publishing subpar work may meet initial clamor, but readers will discern quickly that it's not your best work. And they'll let that be known in social media and reviews, too. Speed is great, but quality is better. You can have both.

Plenty of authors do, including many who have shared their insights for this book. Jennifer L. Armentrout is known for being prolific, so when she talks about the novels that took her a month to write, few are surprised. But then we hear she spent a year on *Half-Blood*. Colleen Hoover has reported that one of her books took her a month to write, and another took six months. She slowed down to work on a tricky character for that six-monther and even set the story aside for a bit. She wanted to get him right. Both authors put those numbers in context by explaining that they write as many as eight hours a day, sometimes up to twelve. Successful NA authors slow down enough to make sure what they slam onto the page in the initial burst of creativity has been pinched and pulled to its best form by the time they send it out into the world.

"The revision part of the process takes longer than the initial writing. The writing usually comes very quickly, then the revision will take two to three times longer than the first draft." —SYLVIA DAY, former Romance Writers of America president and author of the pioneering NA Crossfire series

---

Ultimately, it comes down to you and your readers, as NA always does. The writer-reader relationship is the linchpin of this revolutionary fiction category. You need to be satisfied that you've written the great story you set out to write for your fans, and your readers need to be satisfied that the story couldn't have been any better. Thousands of other novels and pieces of NA fiction are in the market with your work. Your readers' continuing enthusiasm will keep your publishing career alive, so you need to give yourself a certain amount of time to work on your act. You can't look at a block of text on the screen and believe it'll be a book tomorrow. You may be able to pull off a pass of sentence tweaking before the sun rises again, but sentence tweaking isn't revision. That's polishing up a revision.

I'm going to take you into the process of deep, meaningful revision, giving you the tools you need to revise your story effectively as well as efficiently. We'll cover critiquing Big Picture items like character and plot arcs and evaluating more precise items like language mechanics and narrative flaws. I'm including "tests" to help you spot possible weak points and questions that you can ask yourself and pose to your beta readers to make sure you assess all the items you can. I've gathered those questions in a single comprehensive Story Evaluation Questions sheet, which I've included at the end of this chapter. Above all, I'll guide you in devising strategies to fix any flaws you might uncover. You set out to craft a satisfying story about young people struggling through their lives against the backdrop of the new adult experience—let's dive into the final steps of that process.

CRITIQUING: ASSESSING THE BIG PICTURE

As with any creative task, every author forges his or her own distinct revision process over the course of several projects. I recommend a Big Picture critique of your first draft as a separate first step, with you evaluating the cohesiveness, logic, and development of the parts you've loosely tacked together in Draft 1, without regard for individual passages or sentences. You'll use your discoveries in this critique to go back in and solidify those structural elements before you even consider things like narrative voice and evocative language. There's little point in fine-tuning the language of a scene if you may end up cutting out that scene or adding another character to it. That said, if you're one of those creative people who can't proceed to the next chapter without having tight text in place for the current one, your first draft may already have a strong voice evident and you can assess things like dialogue and your execution of narrative beats. I have questions and tests for that level of assessment and revision in the next section, "Deep Editing and Revising," and you may work through those at the same time you assess the overall story structure.

Critiquing your first draft lets you know if the overall story works successfully as it's laid out, with conflicts paced out and characters all accounted for, relationships defined, themes evident, escalating emotions benchmarked, and the ending reached. The draft may be fugly in the extreme, but at least it's all there instead of stuck in your head, and you can finally see if it's working or if significant alterations are needed. That's a perfectly normal and solid first draft revision experience.

Most writers bring in *beta readers*, or early first readers, alongside their self-critique—a decision I encourage. Those objective readers come to the story with no preconceptions about what it's supposed to be. They'll simply react to what it is. I'll provide questions to guide your self-critique and your beta readers so that both produce effective results.

SELF-CRITIQUING

After your first draft is complete, you can take a few days off to clear your head (I recommend it). Then print up your story (yes, PRINT it). Then take that paper manuscript somewhere that you reserve only for reading. Bring a pen and make notes in the margin or on a legal pad. The location and the printed pages provide a "book-reading experience and will force you into a reader's mind-set. Physically turning page after page is very different from working with the pixels on a portion of a page, and that difference is what you seek. All of this forces you to stick to your reactions, fears, and impressions when you might otherwise be tempted to stop and retype lines or entire scenes. That's not what this pass is for; you'll be doing that soon enough anyway. When you're done reading and making notes on your hard copy, ask yourself these developmental and Big Picture questions:

- Is the story about enough? Have you brought out all the facets of the issue that you wanted to explore?
- Is it a new view that gives a fresh approach? Can you easily identify the storyline or other items that will distinguish this from similar titles?
- Are significant conflicts evident?
- Do you feel steady escalation of tension, or do you sense sagging parts?
- Are there any chapters that end without you feeling the urge to immediately read the next chapter?
- Did you make the 'So what?' factor stand out enough?
- Are any of the main characters unsympathetic or predictable?
- Did any of your characters end up doing stereotypical things?
- Did you achieve the growth you sought for your main character(s)?
- Do you want to spend time with this protagonist now that she's written?
- Do any of the characters leave you feeling unsatisfied? Do you feel you captured every one? Which ones make you especially happy each time they're on-scene? Can you do something with the other ones to make you just as happy with them?
- Did you accomplish what you wanted with the relationships? Could any of the characters have worked differently to push the protagonist? In what ways?
- Can you trace the subplots clearly? Do they play into the main storyline? How can you make them more relevant to the story?

- Name the thing your protagonist wanted or needed at the beginning of the book. Do you think your readers have enough information to name that need or want, too? Did your protagonist get that by the end?

If you're finding that your Big Picture elements are holding up to this examination, move on to the questions in the deep editing section below. I recommend that you sit on your findings until you get the feedback from your betas, at which time you can decide what action to take.

BETA READER CRITIQUES

Strong beta readers clearly articulate their reactions to your story and understand the level of feedback you need at each stage. They may be writers; they'll absolutely be readers. Familiarity with New Adult fiction is preferable so that they're aware of category tropes, NA reader expectations, and what's fresh for the market. Establish a due date with your betas before you send it to make sure they're available to turn it around expeditiously.

Betas don't typically address minor grammar, spelling, and mechanical issues. Ask them to focus on the more major items. Encourage them to indicate what's working as well as what isn't so that you can build on your strengths even as you work on your weaknesses. To that end, they should avoid "I like it" responses. Although such sentiment is worthwhile and valid, it isn't what you need when trying to identify what needs revising and how it should be revised. Instead, ask that they lead you to your strengths and weaknesses with "I like it *because* ..." responses that make clear *why* that good thing works or that bad thing doesn't. It may take you a few projects, but work to identify beta readers who can give constructive criticism with a tactful delivery. You can encourage your betas to share any ideas they have, but their goal isn't to solve the problem, just to identify it. As the story creator, you're in the best position to come up with new ideas. That said, a great idea is fabulous no matter where it comes from. Just let your betas know solutions aren't required—and that you may not use them even if they're offered. Reserve your rights as the author up front so there aren't hurt feelings later.

Supply your beta readers with questions to make sure you get the kind of feedback you need at this stage. I've got a starter set for you below, but you may choose to make them story-specific. Be sure the questions are open-ended, following up with "Why?" or "When?" as needed to encourage them to expand. Also, while you want to be thorough, too many questions can overwhelm a beta and shut them down. You can dip into the more comprehensive Story Evaluation Questions at the end of this chapter for those betas who'd find them useful guides as they frame their feedback. You may find that your revision process and your betas' prowess make it possible for you to combine the critiquing and deep-editing pass.

- Is the premise striking enough?
- Did the main character's problem seem important to you?
- Which of the characters seemed like they could be real people? Which did not? What would you change about any of them? Did any of their actions seem unbelievable?
- Did you feel confused at any time in the story?
- Did your mind wander at any point?
- At what point did you start to care about the main character?
- What scene first pulled you into the story?
- Could you predict the ending? Did it satisfy you?
- Was the story about enough?
- Did the characters talk like real people?
- Which settings could use more description?

When you get your feedback, resist any urge to defend yourself or try to explain the items. You won't be there to defend or explain the story to regular readers. If you don't agree with a critique, or think it's overly harsh, instead consider your piece from the critic's point of view—they're trying to help you improve your work. You may ask questions to clarify the feedback, but it is your sole right to privately accept or reject any comment. At times, the feedback may not even apply, as it can reflect personal preferences and styles. Try to be thick-skinned and to separate yourself from your work as much as possible during your critique. Don't be afraid to ask for clarification of comments, though, because you must see your revision path clearly in order to embark upon it.

DEEP EDITING AND REVISING

When you're happy that your story structure is in place and that your characters and relationships are working, you're ready to hold all the nitty-gritty elements accountable. Deep editing and revising has you working on a line-by-line level as well as reshaping scenes.

You may choose to hire a professional editor to help you pinpoint the flaws and suggest revisions. I tell how to find one in Chapter 13. Many people, including agents and successful self-publishers, advocate budgeting money for an editor and a cover designer, if nothing else, seeing those as vital business expenses for those seeking to make a long-term go of publishing. Editors are objective experts trained at identifying and articulating issues and guiding you through the solutions. Of course, I'm an editor so I admit my bias. If you hire a freelancer, you should still do as much self-editing and revising as you can yourself so that you're not paying them to spend time evaluating what you're able to spot and fix on your own. Plus, editing makes you a stronger writer because you learn to identify trouble spots and personal tendencies, making it more likely you'll avoid those things in your future writing. My goal with this section is to help you develop editing skills for your long-term improvement as well as to make your current work-in-progress as strong as you can, regardless of whether you also hire an editor or choose to proceed without one.

"Revising is a learned skill." —**AMANDA BERGERON**, Editor at William Morrow and Avon (imprints of HarperCollins)

The first thing you should do at this stage is adopt the mind-set of a successful reviser, where nothing is off limits and you're willing to do whatever it takes to make your story rock and your readers cheer. Push yourself to go beyond knee-jerk fixes, allow yourself to be experimental rather than playing it safe. Writing is a tough gig, and readers are rightfully demanding. They're spending their hard-earned money, asking for your best in return. That's what you want, anyway, so you're working for the same end.

I'll walk you through this process in the same order we worked through the topics in this book. I'll give you questions and tests that zero in on weaknesses, and I'll accompany those with possible solutions or point you to the chapters that'll help you work through the issue. And of course, as always, we'll keep the new adult experience in our sights as we consider your characters and your readers. Ready? Psych yourself up to be excited about the possibilities rather than overwhelmed by the work. You've finished an entire story, so you've already crushed the hardest part. You can rock this, too!

EVALUATING AND REVISING YOUR CHARACTERS

Let's start the editing fun with your protagonist, since her journey is the primary driver of this story and her connection with readers is essential. They want her to triumph, or to at least come out of these exploits wiser, with some kind of satisfying new maturity. You may have two main characters if romance is an important part of your story. In that case, look for tangible change in both characters. In addition to the character-based self-critiquing questions above, I have two useful character-evaluation tactics for you. The first helps you assess how well you completed your character arcs by taking your characters from the final scene of the book and dropping them back into the first scenes of the book. The second uses a method I call the Stop Looking Test to assess your overall characterization success by checking out the actions you have your characters performing most frequently.

- **SEND YOUR CHARACTERS BACK IN TIME.** Take your main characters out of the final scene as they are with all their new maturity, wounds, healings, and experiences, and drop them back into the first scene of the book. They should act and react quite differently to the situation, showing more maturity or wisdom or patience or whatever it is they attained through their journey. In fact, this more mature character probably wouldn't even stumble into the struggle that makes up this book. She'd solve or avoid or better handle whatever travails sent her over the edge in the first place. If your story were a mystery or thriller, something plot-driven, where outside events are going to happen no matter how she changes, then she'd weather the events more calmly and heroically from the outset, again defying the need for the book. If you've got a series on your hand and this is the first or a middle episode in said series, then your character may not be fully done with her arc but she will still be changed drastically enough that putting her into the first scene will be an ill fit. Physically write the sample scene(s) if you need to, or at least try to do so and see if it becomes impossible because the character is so changed.

You should walk away from this exercise knowing that you've got a more empowered character, one who is willing to take action to overcome her struggles and who has discovered and employed a strength she didn't realize she had at the beginning of the book. She's also actively overcome a flaw in herself. Look back at your Character Thumbnail, which lists her strengths and flaws, and see if you delivered on those. Your next episode in the series may retest her newfound strength and poke at that flaw to make her reaffirm her progress. If your adventure itself hasn't been resolved, as in the case of a fantasy in which the evil enemy remains unvanquished, your character will still have made a vital discovery about herself that launches her into the next installment and makes readers feel a sense of satisfaction as you close this book.

If you don't see evident maturation, then revisit Chapter 7's discussion of provoking characters to make them reach deep within themselves for strength to fight back. You may end up re-envisioning significant events in the book, but that revision is worth the time and effort. It's hard for flat characters to excite readers or carry a series.

- **APPLY THE STOP LOOKING TEST.** When you show up at a workshop of mine, you're almost sure to hear about the Stop Looking Test. It's one of the easiest but most useful "tests" you can apply to your manuscript. It reveals weaknesses in characterization, plus generic language and missed opportunities in dialogue narrative beats. The revision work you do as a result of this test can significantly improve the story and your writing overall. Honestly, it's awesome.

I devised this test after an experience with a writer who had the tsk-worthy habit of using generic actions in the narrative beats (see Chapter 5 for the full lowdown on those). Stewy (not his real name) used the word *look* 398 times in a 352-page manuscript. He used the word *glance* 118 times. Now, I'm a writing teacher, not a math teacher, but even I can do that math: That's 526 instances of characters eye-balling each other, mostly during dialogue exchanges. The rest of the time they were *scowling, smiling, nodding, frowning, turning to,* and *facing* each other. Four hundred seventeen of those, in addition to those 526 eye-ballings. Are you reeling like I was? How many times do your characters look, stare, smile, or laugh in your book? I bet you'd be surprised. I wouldn't. This is a common pitfall, but one I'm happy to find because this tendency means the author knows to put in the rhythmic breaths, which is a very good thing to know. And it's entirely fixable once they're aware of it! Stewy had no clue he was filling his narrative beats with useless generic actions until he ran this test. Once he knew he had this habit, he revised the manuscript to maximize his narrative beats and his writing shot up to an entirely new level. I'm proud to say his published book sits on my bookshelf right now.

The Stop Looking Test has you scanning your manuscript for passive action in dialogue beats using the Find and Replace feature. I've got a starter list for you with common actions; you can add words you know are your personal bugaboos. (Stewy used the conspicuous words *visage* and *countenance* five times each because his storytelling style has an old-fashioned high-fantasy quality.)

look	nod
stare	shrug
glance	sat
gaze	feel
smile	stood
frown	laugh
turn (to)	giggle

Also look for *mean* because frequent use of that word can be an indicator that your dialogue is full of characters reiterating things in order to nudge along the information delivery ("You mean you don't want to go?" and "What do you mean, magic? How is it magic?"). Similarly, I added the variations of *laugh* because that's a major filler action. People don't really laugh and giggle that much in real life; this becomes the equivalent of typing *harrumph* and *huh* into your dialogue. That'll suck the power out of the moments when characters really do need to guffaw. I included *feel* because frequent use of that word can be a flag that you're *tell*ing emotions instead of *show*ing them. It's okay to write, "He felt bad," now and then, but only because you're using a variety of tools, not because telling is your primary way of conveying feelings. See Chapter 4 for ways to embody characters' emotions in their behavior, body language, and dialogue.

You might opt to use a program dedicated to word counting, like the free software TextSTAT (neon.niederlandistik.fu-berlin.de/en/textstat).

So you've spotted this tendency in your draft. How to fix it? One thing you can do is use those narrative beats to sprinkle in setting details (Chapter 11), characterization items (Chapter 4), and exposition or first-person judgments that reveal things about your characters (Chapter 3). That's all great for characterization. Your characters are likely to get a boost from this revision step. Another thing you can do is look at your conversations and make sure you don't have characters just sitting around talking. When they do that, you're forced to add interest to the scene with the *looking* and *turning to* business. Try moving them to another setting or situation entirely for that conversation, requiring the characters to interact with props or respond to things. For instance, instead of having one character report the results of a database search to another character, rewrite the scene with your two characters doing the search in the computer room, one character leaving his post as a lookout to get a peek at the screen, prompting the other character to shove him back as he also fusses with plugs and curses the eye scanner, etc. All the while, they are talking about the database information you need them to talk about. That's a more dynamic scene than two characters sitting at the table. Thus, this Stop Looking Test may reveal a tendency to underutilize settings and props as well as missed opportunities for characterization and atmospheric setting work in narrative beats. (See Chapters 5 and 11 for more on that.)

One last thought about this test: If you want to use all those generic words in your first draft, do so with my blessing. They are solid placeholders to drop in as you plow through your rough draft. Your concern at that point should be pinning those conversations into place and working out the scenes; you don't need to be fussing with narrative beats then. Save that for this revision pass, when you're ready to focus on tightening and perfecting the line work.

- **CONFIRM THAT YOU HAVE NEW ADULT UNDERTONES.** During this characterization assessment step and throughout your editing process, evaluate your characters as new adults, with sensibilities and concerns and behaviors that sync with the life experiences of people aged eighteen to twenty-five. Remember, new adults:

- have high expectations for themselves that don't always match reality
- have a generally positive sense of well-being
- are optimistic about themselves even if they're grim about the world at large
- have a yearning for independence that clashes with their inexperience
- are breaking away from their teen social status, building an identity from scratch
- feel intense loyalties to family, friends, school, and self
- are self-focused
- are experimental and take risks
- are unstructured and working on self-accountability
- have generally shed parental support and thus need support of friends in a new way
- are still undergoing active brain development.

Do you see any of these tendencies in your new adult characters? Universal traits for an age group make them believable members of that age group, even as adding individual traits and personalities make the characters distinct to your book.

EVALUATING AND REVISING YOUR PLOT

In this step, we'll focus on your storyline. We'll make sure you've indeed started as strongly as you intended to, with interesting action that reveals things about your character before you slam the story into gear with the catalyst. We'll also make sure you've marched those characters through a plot that increases their stress. We've got young people here, and we want to be tapping into the natural stress of the new adult time of life. You set out to challenge them with harsh reality, to allow them some victories, to let them get their footing just before every knockdown, and to give them opportunities to prove their mettle and solve their own problems. All the while, you would give something worth fighting for—a goal to be attained, with stakes high enough to push onward no matter what.

I have some ways you can evaluate your plot, along with questions to help you spot weaknesses in it. I offer solutions here, but do take the time to revisit the plotting chapters (6–9 for all stories, and 10 for those with a romance storyline). With the story completed, you now have the perspective to add events that you now see are missing, to remove events that turned out to be unnecessary, and to enhance those events that don't seem to ring as loudly as you intended when you wrote them.

- **CHECK YOUR OPENING.** You've finished the manuscript, so you know a lot more about your characters than you did when you started, even if you did work up a full Character Profile prior to writing the story. You've seen how your characters behave in tough situations; consider using that knowledge to write a stronger, more appropriate opening for your story. Newbery Medal–winning author for young people Richard Peck likes to go back and throw out his first scene entirely, without even reading it. He says he didn't know the characters then, so how could he write them in action? You may not go that far, but do see if your opening scene truly introduces the character you came to know by the end. You may have discovered that he's afraid of the dark; would that information be more useful for readers to learn in the first chapter than the current first chapter showing him loving the beach? If you decide your opening revealed smart information, use your knowledge of the rest of the story to decide if you incorporated elements from that opening into the rest of your story. This will add to the overall cohesiveness.

- **SURVEY THE FIRST PARAGRAPHS.** Assess the plot and characterization progress over the course of your manuscript. Read the first paragraph of each chapter, looking for forward movement in the story. You should be able to clearly see the escalation and stepping-stone quality of your storyline. If you don't see an increase in tension or character progression, your story might be meandering. This will help you spot chapters that you may have slipped in because you like them but that aren't forwarding the story in any way. Perhaps they're even impeding the pacing. Review Chapter 9 for ways to amp up the pacing and increase the tension. You may have to cut some scenes that you like ("killing your darlings," as the writing adage goes). To make cutting easier, put those darlings into a separate file so that you can retrieve them later if you determine that they really were necessary. I'm willing to bet you don't retrieve any. You can survey your scenes within a chapter, too, making sure that each scene feels like a forward step in that chapter. Start by articulating the goal of that chapter to yourself, saying exactly what the step forward should be, and then read the first few lines of each scene only to see if there is tangible forward progress. Do the scene-surveying in a separate step after the first paragraph survey.

- **CHECK YOUR ENDING FOR THE SATISFIED SIGH.** When you were checking your characterization, you did an exercise where you put the protagonist as he is in the final scene into the first scene of the book to see if he'd changed. That will also help you get a feel for the success of your ending. Readers feel satisfied if their character has reached a noticeably advanced state in their journey, even in a series. Your first paragraph survey will help you make sure the tension increases with each chapter, and that there's forward movement in the plot. That helps you determine if everything in the story leads to a believable ending. With your new perspective on the finished book and knowledge of the ending, you can go back and add any foreshadowing events necessary for your ending. Or perhaps you'll see now that you were too obvious, and that you need to remove items or break up info dumps, instead sprinkling the information throughout the story. Also, you can now make sure your protagonist was the one who resolved the story rather than a friend or authority figure, ensuring you have an active hero instead of a passive one. Check that your subplots were all resolved, dovetailing with the main plot as you planned. You may leave some subplots still in progress if you're working on a series, but there has to be resolution of something so that we have a feeling of an episode being tied up when this book ends. For example, a battle may be won with this book, but the overall war against the flying insect men still wages. Without this sense of completion, the reader may feel like you just chopped the story off at a random point because you couldn't reign in your page count. Each book in a series needs readers feeling satisfied that something has been accomplished in the character's journey toward a great wisdom, happiness, or triumph. For more on that, revisit Chapter 7.

EVALUATING AND REVISING YOUR ROMANCE STORYLINE

Did you include a romantic relationship in your NA fiction? Probably. If you did, assess that storyline to make sure it takes into account the unique sensibility of new adults falling in love and to see if you met the challenge of writing emotion that resonates with readers.

First, the love scenes. I hope you'll be able to slip into Reader Mode with the printed manuscript and your special reading-only zone, thus allowing yourself to read your sexy scenes as you would another writer's. Do you forget you're reading and instead feel the heat? Or is it hitting your ear as clunky and leaving your libido unimpressed? If the latter's the case, or if your beta readers are telling you that's *their* reaction, let's get you looking at what surrounds that love scene. Emotions will feel overwrought and thus forced when you don't build up romantic tension and anticipation before you deliver the love scene. I give you a lot of tips for building those in Chapter 10. Have you created enough ebb and flow? Have you attacked the relationship enough? Have you pulled the lovers apart just before they could consummate, taking the tension to its zenith? Try giving them moments of tantalizing touches and looks and even stolen kisses even as you keep them apart for anything more, much to their frustration.

Now examine the characters. Do they feel real? When they're convincing, then the love scene becomes more convincing. Spend time evaluating your characters with the guidance I've provided above. Also examine the relationship between the lovers. Do they feel right for each other? Do they have something in common? Do they have enough reasons to be pulled apart that you truly fear for their union (even though, of course, we all know they'll get together in the end)? If you have dual points of view, giving the narrator's microphone to each of the lovers in turn, are you revealing new insights with each switch? Make sure you surprise readers with those new insights rather than just fleshing out the scene with the other person's perspective. Have you made the dual narrative truly necessary?

Examine your settings with an eye toward making the lovers' time together more interesting. Are they in familiar settings, with nothing exceptional in the props and environmental elements? What if you moved their canoodling off the couch and into a field while on a hiking date? How about that tantalizing lake over there ... might the canoodling fare well with a little water play? Are you working details from one intimate experience into other parts of the story, thus always suggesting, without explicitly stating, that the characters are sexual partners?

EVALUATING AND REVISING YOUR SETTING

Setting is vital for so many things, including creating a sense of atmosphere and the feeling that readers are right there in that fictional realm with the characters. Sensory details are important for this, but too often, writers simply paint a visual picture and move on to the action and dialogue. I challenge you to incorporate a minimum of three separate sensory moments in every chapter, using the techniques in Chapter 11, such as "sprinkling" and prop interaction. Test your chapters by using a highlighter to highlight any sensory stimulation that doesn't involve sight. When you hit three, spaced out through the chapter, then you've probably done a solid job of this.

You'll also be evaluating your setting work when you do the Stop Looking Test, which I detailed in the "Evaluating and Revising Your Characters" section earlier in this chapter. Make sure you don't have story-stalling scenes featuring characters sitting at a table for info exchanges. Revisit my sample scenes in Chapter 11 for ways to use the props and environmental details of their physical space.

If you spot any sags in momentum during your first paragraph survey, or if your beta readers report instances where the pacing slowed, consider relocating your characters to a setting that makes them really uncomfortable or that foils their efforts to do something they need or want to do. Put them in a social situation when they need to be alone, forcing them to fight for solitary moments, amping up the sense of struggle and need.

Lastly, consider your setting choices in terms of familiarity. Have you used familiar settings? If so, do you think you've freshened them up enough to make them interesting to readers as well as to the characters?

EVALUATING AND REVISING YOUR NARRATIVE VOICE AND SENSIBILITY

Finally, remember your mission to convey the sensibility and maturity level of someone who is post-teen and pre-grown adult. Do your characters sound too mature for their age? Read with an eye for comments that are self-focused (as opposed to self*fish*), and make sure you write in moments where young people are unduly optimistic about their ability to triumph. If you don't already do so, slap them down a few times to make sure they understand that hard work is going to be necessary, that they won't triumph simply because they're sure they will. That's part of the new adult maturation process. Revisit the section "Cultivating New Adult Undertones" earlier in this chapter and see if you've done all you can to make sure they don't sound "like a child or like a jaded adult," as author Jaycee DeLorenzo puts it. And if your betas are reporting that any of the characters feel a little distanced, be brave and try this experiment: Rewrite a chapter in a different tense. Switching from past tense to present, or vice versa, might be just the change you need to get that sense of immediacy.

EVALUATING AND REVISING YOUR DIALOGUE

Strong dialogue is the result of balancing many storytelling elements. Is there enough variety within your conversations, and from conversation to conversation? Are your characters having a logical, straightforward back-and-forth every time they interact, or do you sometimes have them not answering questions directly or cutting each other off to convey discontent in a relationship or the sense of being rushed? Do you have your characters sometimes double-back on their words and repeat things for emphasis rather than relying on exclamation points and dialogue tags like "he shouted"? Going for the straightforward exchanges in your first draft is fine, as you plug in the conversations and get a feel for your characters' dynamics, but during revision you can add nuance to the exchanges and work up the content of the narrative beats to enhance what's being uttered aloud. If you've already applied the Stop Looking Test I explained earlier in this chapter, you've got your eye on those narrative beats by now. Do you now see opportunities for subtext? Do the things your young characters say sound like new adults, revealing the new adult mind-set and priorities that we covered throughout this book but particularly in Chapters 2–4? Look for long passages of dialogue that might be info dumps. Can you work some of that information into a dynamic conversation, with interruptions and prop interactions and strategic narrative beats? If you have long passages of dialogue, experiment with moving some of the info in that dialogue to the narrative for a more balanced flow.

EVALUATING AND REVISING YOUR LANGUAGE MECHANICS

This is the time to make your language tight and personality-laden. Check to see if your narrative language has flavor or personality by moving through the manuscript a chapter at a time, looking for common phrases or clichés. Replace expected phrasings with direct word replacements from the thesaurus, choosing more evocative verbs where possible, or with entirely different and unexpected phrasing when possible. For instance, "He came over after work" could be replaced with "We kicked back for half the night." Or you could create flavor by being specific, as in this replacement: "Having him on the futon after work every night was awkward."

You'll also be evaluating your language work when you do the Stop Looking Test. If you've noticed any places in your story where the pace seems to be slacking, then you've probably spotted opportunities to trim the language into direct sentences and short paragraphs instead of long and complex sentences. That'll goose the pace. If you feel like a section is rushing when you really want to focus on something, perhaps with a love scene, revise the language in the scene to include longer sentences, with commas and clauses, and to have thicker paragraph blocks on the page, giving the manuscript a denser feel.

Now take a step back and scan the chapters. Do you see a lot of dialogue? Does that suit the nature of your story as you know it now that you've finished crafting it? Or do you need more introspection, which you can get with more narrative and indirect thoughts than dialogue? See the end of Chapter 5 for ways to use indirect thoughts and internal dialogue to add immediacy and intimacy without relying solely on dialogue.

If your beta readers are reporting choppiness rather than a nice flow in the reading experience, revisit Chapter 8 to make sure your transitions between scenes and chapters are smooth, and work on sentence variety within the scenes. Also see how many dialogue tags you can remove, since going too heavy on those puppies creates a staccato feel.

KNOWING WHEN YOU'RE DONE

Probably the hardest part of revising is knowing when you're done. If only there were a fill line or some other empirical marker to clue us in! Alas, we must rely on our best judgment. I believe that your best judgment, combined with this chapter and your beta readers, will do the trick for you. I recommend you work through at least two rounds of revision—the critiquing round and the heavier editing and revising round, although those may fuse into a single pass for you depending on your revision style. You'll likely do more than two passes, though, as the heavier revision work may have you going through the manuscript in phases, with a full pass just for character assessment and revision, one for narrative beat work, and so on. Ultimately, you'll have worked through all the items in this chapter. When you get to that point, I recommend having your betas, or perhaps entirely new readers, read through the manuscript one more time to see if their concerns were addressed. You need to know if you hit all the marks, and this deep immersion you've just done sorely limits your ability to determine that on your own. This would be a great time to bring in a freelance editor and then address any items she calls to your attention.

When you've reached the point where you feel you're just futzing with the lines and that substantial changes aren't going to happen, that's your stopping point. Run your spell-check, then have someone proofread it for typos that the spell checker can't pick up—and you know those always creep in despite the seeming infallibility of technology. Even in major publishing houses typos creep in, and that's with a minimum of three sets of eyes on the manuscript, including the editor's, the managing editor's or copyeditor's, and then the proofreader's. As readers we've all encountered them. At that point, you've got your finished manuscript and are ready to work on submission or self-publication.

Do give yourself the time to work on the revision. It's not going to be a finished book by tomorrow, no matter how fast you write—nor should it be. You're building a career and stoking a fan base. A few weeks could be the difference between a good book and a great one; I encourage you to always err on the side of great.

CRAFT CLOSE-UP: STORY EVALUATION QUESTIONS

- **CONCEPT:** Is the premise striking? Is it a new view that gives a fresh approach? Where is the story's heart—in the action, in the characters, in the relationship? What is the "So what?" factor? Would anyone care about these characters?

- **CONFLICT:** Are significant conflicts evident? Do you sense the conflicts escalating? Do they escalate enough? Does the main character's problem seem important to you? Do you see potential to provoke an emotional response in readers?

- **CHARACTERIZATION:** Do the characters seem real with depth and emotion, or are they recognizable stereotypes? Are the motives of the characters understandable and logical to the story? Do you want to spend time with the lead characters? At what point do you start to care about the main characters? What would you change about any of the characters? Do any of the characters do stereotypical things?

- **DIALOGUE:** Does the dialogue seem natural and realistic? Do the characters talk like real people?

- **SETTING:** Is the atmosphere in the story allowing the reader to experience what the characters experience? Can you imagine the location clearly? Which settings could use more description?

- **POINT OF VIEW:** Is the POV consistent throughout the piece? Is this the best POV to tell this story?

- **PLOT:** Does the story develop logically, or does it make sudden leaps that confused you? Can you predict the ending? Does it satisfy you? Is the story about enough? Are significant conflicts evident? Do you feel steady escalation of tension? Are there any chapters that end without you feeling the urge to immediately read the next chapter? Did all the storylines feel wrapped up at the end?

- **PACING:** Does the action progress slowly or quickly? How long does it take for the story to be set up? Which scene first pulls you into the story? Do the chapters end in mini-finales and/or cliff-hangers? Does your mind wander at any point?

- **MECHANICS:** Is there an effective variety of sentence lengths? Did any of the passages confuse you, causing you to reread them? Does the author show instead of tell?
- **VOICE:** Does the text have a distinct narrative voice or personality? Is it consistent throughout?
- **LANGUAGE CHOICE:** Is the language unexpected? Has the writer avoided stock phrases and clichés? Are the words dynamic? Is the language choice appropriate for readers of New Adult fiction?

CHAPTER 13

Self-Publishing Your New Adult Fiction

*S*elf-publishing worked for New Adult bestsellers Tammara Webber, Abbi Glines, Jessica Park, Colleen Hoover, Jamie McGuire, Cora Carmack, Sylvia Day, and Gayle Forman. Can it work for you? Perhaps. Beyond the glamour of these Cinderella stories lurks a lot of hard work. In this chapter I'll walk you through the self-publishing process so you can prepare for the bumps even as you set yourself up for smooth sailing, determine your budget and goals, and produce and publish the awesome NA fiction you've so carefully yet passionately crafted.

"E-NA": NA FICTION'S LOVE AFFAIR WITH E-PUBLISHING

New Adult fiction exists primarily in the virtual word. The category's very existence owes itself to the individual writer's ability to self-publish e-books, coupled with readers' ability to cheaply and easily download those books into their e-reading devices. You can format your manuscript on any computer, with minimal programming know-how, in a very short time and in any story format, from novellas to short stories to collections and even anthologies with fellow NA writers, all at any price you want. It's easy to see the appeal. Some adventurous souls do go all-out and form their own small indie publishing companies to deal in big print quantities with distributors like Ingram, but most commonly, NA self-publishers go the solo, smaller-scale digital route, so that's my focus here.

Even traditional publishing houses, who specialize in bound book publication, publish most of their NA fiction as e-books. They crank out big print runs only when enough e-copies sell to convince them (and the store book buyers they'd have to sell to) that an audience for physical copies lurks out there, too, or when an author is "brand name" enough to prompt physical bookstores and mass merchants like Walmart or Costco to take a chance on stocking the physical book. At present, the latter are the less common breed of NA author. The rest of the NA gang functions digitally. E-books, e-publishing, e-publicity ... NA could be called e-NA.

UNDERSTANDING THE PROS AND CONS OF DIGITAL SELF-PUBLISHING

Self-publishing is the perfect business decision for many writers. You're in total control, you keep all the profits after expenses, and you can publish as many new stories as you want, as quickly as you want. You're no slave to the comparatively slow-moving wheels of traditional publishing houses with their lists, seasons, production schedules, marketing roll-outs, and printing and shipping schedules. If you score it big, you can establish a writing career and maybe those traditional publishers will come a'ringing your phone. Ask Molly McAdams and Tammara Webber about getting those phone calls.

But there's no guarantee that you will get that call or those sales, or that being in control will be so peachy keen. Go into this endeavor understanding that total control means total responsibility for the final product, including selling it through to customers and taking returns, all of which may require significant research into the market, players, and processes. You assume all the financial risk. You must make all the time necessary to pull off this venture, and life doesn't always make that easy. Lastly, if you don't score those sales that lead to those calls, you could risk shooting your traditional publishing aspirations in the foot. Agents and publishers can hold low sales—or worse, bad reviews— against you during submission because (1) it's hard to build momentum on a book that never had momentum and (2) those bad reviews never go away thanks to the same virtual world that makes e-publishing and promoting possible.

Self-publishing is a big venture, for sure. My goal with this chapter is to give you a solid sense of what it entails before you make a decision about pursuing this path. It's entirely possible that you'll decide you'd much rather go traditional publishing all the way or at least start there, and that's okay—working with a publishing house can be pretty fantastic, too.

"This is my career, and I make decisions about my career just as everyone else does: by weighing what I stand to gain financially, and where my family and personal time are concerned. I analyze the stress level involved and whether I think I can handle it or not. As a writer, you've got to do what's best for you, and give no apologies for it." —**TAMMARA WEBBER**, *The New York Times* and *USA Today* best-selling author of *Easy* and the Between the Lines series

---

CREATING YOUR SELF-PUBLISHING STRATEGY

Many NA authors go into self-publishing committed to sticking with this path unless bestsellerdom strikes, at which point they'll weigh the pros and cons of signing with an interested traditional publisher. Other NA authors intentionally pursue self-publishing as a back door to traditional publication. They want to work hard and sell well enough to gain a publisher's confidence, at which point they intend to hand over the heavy lifting to the house. I'll talk about the potential of that strategy in the next chapter when I explain how editors make their acquisition decisions. With either mind-set, you're going through the self-publication process and need a strategy for attacking that work. You have three options: doing it all yourself, heading a team of experts for each part of the process, or hiring an author services company to do it all for you.

OPTION 1: DOING IT ALL YOURSELF

In this option, you create, gather, and assemble all the pieces of the book in electronic form yourself, then upload the digital files to each online e-book retailer website (the big ones being Amazon, Barnes & Noble, iBooks, and Kobo) or to an e-book distributor website like Smashwords, which for a fee formats and distributes your books to the major retailers in a single swoop for you. This chapter covers the tools you'll need for this option.

If you want to self-publish bound books in a traditional bulk-printing manner, you can work directly with a print-on-demand (POD) printer like Lightning Source, the printer that most self-publishing entities use to print their POD books anyway. Then you arrange for shipping and warehousing. Some self-publishers go the extra step of formalizing themselves as independent publishers, getting a company name, and sometimes even publishing other authors' books. Aaron Shepard is an established proponent of this method; you can learn the process through his books and website (www.aaronshep.com). There's also a Yahoo group focused on POD publishing with Lightning Source: finance.groups.yahoo.com/group/pod_publishers.

OPTION 2: HEADING A TEAM OF EXPERTS

You can act like a general contractor and hire experts for each element of the bookmaking, then upload the final assemblage yourself directly to the e-book retailers or to an e-book distributor. You can publish bound books through a POD printer, or your experts can help you work with a traditional press printer, or some combination of these entities. I'll cover all the experts and what they can do for you later in the "Building Your Book" section of this chapter.

OPTION 3: HIRING AN AUTHOR SERVICES COMPANY TO DO IT ALL

This is the one-stop shopping version of bookmaking. Author service companies pull all the pieces together for you in return for a fee and/or a cut (*royalty*) of each book sold if you choose to do the entire publishing process through them.

You can hire them for as few or as many services as suits your strategy: editing, cover and interior design, printing and e-book setup, listing with online sellers, and marketing and promotion packages. You can't choose your editor or designer, so your ability to control and customize is limited, but this simplified process appeals to many authors.

There are new entrants into this exploding vendor community all the time, but the most popular are CreateSpace (an Amazon company used primarily for paperback POD copies, but their formatting program yields e-book files that you can upload to Amazon's e-book arm, Kindle Direct Publishing); Author Solutions (owned by the major publisher Penguin Random House); Lulu; Aventine Press; BookLocker; Dog Ear Publishing; Infinity Publishing; and Outskirts Press. Do your homework before you decide on a company, as their pricing packages can be complex, and you need to navigate fee structures and understand how much royalty the company receives on each book sold. It has traditionally been considered unethical for a publisher to make the author pay for manufacturing costs and to also demand a portion of the proceeds (a model that was pejoratively dubbed "vanity press") because then the publisher has little motive to promote the books—they'd make all their money in the creation of the book, never banking on significant sales of your actual book. Today's author services companies blur that line with their mix of paid-for services and royalty requirements. In fact, a notable class-action suit against Author Solutions reveals just how thick and potentially unsavory that blurring can be. Read your contract language carefully to make sure you understand what services you are getting. Don't be swayed by enthusiastic pitches for marketing and promotion programs. Always consider the marketing of your book to be completely on your shoulders unless you explicitly hire a publicist/marketer who is devoted to your book.

Another reason to scour your contract with an author services company is to make sure you aren't signing away your rights to the content. Believe it or not, some companies will try to fool writers into giving them exclusive publication rights, for short periods of time or even forever. Yikes! Those are the cretins who still fall solidly into the inscrutable vanity press practices. To research your company, use simple web searches, writers' forums, the Preditors & Editors website (www.pred-ed.com), the Writer Beware website run by Science Fiction & Fantasy Writers of America (www.sfwa.org/for-authors/writer-beware), or hire an experienced publishing attorney to review the contract. You can also check *The Independent Publishing Magazine* site for author services company reviews (www.theindependentpublishingmagazine.com) and often your preferred writers' organization.

Note that you don't have to use an author services company to publish to the major e-book retailers. For example, you aren't required to use the author services company CreateSpace to upload your e-book for sale on Amazon, or the author services company Nook Press to upload to Barnes & Noble. You can create the files yourself and upload them to the retailers' websites after meeting their formatting and file specifications, which they make available on their websites.

You may find your feelings about these options will change with each book you self-publish. After all, your experience is growing and you're learning what works for you and what doesn't. Thanks to the Internet, you can research other writers' self-publishing experiences as well as reach out to writer friends for their insights and recommendations. There are organizations and publications that can put a wealth of resources in your hands, including the Independent Book Publishers Association (IBPA, www.ibpa-online.org), which is a not-for-profit trade association representing independent book publishers; *Independent Publisher* online magazine (www.independentpublisher.com), which covers self-publishing as well as the rest of the publishing industry; and Digital Book World (www.digitalbookworld.com), which covers electronic publishing on its website, in e-publications, and in professional gatherings.

MAKING YOUR BUSINESS PLAN

Regardless of the option you choose, you need to do some things as a business-person that are vital to executing a successful strategy. I've laid them it out in six steps.

1. Set Your Career Goal

It's time to quantify your goal. Are you building a long-term writing career? If so, you need to think about branding yourself rather than your books. You'd do well to create an overall visual style for your covers that can be adapted for each series as well as for promo materials and your website, which is an essential billboard for your business. Do you plan to stick within a genre or to diversify? That will influence your branding strategy as well. I'll get into that in

Chapter 15 on marketing. For now, knowing your career goal helps you devise an overall business strategy.

Do you plan this as an interim step toward traditional publishing? If so, you need to sell enough books to get a publisher's attention. But what's "enough"? There's no solid number, but you can show publishers modest success when you start moving up through the five digits, impressing them around 30,000 or 40,000. For context, consider that to get on a mainstream bestseller list like *The New York Times* or *USA Today*, you've got to sell six or seven thousand copies in a week to beat out the other top-performing authors for that week. Publishers want to sign up self-published books that have gained momentum on their own, demonstrating that there's a market for that story, and then they can use their powerhouse resources to build on momentum. At best, sales in the hundreds can do nothing for you when you pitch to agents and publishers. You've created a quality book and gotten good reviews, but you just couldn't rack up sales. No boost, but no harm done, either. If it was done with quality, the publisher may be willing to try you out if you remove the book from the market and they can launch a newly packaged and likely newly edited edition. In the less palatable but still real scenario, they may just see the low-selling book as old and unable to compete, certainly lacking in momentum, and quickly pass. Unfortunately, sales in the hundreds that come with bad reviews and low quality in story and production can hurt you; the book is now damaged goods. *You* may be damaged, too. Nothing disappears from the virtual world, so doing a search on your name will turn up those disappointing outings forevermore. So, if you aim to self-publish as a way of getting your foot in the door at a publishing house, your first task is to create a professional-quality product that can't hurt you, and your second step is to sell, sell, sell to establish momentum.

2. Establish Your Budget

You can self-publish cheaply, or you can invest significantly; the financial decisions are all yours. I know authors who've spent a few hundred dollars to make e-books available, and I know others who have spent upwards of $30,000, going all-out with bound books and full-scale marketing campaigns run by experienced publicists. Know up front exactly how much you're willing and able to invest, then build a strategy around that. I can't feed you specific numbers to plug into a starter budget, as author services companies continually update their fees, royalty rates are an evolving factor, and even within your own day-to-day, book-to-book business, you'll be changing your price points. Let your budget strategizing start with the services and items you believe are essential to your vision of success and then research those for sample pricing or ranges. Many experts include professional editing and professional cover design among the essentials for every self-publisher. It's prudent to also set aside specific amounts for promotion since it's easy to lose track of your promo spending as you piece it out over weeks, months, and even years, ending up with more money spent promoting than made selling (I list core promo items in Chapter 15). There will be trial and error over the course of books—that's inevitable. Be stingy about adding to your list beyond essentials so you don't nickel-and-dime the daylights out of your wallet with making and promoting the book. Note the $30,000 I talked about above. Few of us have *carte blanche* to do all the things we want to do for our books. Budgeting helps you establish your priorities.

3. Pick Your Format and Price Point

Your costs depend on your format, so you need to know up front if you want to stick with e-books or if you need some bound books. The digital-only strategy is the most cost-effective since you don't have to pay anything to upload your files to e-book retailers, and readers' costs stay low since they pay only your set price to download the e-book file to their e-readers. You make your money from the royalty set by each e-book retailer. If you make printed paperbacks available to readers, you will pay the cost of the paper, printing, and binding of each book as it is ordered, and then take your royalty from the profit you get marking up the price from there, with your readers paying shipping on their purchase. Some authors choose this option to give their readers choices as well as to make sure they can have physical books for signings and events, although your profit on at-event books may be minimized after you've paid for the book to be made and shipped to you. (You can trim that expense by buying your paperbacks in bulk to take advantage of some retailers' free shipping policies, and retailers often give you a discount when purchasing your own book.)

Clearly, your format choice will influence your price point. E-books sell for much lower prices, usually in the $2.99 to $6.99 range, although traditional publishers can command $9.99 for big-name authors. Hardcover books can handle higher price points, from $12.99 to $24.99 for bestsellers. Paperbacks, which are the go-to choice for NA bound books even with publishers, range from $11.99 to $16.99, with the book buyer also paying for shipping on top of that. Self-publishing authors will discount their early titles, or perhaps the first book in trilogies and series, to as low as $.99. Or they may temporarily set a $.99 price point for a book as a promotional strategy. Many NA authors are finding, though, that readers will wait for that temporary low price point, expecting that the author will drop to $.99 sooner or later and choosing other books while they wait. Knowing your discounting plan will factor into Step 4 below. Digital Book World (www.digitalbookworld.com) keeps tabs on price points for electronic books, announcing the current popular price in its free daily e-newsletter. E-book price points can be reset easily and frequently, so you're not setting things in stone.

4. Calculate Your Costs and Sales Goals

If you do absolutely everything on your own, your book doesn't have to incur any up-front costs (with the exception of buying a copy of your print-on-demand paperback to review before approving that edition for sale). You'll upload the properly formatted cover and interior files as specified by each retailer's site, paying that site a percentage of the net sale price only when a book sells. This makes self-publishing an attractive choice for authors. It can also lull writers into not considering costs they *could* incur, which do exist and depend on their needs, skills, and vision for the book. Here are some items to consider when figuring your potential book production costs:

- professional fees, such as editing, author services company fees, attorney fees for reviewing contracts
- book design costs, such as stock photos, design services, or software
- publication costs, such as digital file creation and uploading, ISBN/barcodes
- printing/binding/transportation/warehousing if you want bound books
- copyright registration

The e-retailer's royalty is your payment to them for their providing their sales platform, point-of-sales cost, money transfer fees, and online customer service. Each e-retailer's royalty is different, but generally you'll pocket about 40 percent of each print-on-demand bound book sold and either 70 percent or 30 percent for each e-book, depending on the price point you choose. The 70 percent may require you to pay a "delivery fee" for the book to be sent on the store's wireless network. It's worth studying the rates on major e-retailer sites in this step for the sake of your calculations, including Amazon (Kindle Direct for e-books, CreateSpace for POD bound books), Barnes & Noble (Nook Press), iTunes (iBooks), and Smashwords. They'll send you your share of the money on a monthly or quarterly basis. (This is different from the twice-yearly royalty payment system used by traditional publishers.)

Once you have an idea about your costs and the most likely price point of your book, you can work out how many books you must sell to break even and then beyond that to make a profit. (Don't forget to figure a marketing budget into your calculations; see Step 5.) You may have to play with the price point until you've got realistic numbers that give you enough comfort to move forward.

5. Strategize a Preliminary Marketing Plan

The world can't buy your book if they don't know your book exists. You'll need to build a marketing plan that will, at minimum, sell your break-even number. Perhaps you'll give away books ("freemium") or sell them for $.99 in order to build buzz that will result in sales. This isn't something you can escape—you must self-promote whether you self-publish or traditionally publish. Have no fear, there are tools for you regardless of your comfort with self-promotion, and I've packed Chapter 15 with them. At this early stage, give thought to what your comfort level is with promotion, determining if you'll DIY it, if you'll do it primarily online, if you plan to finance giveaways, and if you'll hire marketing experts. Then, set aside a portion of your budget for marketing. You can get more detailed about your campaign and finalize your budget after you've worked out the details of your book production.

BUILDING THE BOOK

In this section I walk you through the steps of turning your manuscript into a sale-ready product by yourself, pausing each time to tell you what an independent expert could contribute should you decide to hire out that step. There are plenty of knowledgeable book-loving professionals whom you can enlist on a freelance basis. Besides just building you a quality product, they offer you industry expertise and a creative sounding board. You can bring in as many or as few pros as suits your budget and vision, pricing them out on their websites or contacting them for estimates based on your project's specifics.

Regardless of whether you hire a pro or DIY, commit to creating a professional-looking product. Approximately 235,000 print and e-books were self-published in 2012 alone—New Adult fiction's breakout year—and hundreds of thousands more get published each year. To make your book stand out and hold up against competition from both self-pubbers as well as traditional publishers, don't compromise on quality. Self-publishing may have come a long way in terms of reader acceptance, but a stigma remains and won't disappear as long as writers churn out amateurish stuff. Editors and agents certainly note the professionalism of products and self-marketing when they consider signing previously self-published authors.

GETTING EDITING HELP

I devoted Chapter 12 to the revision process, so here I'll focus on the option of hiring a professional editor to guide you in realizing your vision for the story as well as building writing skills that will serve all your future books.

I admit my bias as a veteran in-house editor and then freelance editor even as I say that the most basic element of a professional-quality book is a strongly edited and revised story, so do budget for and hire an editor. If the story doesn't hold up, no amount of pretty packaging and masterful marketing is going to make up for it. A few readers may pick up copies, but the negative reviews will land on Goodreads and online retailer sites and in blogs and social media and then you'll be screwed. Your critique buddy can help you, and the revision checklists in this book are powerful tools for you, but you'll be best served by an objective expert trained not only to spot what isn't working but to articulate the absence in a way that you understand, and then envision what could make the difference and guide you there with tangible recommendations while keeping the NA audience and marketplace in mind.

You hire editors for content editing and for proofreading; some can do it all, although they may specialize. Content editing can start as early as the concept stage and will include discussion of marketplace and reader expectations (editors may specify this as *developmental editing*). You work out the storyline and find your voice and narrative style as you shape the concept into a viable rough draft. You may work through a first draft chapter by chapter with your editor in this kind of editing. Or, you may start with a *substantive edit*, which is appropriate for a finished first draft, with the editor critiquing the draft in order to advise you about Big Picture items like voice, plot, characterization, pacing, scenes, and opening pages. You'll walk away from that edit with a revision strategy so that you can start the next draft. You may be happy with your next draft and go right to publication, or you may go through this phase several times, depending on your preferences, budget, and confidence in subsequent drafts. This is the most common type of editing I do as a freelance editor, as writers often like to produce a first draft on their own or with trusted beta readers, then get my advice and revise on their own based on what I bring to their attention. If you don't have a lot of Big Picture work to be done, the editor may go right into *line editing*, where line-by-line word massaging happens. When no more tinkering is needed, hire a proofreader to cast fresh eyes on the manuscript in order to spot typos or misspellings. A copyeditor can also do this, as they specialize in fact-checking, grammar, and generally making every word and letter on the page earn its keep. Even if you don't hire anyone for copyediting or proofreading, do *not* proofread the manuscript yourself. You're too close to the text to catch the typos—you've read it too many times, plus you're likely to rewrite lines, passages, or whole chapters during what should be a hands-off pass. Make sure to have the final manuscript reviewed by someone who hasn't read it before—better yet, multiple someones. The more eyes the better. And tell them that they cannot make content suggestions at this stage.

You find qualified editors by asking writing pals, by consulting online searches and writers' forums, by seeking references from your writers' organizations, or by consulting the Editorial Freelancers Association (www.the-efa. org). When you get a specific name, research the editor online. Read interviews with her to determine her editorial experience, sensibility, and interest. Review her website to see the kinds of books she specializes in. Find out what services she recommends based on what you think your needs are and perhaps on a preliminary review of a portion of your manuscript. Ask about her availability and turnaround time, and find out her fees and payment structure (some editors charge per word or page, others per hour or per project, and some require partial or full payment up front). Before you sign any contracts, make sure that the copyright for the editor's comments on your text belongs to you, the author.

That way, no matter how extensive the edits, you have the right to publish the work under your name alone.

DESIGNING THE INTERIOR

Most writers know to give careful attention to their book covers, but a well-designed interior also contributes to a professional-quality finished book. You can have your author services company design the interior for you, you can use their software to do it yourself, or you can go straight to your e-retailer and use their software before uploading to their site.

You can build e-books in many formats including PDF, MOBI (which is primarily for Amazon's Kindle devices), and EPUB (which is more universal and so compatible with a broad range of e-retailers and reading devices), but it's beyond the scope of this book to detail each of those. The basic process has you converting your Word files into text files that you'll then clean up for uploading into the e-book conversion software for each e-book distributor. As I mentioned before, you could choose to upload to Smashwords, an e-distributor that, once you meet their formatting specs, will convert your files into acceptable formats for each of the major retailers and then will distribute those files to those retailers for you and sell your e-book in its storefront. Often self-publishers handle all the uploading for Amazon, Nook, and Kobo on their own, then use Smashwords for the rest of their e-retailers, adding in CreateSpace for the printed version. See the Smashwords website, www.smashwords.com, for its most current retailer distribution list.

Read your conversion instructions carefully, and spend time reading articles about "formatting your manuscript for e-books" so that you can know the latest needs. It's best if you get specific with your conversion goals in your article search once you know your retailers (example: "formatting your manuscript for Kindle"), as conversion software is frequently updated. Things you'll do in the formatting stage to clean up your manuscript for uploading include replacing # or *** scene break markers with double spacing to create the scene break treatment that traditional books use, and revealing and removing hidden formatting so you can look for extra line spaces and tabs and returns in order to delete them. After you clean it up, you'll pretty it up, adding decorative elements and spiffy chapter title treatment to the file using formatting style options. Don't go overboard with decorations, though—your primary commitment must to be legibility and easy reading. You'll add your author bio at the end of your book if you choose (*back matter*), and insert a title page, copyright statement, disclaimer, and prologue if you've got one to the *front matter*. Ultimately, you'll upload the Word file for the interior document.

Be sure to view the final result in various ways before approving it: Download the e-retailers' apps onto your laptop so you can view your book on your "big" screen and onto your smartphone so you can view it tiny; send the PDF/MOBI/EPUB files to all of your e-reading devices/apps and your retailer-specific files to those dedicated e-readers if you've got them so you can view them there. And if you're doing a POD paperback, order a copy so you see it on paper. Read one or more of those previews entirely to spot any lingering, sneaky typos. Your cover will be a separate JPG cover file, with e-retailer instructions for that, too. Make sure you get the files sizing correct for resolution purity.

As you might suspect, this can be time-consuming and, depending on your skill set or interest in expanding it, potentially frustrating. You could instead hire a freelance book designer to take your finished, proofread text and set up the files, laying out the design of the book with e-readability in mind and even uploading for you. Some authors have proofreaders review the manuscript after layout to help spot formatting problems. If you're printing and binding in significant numbers, not just through single-copy POD orders from an online retailer, you'll benefit from having a book designer to communicate with the printer, using all the right tech-speak to get the book printed the way you want and helping you understand your options.

You find book designers through recommendations in your writing community, by Internet searches, and through writer or self-publishing organizations. The Independent Book Publishers Association has an extensive suppliers and services database. Pay attention to book design awards like the Indie Book Awards for cover design and interior book design: www.indiebookawards. com/awards.php. All freelance designers will have galleries on their websites so you can see their style and design sensibility. Ask for references, establish if their current turnaround time works for you, and understand what services they offer for their fees. As with editors, make sure the contract stipulates that you own the copyright in the book's final design.

COVERING YOUR BOOK

A reader makes a judgment about a book in less than ten seconds, with some experts claiming it's as little as three to five seconds. In that time, the reader processes all the factors, including the title, author, and cover elements. Thus, you must aim for a cover that instantly stirs curiosity or piques an emotion, giving readers cause to find out more about your book. Whether you DIY or hire a pro, you've got to have a striking cover.

You can design your own cover using Adobe Photoshop. That program isn't cheap and requires training, but it allows for some serious awesomeness in designing. There are a number of resources online with Adobe book design templates—do a search for "book design templates" to check them out. Or you can use the software provided by your author services company or online e-book retailers (Amazon's CreateSpace offers online book design software), or you can use freeware like GIMP or Paint.net or even the standard PowerPoint program.

I believe that unless you have graphic arts training or related expertise, hiring a cover designer is an essential self-publishing investment. Cover designers are experts at helping you make your vision a technical reality and possess the expertise with software and training in graphic design. They understand composition, readability, and visual appeal, and work to make the many elements like images, title, author name, and decorative or digital affects cohesive. They keep printing compatibility in mind to make sure your printed book cover will be exactly as expected no matter how you reproduce or print it, taking into account things like file formatting, color consistency, bleed, banding correction, and overall image integrity.

You find cover designers through references or through the IBPA's suppliers and services database. Some writers are finding designers through crowdsourcing sites, where you post your project and price and then designers bid on your job. If you see an impressive cover on someone else's book, find out who designed it, then scour their website to learn more about the designer's style and sensibility. It helps if you hire a designer who knows the NA market in particular, as each market has reader expectations and standards, such as NA's favoring of photographic, character-centric covers. A good designer can create something distinct and eye-popping without straying from the understood tone of the covers in your market. Discuss their sourcing of photographs, making sure you understand the conditions of the images' licensing and letting them know your preferences and image budget. Determine how much input you have on the final design and what kind of design credit they might require on your website and on the copyright page. Often they or the image creator will request particular crediting verbiage. As with every element, make sure you hold the copyright in the final cover design.

Hiring a pro does not mean handing over control of this vital part of your book. As both author and publisher, you have an enormous say in the final cover. In fact, the vision for it begins with you. You may not have a specific image in mind when you talk to your designer (although you just might!), but do be able to provide some adjectives that convey the tone you want, the mood and personality and feel of it. Also provide the designer with a slim synopsis so that she can help you decide the physical elements to include in the pictures and any decorations or symbols and font style that would suit your specific tale. Pointing to comparative covers is also helpful.

To help you understand your designer's approach to embodying your vision or to augment your DIY efforts, here are some generally accepted principles of cover design. All of them revolve around three tenets: make it distinct, make it clear, and make it something people can connect with.

- **DESIGN FOR THUMBNAIL VIEWING.** Remember that this cover will be viewed at thumbnail size more than any other, and on some e-reading devices that thumbnail will be in black-and-white. The elements need to be distinct to be viewable under those circumstances. You want your title, author name, and the concept or genre to be clear in that split-second glance.
- **READABLE TYPEFACE IS ESSENTIAL.** A flourishing font can be pretty, but it's not your best friend when it comes to legibility. Always choose legibility over aesthetics—this is a product that must sell, and readers won't buy if they can't work out the title.
- **COLOR MATTERS.** White is a perilous cover background choice. Against a white background, which is the background of many e-retailers, a white cover risks getting lost. Bright colors pop on thumbnails and suggest moods—and moods are emotions, opening doors to emotional connections with readers. If you need a very light background, pick a faint color

shade with texture, and then make the primary images really pop visually to make sure readers' eyes are pulled to your thumbnail.

- **BE DISTINCT.** The idea of being distinct is particularly important for you as an NA novelist. Early on, NA book covers developed a general categorical feel, much like you can tell a paranormal from a thriller. They tend to feature one or two characters, are usually photographic, and favor swooshy title type. There's often a dreaminess about the photographic people, and those with a strong romantic theme tend to follow Romance Lit's example of clasped couples showing dreaminess or smolder. So your task then is to figure out how to be distinct within certain standards that took hold. Perhaps that means breaking away from those models completely and deliberately, going for something surprising, unexpected, yet attention-catching and intriguing. The more that happens, the wider the field will open up. Or maybe that means accepting those rules but pushing beyond them, perhaps putting emphasis on the pieces not normally emphasized or adding color splashes in surprising ways.
- **REFLECT YOUR BOOK'S HOOK IN YOUR COVER.** Tell readers visually, at a glance, what makes this book special from all the other NA books with character-centric photographic covers. Doing that means understanding what it is that distinguishes your book. Revisit Chapter 6 if you haven't already worked that out. Convey the most important, meaningful elements.
- **LET LEGIBILITY LEAD YOUR SPINE DESIGN.** Printed books have a spine. What will yours look like? Reflect the style and overall design of the front cover, but keep the title type easily readable, meaning simple and without interference or distraction by other elements, like fussy decorations. Logos need to be simple, too, as they are going to be tiny on the spine. Think "thumbnail principle" again with that element.
- **KEEP YOUR BRAND IN MIND.** Pull out your crystal ball and think about the covers for all those books you haven't written yet but will. Do you want a branded treatment for your covers? If so, read cover designer Robin Ludwig's advice below about covers and author branding.

INDUSTRY INSIGHT: AUTHOR BRANDING THROUGH COVER DESIGN

BY ROBIN LUDWIG

In any marketing campaign, a good first impression is invaluable in creating a brand for your author identity. For a book, a cover is that first impression. The key to branding yourself through your cover design is to create interest in your writing from a glance. An appealing design sticks with your fans and gives new readers more confidence about trying an unfamiliar author.

Your cover design can serve as inspiration as you establish a professional identity for your author name, so make sure that the brand you create with your cover translates to your readers and your future writing goals. Whenever possible, repeat elements of your brand into future cover designs. These elements can be a font, the layout of your design, a specific image, coloring, and the tone of the design. Your goal is for readers to recognize the publisher, author name, design style, series, or characters. Even when they don't recognize specific branding, they may be drawn to a book simply because it has a similar look to books they are familiar with, so make sure your cover fits your genre, target audience, and the current tone of the market. A professional cover designer can help you visualize your idea into a cohesive design with respect to current trends.

Extend your author branding by promoting your book in teasers using portions of your cover artwork and by repeating elements of your design on your blog and networking channels. You can also use your cover design to further your recognition with readers through swag, book trailers, marketing campaigns, and custom graphics. As your readership grows and the publishing industry changes, you can make subtle adjustments to refine your brand.

Robin Ludwig is an award-winning book cover designer and president of Robin Ludwig Design, Inc. www.gobookcoverdesign.com; coversbyrobin.blogspot.com

Obtaining Cover Images

If you want to design your own cover, there are plenty of online stock photo websites. Some allow free use, others license their images for a fee. You get more images to pick from if you pay licensing fees, of course—a choice that also cuts down on the probability of your cover image appearing on a competing novel. Multiple authors using the same image is okay from a legal perspective since those authors don't have sole right to the photos, but you'll need to decide if you're okay with the marketplace repetition.

Before you choose your final image, read its licensing agreement to see what uses the image owner allows. Make sure they have model releases and property releases, as some sites leave that up to you to confirm. You don't want to mess with that detail, and you don't want the models in the photos suing you over use. No image is worth that risk, hassle, and expense, no matter how good it is. You can find another that is worry-free.

Obtain the largest size, best-quality image you can. You'll likely find yourself blowing up your cover image for use on large banners or projected onto a screen at book signings or other events. Don't risk losing resolution over a few dollars in the image-buying phase. This can be an issue even with promo items like postcards or T-shirts. You certainly don't want any nasty surprises when your cover is printed on a bound POD book.

If you're able to take professional-quality photographs, you can spare yourself licensing hassle by taking your own photos, being sure to have your models sign waivers giving you all rights to that image. But only choose this option if you're sure your photos and your models won't look amateurish.

Back Covers

Printed books will also have a back cover, so you'll need to design that, too. Handily, what you write for your back-cover blurb will be adaptable for your query letter should you decide to submit to agents or editors (next chapter) and for your sales blurb in bookstore listings and on your website. This is going to be your go-to sell copy.

As you decide what to put on that back cover, resist the temptation to pack it margin to margin. An info-packed blurb, clever taglines, enticing reviews, *and* your notable bio may all be enticing, but a big block of stuff can overwhelm, pushing readers' eyes away. With sell copy, less is more. Be selective about hitting the key interest points, hit them clearly and well, and then stand back and let the reader absorb that hit.

To help you do that, pick up that hook you wrote back in Chapter 2 or set about writing it now, and lead with that. It tells you the essential selling points of your story, which you'll want to emphasize on the back cover. You may decide to place the hook directly on top of the back cover, with some massaging for dramatic flow, as in this example:

> Determined to expose a secret thrill-betting network that offers big payoffs to desperate students, USD freshman Sharia accepts a dare to ocean dive from the hood of a car—as it's shoved off the cliff.

You'd then give some flavorful and informative context in a longer blurb right below this. Readers could pick up this hook statement and use it in their social media when they tell their friends about the awesome book they just read. Or you can get more dramatic, moving the information from this hook statement to the main blurb and instead turning this lead-in, top-of-the-cover space into a moment of drama, a sort of glimpse into the story itself. Some writers like this approach, although it does sacrifice the line that readers can cut-and-paste to pitch your book. Here's the more dramatic approach (bolded here and often given special type treatment on a cover to distinguish it as something special and glance-able for readers), which I've followed with the main sell copy:

> **She knows she'll do it. She'll nod her head, the signal to shove her car over the ocean cliff, then she'll jump from the hood, arms outstretched, and plummet to the crushing waves below. She'll do it. She'll take the dare.**
>
> Sharia Santanillo is devastated by the senseless suicide of her best friend. Sure, Carlo was exhausted, working three jobs to put himself through school. But he loved life. He was invincible. Yet nothing he'd done that week made sense. He'd given her a wad of money and told her to meet him at the bank in three hours and if he didn't show up, to give the cash to his mom. He had shown up—shaking, bruised, with $90,000 more. Days later, sleepless, skittish, refusing to talk about the money, he'd jumped from the school clock tower. With Carlo's brother Victor, Sharia discovers her friend had been recruited by a thrill-betting

ring that preys on desperate students. She and Victor blood-swear to find the scum who recruited Carlo. Dark, chiseled Victor is methodical, fierce, and passionate; she can't resist him any more than she can resist her yearning for revenge. Yet she's sure Victor is wasting precious time, that a desperate kid will take the next horrific dare so some rich bastards can get a power thrill. So Sharia hatches a plan: She'll take the next dare herself.

That longer copy fleshes out the context you introduced in the hook, conveying the main themes and main problem that'll play out, using language and delivery that suggests the mood, story, and tone of the narration. I'm going to use this same book concept for my sample query letter in the next chapter so that you can see the kind of massaging that you can do to this blurb to make it useful in different situations.

The fewer words you can use in your blurb, the better. That'll leave you more room for your barcodes and any review lines or decorative elements you want to add. My blurb emphasizes that this is a New Adult novel by calling out the new adult traits of college and breaking from a limiting past. Also look for ways to convey the genre of your story so that fans of that genre will recognize elements and themes they like. You can find a bazillion other back-cover examples in bookstores—and I recommend you do. Just as reading great fiction trains your brain to write great fiction, reading effective sell copy trains you to write effective sell copy.

OBTAINING ISBNS AND COVER BARCODES

Each of your books needs its own unique thirteen-digit ISBN (International Standard Book Number) to identify it and its publisher. You can buy ISBNs singly or in bulk from Bowker, the official ISBN agency for the United States. Bowker explains ISBNs and the buying process on its website, www.isbn.org. If you use an author services company, that company will assign you one of the ISBNs it's bought in bulk, but understand that the ISBN they assign identifies *them* as the publisher of that edition of your book. ISBNs can't be transferred or assigned to any other books.

Your printed-and-bound books need barcodes that make the ISBN readable by store scanners. You buy barcodes from Bowker, too. Some author service companies will offer package deals of barcodes and ISBNs, as well as LCCNs (Library of Congress Catalog Numbers). You only need an LCCN if you think your bound book will be stocked in libraries, which isn't common with self-published NA novels. You can obtain LCCNs on your own at www.loc.gov/publish/cip.

ROUNDING OUT YOUR SELF-PUBLISHING TEAM WITH AN AGENT

Believe it or not, agents can play a part in a self-publisher's career. If you've sold enough books to make publishers take notice or already have interest from potential licensees (such as a foreign publisher or a movie producer who sought you out), a literary agent is a smart partner to have in your corner. Your agent would likely have a sub-agent specializing in film/TV rights or licensing deals, whom she'd pay from her agency's cut of your royalties or licensing deals. That would all be spelled out in your literary representation contract.

Presently, the industry standard has agents taking 15 percent of domestically distributed book royalties. Be sure to choose agents who are part of the Association of Authors' Representatives (AAR), which is the primary professional organization for literary and dramatic agents. AAR members agree to a Canon of Ethics, established to protect you from unscrupulous agents who would do dodgy things like charge you reading fees. Don't ever pay an agent to read your manuscript or pay for them to edit your manuscript. She represents you to others, taking a cut of what she makes selling your work, not on selecting or developing your work. I tell you how to find, vet, and submit to agents in Chapter 14.

LEGAL CONSIDERATIONS FOR SELF-PUBLISHERS

Because U.S. copyright law says that as soon as you type your story into creation (or somehow put it in a fixed form, on canvas, on disk, on lined paper in scrawled print even) it belongs to you and is protected from others' use. Thus, you don't technically have to register your copyright with the U.S. Copyright Office. But you should. That way, if someone tries to pull a fast one on you by plagiarizing your work or accusing you of plagiarizing *their* material, you can provide legal proof of ownership of your intellectual property. Registering will cost you a few bucks, but it's cheaper than hiring an attorney later to defend your ownership. Get registration forms and instructions at the U.S. Copyright Office's e-copyright page: www.copyright.gov/eco/index.html. Your author services companies may register the copyright for you; just be sure that they're registering it in *your* name. Unscrupulous companies may try to register it in their name.

Also protect yourself by getting written permission for any material you include in your fiction that belongs to other content creators, such as passages from other books, song lyrics, and poems. This will prevent lawsuits for copyright infringement or perhaps even plagiarism. Plagiarism is when you reprint someone else's words or ideas and pass them off as your own. Don't think you won't get caught. In a 2012 instance of an author plagiarizing several best-selling NA authors, fans spotted the plagiarism in the offending books and broadcast it all over the Internet. There's no undoing that kind of damage, not by claiming you rewrote the other person's material enough to make it a "new" piece, by calling it "fair use," by trying to pitch it as publicity for the other person, or by simply saying, "Sorry, bad call."

Fair use is a notoriously misunderstood term. Fair use allows you to print portions of someone else's work in certain circumstances, such as in teaching materials and scholarship, criticism, commentary, news reporting, and research. None of those sounds like an NA novel, does it? Some people think there's a word count limit that draws the line between fair use and copyright infringement, but that's a myth. Judges weigh four different criteria when deciding if a use is fair, which you can find in Sections 107 through 118 of Title 17, U.S. Code:

1. the purpose or character of the use, including whether such use is for commercial or nonprofit purposes
2. the nature of the copyrighted work
3. the amount and substance of the portion used
4. the effect of the use upon the potential market for, or value of, the copyrighted work

There's a huge amount of discretion within these criteria, and every case has its particulars that make it unpredictable.

Writers often wonder when they must get permission. I recommend you cover your butt and ask permission whenever humanly possible. Even if a source wouldn't win a lawsuit, they can still *file* suit (or threaten to do so), causing you stress and legal expenses as you defend yourself. Make your best efforts to find the copyright owner and secure permission. If you're wondering whether you're crossing the line or not, chances are you're in the risky gray zone. Make your life easier by simply making up your own song lyrics and your own poems. Or refer to the songs or poems by name and artist and let that be enough without quoting content (titles aren't copyrightable, with the exception of those songs that have become popular identifiers of a music group, as with the most popular Beatles songs). Or you can ask permission, and if you don't or can't get it, then use public domain material. *Public domain* is work that has gone out of copyright and is now fair game for anyone. U.S. copyright law sets the term of copyright for works created after 1978 at the author's lifetime plus 70 years (www.copyright.gov provides full information about right, no matter when the work was published). After that, no more copyright protection, so you can use that material within your novel, crediting it on your copyright page, of course. The law doesn't require you to add that credit, but professionalism does. Give credit where credit is due. Also, know that putting public domain material into your copyrighted fiction does not put that public domain material within your copyright. It remains in the public domain.

So how do you get permission when you want it? If it's material from a book, you can contact the author in the case of self-published works or the publisher if that book was released through a traditional house. Publishers post their Rights and Permissions Department's contact information on their websites and on the copyright pages of their books. Let them know exactly what you want to publish, the way you'll use their copyrighted material, the number of books you plan to publish if you plan a bound book run or the estimated sales for e-books, your intended price for the book, and your publication date. They will charge you a permission fee based on those factors and lay out their rules for use of that material. Usually it's for a limited time, number of printings, or number of sales, but it can be *unlimited*, which lets you use that material in as many printings of your book as you want, as long as you want. They'll also provide you with the wording you're to use on your copyright page to credit the material. Expect this process to take four to six weeks from your initial date of contacting the publisher.

Asking permission can get tricky with nonbook material, such as song lyrics, film dialogue, or photographs. A physical music CD will probably have copyright information on the CD's liner notes, or at least a point of contact for your search to begin. If you don't see that or it's not available because you're referencing a digital version of the song, look on the artist's webpage for the information or to find out the name of his agent. The agent can point you in the right direction in the case of songwriters who retain lyric rights, etc.

Another source for information is the U.S. Copyright Office's online database of copyright registration at www.copyright.gov. Keep track of your search efforts so that you can prove due diligence should you be unable to locate the copyright owner and decide to use the source material anyway. That's a risky call since you're still open to lawsuit, but if you show that you made best efforts, the issue may be settled more smoothly. You'll credit all your sources on your copyright page; most will provide you with the language they want cited.

Lastly, that whole "inspired by a true story" thing: You've got to be careful when basing stories, situations, or characters on real-life examples. *Libel* is the legal term for making false statements about someone, either in print or broadcast, that damage that person's reputation. There are all kinds of gray areas in libel law. And remember that you don't have to actually libel someone to be sued and forced to defend yourself. You've got some wiggle room to write about public figures, but what you say has to be true to be deemed not libelous, and you have to be able to prove it when challenged. Using a nonpublic figure isn't any easier—in fact, it can be even more booby-trapped, as those folks can claim invasion of privacy. Relatives of deceased nonpublic figures can even sue for that!

If you're inspired by real life, I advise the amalgam approach, where you make brand new characters by merging traits and facts from many different real-life people for a final character who can't be identified as any single person. That would probably be more interesting to you as a novelist anyway, as you'd get a character who is wholly your creation and has plenty of room to grow into a rich being all his own. That is, after all, the spirit of new adulthood: young people leaving behind personas defined by childhood social circles, now blooming into fully formed, stunningly original selves.

BEYOND THE BOOK: CREATING YOUR OWN AUDIO BOOK

BY ALANA ALBERTSON

So you wanna make your book available in audio? Don't be intimidated—it's easier to do than you might think. You can produce your own in ten straightforward steps.

1. **LOGIN TO WWW.ACX.COM.** ACX is an Amazon company that specializes in producing audio books.
2. **FIND YOUR BOOK.** Search for your book and claim it.
3. **DECIDE IF YOU WANT TO DO ROYALTY SHARE OR PAY BY THE HOUR FOR NARRATORS.** In a royalty share, the narrator will take 50 percent of the profit of the book. In the hourly rate, the author will pay the narrator to record the book. I chose to pay my narrator by the hour because I was committed to the long-term promotion of my audio book and wanted to keep the profits. But royalty share is a great option for authors who may not have any money to spend out of pocket.
4. **CREATE A PROFILE.** Describe your story to potential narrators to get them interested in auditioning for your project. Narrators will search available projects and submit their auditions. What makes your story special? Pick a one- to two-page section of your book to submit as your audition script. Set your criteria for a narrator. Would you like a male narrator or a female narrator? Sexy or serious?

   TIP: Don't limit the auditions. I was *positive* I wanted a female narrator for my book so I only posted for female auditions. But an audio producer contacted me and let me listen to samples of the voice actors that worked for him. When I heard Grant George's audition, his sexy voice leveled me. I knew he was perfect for Bret.
5. **SIT BACK AND WAIT FOR AUDITIONS TO ROLL IN.** It was so fascinating to hear all the amazing narrators reading my book! If you don't

seem to be getting many auditions, you can search for narrators by age, gender, and dialect and ask for narrators to audition for you.

6. **CHOOSE A NARRATOR.** This was difficult. I had many talented narrators audition, and I hated rejecting narrators who had spent the time doing so. But this is your production, and you need to pick the voice that best represents your story and appeals to your audience.

7. **REVIEW YOUR SAMPLE RECORDING.** The narrator will produce an initial fifteen-minute clip for you to approve. Be sure to bring up any concerns. I provided a character list and pronunciation guide.

   TIP: Communication is key. My narrator/producer was wonderful about giving me updates.

8. **LISTEN TO YOUR AUDIO BOOK!** This was the most exciting part for me—hearing my words come to life. I recommend listening to it at least three times. The first time without looking at your book, just to listen to it as an audio listener. Make sure the tone is correct. The second time with your manuscript open. Make sure pronunciations are correct, no words are skipped or repeated, and no background noises are audible.

9. **APPROVE AND PAY.** Once the producer receives the payment, your book will go through a final vetting by ACX before release.

10. **PROMOTE YOUR AUDIO BOOK.** Congratulations! You have a completed audio book and one more income stream. You'll receive samples from ACX. Send the audio book to bloggers, use it for giveaways, and share it with the world!

Alana Albertson is the author of the New Adult series Dancing Under the Stars and the Trident Code and is the former president of Romance Writers of America's Young Adult and Chick Lit chapters. www.alanaalbertson.com.

CHAPTER 14

Casting Your Lot With a Traditional Publisher

*M*any New Adult best-selling authors, including Jessica Park, A.L. Jackson, Abbi Glines, and Tammara Webber, originally self-publish then sign with traditional publishers like Penguin Random House and Harlequin, a division of William Morrow. Others publish traditionally from the get-go, either with big houses or smaller publishers like Entangled Embrace, the New Adult fiction imprint of Entangled Publishing. There are even some authors who straddle the two models, publishing some of their novels through established houses while self-publishing other work, earning the moniker *hybrid author*. Our post-digital revolution publishing world—and the digital focus of the NA marketplace in particular—offers you opportunities to pursue a model that best suits your publishing situation.

Being signed by a traditional publisher requires submitting your fiction to editors, with literary agents often playing the middlemen in that hookup. In this chapter I'll help you understand the strengths and weaknesses of traditional publishing, then formulate a strategy for submitting to agents and editors if you decide that's the path for you. Then I'll walk you through the process of writing an effective query letter and synopsis so that you can submit with confidence.

TRADITIONAL PUBLISHERS AND THE E-CENTRIC NA MARKETPLACE

In December 2012, Penguin Random House (at that time just "Random House") announced the creation of Flirt, a combination NA/YA "digital first" imprint that signaled a bold Big House commitment to the new fiction category. In one swoop, New Adult fiction jumped miles ahead in its quest for legitimacy as a full-fledged category with long-term potential. In the previous year, publishers like Harlequin and Simon & Schuster had declared their interest in a less full-throated manner by signing some self-published NA successes to traditional bound book deals. Capitalizing on the momentum the authors build, these publishers not only promote (and in some cases distribute) the existing e-books, but also push bound books online and onto the general fiction shelves of brick-and-mortar stores. The *digital first* twist at Flirt means that the new imprint focuses almost exclusively on e-book formatting, only producing bound books when a title's popularity warrants the additional format. Such two-pronged bound book/e-book strategies meet the needs of a readership that primarily searches for their e-books online, buys them from e-retailers, and downloads them into their e-reading devices. E-centric publishing strategies for an e-centric marketplace.

This e-centrism of the NA fiction realm is also of interest to publishers open not just to alternate publishing strategies but to alternate publishing *models*—such as foregoing advances at the time of contract and instead offering higher royalties on copies actually sold—and to alternate submission tactics, such as crowdsourcing sites like Macmillan's Swoon Reads, which is a website (www.swoonreads.com) onto which writers upload their manuscripts for visitors to read and comment on, with the "most Swoon-worthy" manuscripts getting looks from the site's "publishing board" and, for those that continue to stand out, standard publishing contracts.

THE TRADITIONAL BUSINESS MODEL EXPLAINED

What makes a publishing company "traditional," be it a big or small company (or *house*), is the long-standing business model of an author selling an editor the right to publish his manuscript as a book. The author's payment is a minority percentage of the profits from the book's sales—the *royalties*. The house keeps the larger percentage of the profits in exchange for funding and executing the design, printing, binding, shipping, and warehousing of the book, all while sales reps work with store retailers' buyers to stock books from each new season's offerings and replace stock from the backlist catalog. To help them make their decisions, chain book buyers consult computer databases for a chain-wide sales history of every author. Because online retailers theoretically have every in-print book "in stock," their distributors place printed book orders with publishers in order to fill their book warehouses and have stock at the ready. Through all these shifts, the editors' front-end buying of rights and the subsequent in-house production of the book has remained constant.

We're seeing some alterations in this model as the digital publishing revolution plays out, though again not generally enormous changes. First, the standard royalty structure now includes e-books. Industry standard royalty structure usually calls for 10 percent of the net profit of each hardcover sold going to the author, along with 6 percent to 8 percent of each paperback and 25 percent to 30 percent of each e-book. That e-book royalty is where the knuckle clenching occurs. Authors and agents want that royalty to be much higher than 25 percent, pointing out that e-books don't cost much to make because there are no printing and binding, shipping, or warehousing costs. Publishers counter that e-book-only titles incur the same in-house production and marketing costs as any physical books and so e-books cost more to make than you'd think. Plus, they say, simultaneous bound book/e-book publishing means the costs should be spread out across *all* the formats, just as they are spread across the hardcover and paperback formats. Publishers who've shown interest in finding new models for e-publishing may offer e-book royalties of 40 percent and even 50 percent, sometimes basing each individual e-book sale's royalty on whether the book is sold through their site or other retail sites so that you'll make more on one than the other.

While royalty rates are essentially non-negotiable, even for agents, you can negotiate for a royalty *escalator,* which means that higher sales are rewarded with higher royalties. A common escalator gives you 10 percent on the first 10,000 hardcover books sold, then 12.5 percent on the next 5,000 copies, then 15 percent thereafter. Since escalators are based on real sales instead of predictions, publishers usually agree to that request. Some agents and authors negotiate escalators of e-book royalties that raise the royalty up to 50 percent once you hit a certain sales number.

Publishers are tighter in their negotiations of your *advance against royalties*, or simply *advance*. The advance is a sum of money they pay you up front, even before the book is made. You start receiving your royalties only after your book has sold enough copies for the publisher to make back the money they advanced to you. Advances differ for every author and every book, as the publishers estimate how many copies of your book they'll sell. Obviously, a well-known author is likely to sell more books than a newbie, and that'll be reflected in the advance offer. Usually you get half of your advance upon signing the contract and half upon delivery of the full manuscript, though the contract may break that second half into smaller payments due upon delivery of things like half of the manuscript. If for some reason your book doesn't sell enough copies to break even, you don't have to return any of that advance, so it's in the publisher's interest to keep the advance as low as possible. Some authors push for the biggest advance they can get because they want the sure money and they believe that publishers will work harder to market books if they invest more up front, while other authors strategize that lower advances lessen the publisher's break-even risk, thus increasing your chances of scoring future contracts with that publisher. If that latter case were your preference, your strategy could be to accept a lower advance but negotiate an escalator.

The newer payment model that has publishers skipping advances completely in favor of higher royalty rates—sometimes as high as 40 percent or even 50 percent of the e-book cover price, with 8 percent on print copies—pins everyone's wallet pleasure on real sales instead of predictions and in theory has all parties more motivated to push for high book sales. Houses that offer this "no advance/higher royalty" model usually call it out on their website.

REASONS TO GO TRADITIONAL

When people hear the difference in royalty rates between self-publishing and traditional publishing, they might look at you like you're crazy for even considering letting anyone have money that you could be making yourself. But there are plenty of reasons to make a play for traditional publication:

1. **CREATIVE TEAMWORK WITH VESTED EXPERTS.** A publishing house gives you editorial, design, and production expertise and resources. Writing is

hard work, and publishing your own book is another can of hard work worms. Publishing with a house puts you on a team with professional, experienced editors and designers who know how to physically realize the vision of a story and spark readers to buy it. Publishers have a vested interest in your book's sell-through success, as opposed to author services companies who make the bulk of their money on creation services for the books, not on the actual sales of the books. Thus, the publisher's employees conceivably are vested in your book as moneymakers for their company. In the case of editors, their own careers are defined by the fates of the books they sign up (which accounts for their super-duper care in acquisitions).

2. **SALES, DISTRIBUTION, AND MARKETING EXPERTISE AND RESOURCES.** A publishing house gives you national distribution and access to brick-and-mortar stores, as well as the development input of sales reps with marketplace experience. If you're a new or mid-level author, physical distribution may not be a big draw for you because your NA novels are sold mostly as e-books; the lack of NA-dedicated bookshelves almost guarantees that. But getting the muscle of a marketing department behind your book can be significant. In theory, the greater distribution and increased marketing efforts will result in more sales than you could earn through self-publishing and thus the royalty discrepancy argument becomes less clear-cut.

3. **DREAMS.** Many of us have spent our lives dreaming of our names on the cover of a book, and even if self-publishing makes that possible, the ultimate peak of dreaming is having our name on a book published by a well-known, established publisher. This is the same dream that has our names on bestseller lists and on marquees for book tours. Dream building is a powerful motivator, and many writers don't consider their dream truly fulfilled without that final validation of being published by a house.

4. **CREDIBILITY.** The issues of legitimacy and value continue to be debated even as more and more people buy self-published books. But when a publisher calls a book good, it must be good, right? Maybe. Fair or not, many readers believe this, and you may, too, even just a little bit. So publishing with a traditional publisher can validate your story and make some people trust and even respect you more deeply as a storyteller.

5. **FOCUS AND WORKLOAD.** The simple amount of work involved in self-publishing versus traditional publishing is something to consider. You saw how much work goes into self-publishing a book in the previous chapter.

Plenty of authors would be happy to let someone else deal with the bulk of that. Perhaps the most famous case of a best-selling, self-published author going traditional is Amanda Hocking, whose paranormal YA novels were selling in the millions *before* she signed with a publisher. She was one of the first self-publishing boomers, so she remains an entrepreneurial icon to many, quite a few of whom felt betrayed when she signed with Simon & Schuster in 2010. Amanda was exhausted with all the nonwriting work required and wanted to hand that over to others so she could focus on the stories.

There are cons to traditional publication, of course. There's the money issue, but as big as that, for many, is the issue of control. The thing many authors worry about is that you cede almost all cover control to a publisher, which is usually spelled out quite clearly in your contract. The idea behind that arrangement is that just as you benefit from a marketing and sales teams that knows the market well and will do what it can to position your book for success, those professionals can apply their expertise to the packaging of the product—particularly the cover. You may be able to negotiate "cover consultation," although publishers can stand tough on even that point. Bestsellers with the clout to make the demand may be able to negotiate "jacket approval." That said, no one inside your publishing house is looking to make you miserable. They'll have discussions with you about vision and positioning and want you to be happy with the final result. If you pursue traditional publishing for your book, you must be open to them applying their expertise to your cover.

The same fear of losing control can make you worry for your story, too. Will an editor insist you change something? What if you don't want to? Yes, there are cases of this happening, but they are rare in comparison to the scads of authors who are thrilled to have a trained, articulate, visionary editor guiding them to their strongest possible final story. Plus, your editor isn't going to sign up your book if she's not crazy about it and isn't confident in its potential to please readers, review well, and sell well. She wants a long, productive, happy relationship with her authors, and in offering you a contract, she's betting her company's money, her co-workers' time and energy, and her career on her belief that you and she will have that kind of relationship.

Another less than savory thing to consider is that most traditional publishing houses pay out royalties twice yearly, while self-publishers get their profits from e-retailers either quarterly or monthly depending on the organization's current policy. This is a long-standing practice that frustrates agents and authors, and it's wrapped up in another long-standing practice: *holds for returns.* Publishers' contracts allow them to hold back cash reserves from your book sales on the chance that your physical books, which are sold to bookstores but not to readers themselves, get returned by those bookstores for full credit if the books don't sell through to the store's customers. This returns policy became entrenched after publishers used it during the Depression Era to encourage stores to take risks on unknown authors. The policy is now considered by many to be a poor business strategy that encourages unrealistic orders. Periodically the cry goes up to abolish it, but for the moment it stands. Some publishers are starting to revamp their twice-yearly payment schedule or at least are adapting it to allow for more immediate royalty payments for digital book sales.

INDUSTRY INSIGHT: BREAKING INTO THE TRADITIONAL MARKET

BY EDITORS KAREN GROVE AND NICOLE STEINHAUS

What does it take to break into traditional publishing? The truth is, nowadays, good isn't good enough; exceptional is what sells. So what makes a story exceptional?

Standing out with an unparalleled premise is a must. Editors (and in the end, readers) slaver over the thought that they've stumbled upon something groundbreaking. Big shoes to fill, right? It's actually quite simple and begins with the use of unexpected characters and unpredictable twists. There are only so many storylines, but molding characters so they gnaw at readers even when the book is set down and kinking the plot in a way that feels like it's never been done before is a surefire way to get your story to stand out.

A fresh voice is also essential. Whether it's light and airy or hauntingly dark, the voice should pop off the page from line one, and this doesn't only mean with witty dialogue and well-crafted prose. A quality of voice most overlooked is tapping deep into the readers' emotions, pushing them to hurt, laugh, and hope alongside your character.

The business side also comes into play. "Good" sells for self-publishing, but only "great" will break through the walls of a traditional publisher. Why? Because we see hundreds, if not thousands, of manuscripts a year. We know what's out there, what's selling, and what's not. Time is also at a premium, and we need to focus our time on books we believe will sell well because traditionally published books must retail at a higher price point. There are editors, designers, publicity and marketing staff, and sales reps—in addition to the author and agent—who must earn a living. We look for books that are able to carry that higher price point and still sell in large quantities.

So our decision to sign a book is both from our hearts and from our heads. We look for books that move us to sit up and take notice, to feel emotions deeply, to challenge us mentally, to give us something unexpected and stick with us long after we've turned that last page. And then we must weigh that against the business side—will it sell? And sell in quantities large enough that we can afford to spend the time and energy and expense in publishing it? What's its hook? The thing that will make readers want to pick it up and savor it? When heart and head match up, then we have a manuscript we can sign.

Karen Grove is Editorial Director and Senior Editor at Embrace, Entangled Publishing's New Adult fiction imprint. Nicole Steinhaus is Associate Editor at Embrace. www.entangledpublishing.com/category/new-adult

THE ROLE OF AGENTS IN TRADITIONAL PUBLISHING

There are many reasons to seek literary representation if you plan to publish traditionally. The most obvious reason is to get help submitting your manuscripts to a publisher. An agent can get you around the "no unsolicited mss" policies of the big houses, which turn away all manuscripts that don't come from agents.

Agents know all the editors and their tastes and can dial them up or shoot off an e-mail, and they get a faster response than you would because editors want the agents to keep the manuscripts coming. Also, editors are thankful for the role agents play in parsing submissions, sending only the best stuff they can find.

"Editors are expecting a certain quality of storytelling and writing and skill. Agents have to go in there and assess the story for the qualities that would be expected by publishers." —**STACEY DONAGHY**, Agent, Donaghy Literary Group

---

The agent gets paid only when he sells your work, taking his 15 percent commission from your advance and then from your royalties as long as that book is in print with that publisher.

But beyond the obvious submission factor, there are some other benefits that may be unknown to writers new to the publishing business. Here's what agents do:

- **SUBMIT AND FIELD OFFERS.** They create a submission list for you that's more targeted than you could make, because they know what each editor is looking for, buying, and has published. They can submit your manuscript to multiple houses as an "auction," having editors bid for a much-desired project. They can help you pick the best editor for your personality as well as your work. If editors are contacting you directly, you can usually secure an agent who will then help you vet that contact and negotiate the intricacies of deal with your interests at heart.
- **HANDLE THE BUSINESS.** Agents negotiate the deals, reading and working the contracts to your best benefit. In fact, agencies have "boilerplate" agreements with most publishers, which means they've already negotiated good deals for their clients and you get in on that, tweaking the details as necessary for your specific project. Agents handle all monies coming in, taking out their percentage while translating royalty statements to make sure you get all you're due. They chase down editors for payments so you and your

editor can keep strictly to the creative work. Agents also peddle and protect your subsidiary rights. *Subsidiary rights* is a broad term encompassing all those nonbook things you can license out, like the right to create a movie out of your book, or to create merchandise like clothing, or even to publish foreign editions. Publishers will peddle your subsidiary rights for you with their in-house subrights staff for a cut spelled out in your contract; that leaves the agent out of the deal, so most literary agencies contract with sub-agents who will peddle those subrights for you, with the two agents splitting their piece of the sale.

- **STRATEGIZE AND MANAGE YOUR CAREER.** Agents help you decide which stories to write next and help shape your overall career. They are your business partners. I've heard plenty of cases where agents have told their author, "That manuscript isn't your best work, but this one is, so let's lead with this one." That's how so many second manuscripts become the first ones published. Your agent will also educate you about how the business works and point you to opportunities you weren't aware existed. Through their networking with editors, they may find a desired story topic that suits your style and interest and then bring that idea to you, giving you the opportunity to shape a project with an editor from the outset.

A funny little catch-22 about getting an agent is that it's easier to get one if you already have an editor. It does happen that way sometimes, though. I advise you to submit to agents and editors at the same time, and it just may be that an editor bites first. In that case, you let agents know you've got editorial interest and want representation before you sign. They'll likely take a quick look at your submission. And I do recommend that you get an agent even if you no longer need her to open the publisher's door; all of those other reasons for getting an agent still stand. At the very least, it's worth your money to have the book contract reviewed by a publishing attorney experienced with publishing contracts. That experience matters now more than ever, as publishers are radically updating their contract wording to account for new and potential format rights. You don't want any surprises later, even with a good relationship.

You can vet agents through your writers' community, online research, Preditors & Editors (www.pred-ed.com), and Writer Beware (www.sfwa.org/for-authors/writer-beware). Interviews with agents abound on the Internet, and all agencies post their preferences and submission rules on their websites. Check out who they represent to see if they're a match for you and if they're open to submission from self-published authors. Most are, but you'll have to prove your book to them.

SUBMITTING TO AGENTS AND EDITORS

Being in business for yourself is all about strategizing your business, and that carries over to identifying the right people to work with. In your case, you're looking for the right publisher and agent for something that's more than just a "product" to you. So you want to pick agents and editors who will share your vision and enthusiasm for your book and your career, and who will be pleasurable partners in the trenches. There's no sense in hiring someone who's good at what he does but who makes you miserable or angst-ridden. I realize it seems like writers get the luck of the draw, being plenty happy to take any agent or editor who will have you, but there are ways to vet a pro's personality and sensibility.

Submitting is basically the same with both agents and editors: You submit the same materials, pitched in the same manner, and you go about finding the right people to submit to in the same way. The real difference is that more agents have wide-open submission doors. Some of the more veteran agents may have a pretty full stable with the authors they already represent and so only take submissions through personal referrals, but the rest are actively reviewing submissions. Agents want to see everything as long as it meets the criteria they lay out in their guidelines, which are posted on their websites. Look specifically for NA fiction interest on those websites.

Some publishing houses set *no unsolicited manuscripts* rules that prevent you from sending to generic "Dear Editor" or "To Whom It May Concern," but many NA imprints are exempt from that. The imprint's submission guidelines will spell out exactly what kind of work can be submitted and how it should be done. Often individual editors will invite submissions through contests and at speaking appearances and in interviews. Those opportunities take a little more searching-out than simple webpage guidelines. Note that younger editors tend to be particularly active in making the rounds to blogs and writing conferences. This works in your favor, as they're in active list-building mode while the veterans with the corner offices already have a cadre of writers supplying them with great books. Young editors have the same experienced production teams and veteran marketing teams in their corners and are usually mentored by the hotshot bigwigs anyway.

In this section I'll help you find, vet, and pick the pros you want to work with, then I'll help you develop fabulous, intriguing query letters and synopses to get those pros to read your sample pages, which, thanks to all your work in the rest of this book, will compel them to request the full manuscript and then fall in love with it.

BUILDING YOUR SUBMISSION LIST

To strategize your submission list, first locate the names of NA-interested agents and editors/publishers, then pick who among those would be most likely to click with you and your project. Ultimately, you can't know you've got a match until the editor and agent weigh in with their subjective tastes, but you can develop a sense about it. I'll help you do that.

Here's how you can identify agents and editors interested in NA fiction, then research them to learn about their tastes through their interviews and their client lists:

- **WRITERS FORUMS AND CRITIQUE CIRCLES.** Your fellow NA writers are doing the same thing you're doing. Ask who they are submitting to or if they've heard anything good or bad about the people you've identified.
- **DEAL ANNOUNCEMENTS.** Subscribe to *Publishers Weekly*'s free weekly e-newsletter "Publishers Lunch," which announces pub deals made the previous week, listing the authors, agents, and editors involved in each deal. See whose names turn up in association with NA projects. If you go the extra step of paying for premium subscription, you get access to their deals database in which you can look up the latest deals by category and date and see a list of them at once. From that you can start your website research and build a targeted submission list that has better chances of return, and you can do it more quickly than waiting for deals to show up randomly or floating around websites.
- **PUBLISHED AUTHORS.** Go to the websites of authors whose books are comparable to yours and see who they list as their agents. Check their books' copyright pages or spines for their publishers and imprints. Look in their

books' acknowledgments pages and see if they called out their peeps by name. You can also just flat-out ask them who their agent is on social media, if they're active there. Most authors will share that information even if they can't provide introductions or referrals.

- **SOCIAL MEDIA.** You can follow many editors and agents on social media to get an idea of their tastes, sensibilities, and personalities, although few appreciate being contacted through social media for submissions. It's helpful to be able to say in your submission query letter, "I saw on Twitter that you are looking for more books like So-and-So's, and I think I've got that for you." This shows you're doing your homework and really think there's potential for a match, which could incline them to look more carefully. Through social media, you can find out where agents and editors are going to speak, and identify blogs they've visited or the authors whose books they promote. You can get a feel for their personality here, as some will extend beyond the professional pail a bit and mention their likes and activities. Social media is also a great place to hear about submissions contests, new interviews, etc.

- **CONTESTS AND OPEN CALLS.** New NA imprints are building their lists, which means they want as many submissions as they can get. Those imprints will announce open calls and contests like pitch contests and first pages contests on blogs or websites. To hear about those, subscribe to their e-newsletters, follow major NA websites like NA Alley, take part in #NAlitchat on Twitter, follow New Adult Authors on Google+ and the various New Adult groups on Facebook, and keep your eyes open in your writers' forums.

- **BLOGS.** This is a great source for vetting your prospective editors and agents. When you do general online searches, you're bound to turn up blog interviews with editors and agents—literally type in "Interview agent New Adult fiction" and the like. Some agents even host their own blogs, where they write more extended thoughts about publishing or whatever rings their bells, revealing their personalities and interests. NA Alley is one of the first and most prominent New Adult–dedicated blogs and, as a result, carries a lot of exclusive interviews and contests from publishers and agents.

Most of those steps involve going online. The Internet makes it easier for you to identify editors and agents than any other generation of aspiring writers, but with that comes a new challenge just for you: trying not to feel overwhelmed.

PITCHING YOUR BOOK

Now it's time to formulate your pitch and shape it into a query letter and prepare the rest of the materials for when agents and editors request more material. In most cases, submission guidelines instruct you to query via e-mail and attach a few sample pages. If you're instructed to submit only a query, then you send in your query letter pitch and hope for a *request for partial*, which is the first pages, usually the first ten. Don't insert your ten pages of text into submission fields unless told to do so. Your next step is a *request for full*. Sometime in that process they're likely to require a synopsis, which I'll cover here, too.

Your overriding philosophy during submission should be to keep everything as easy on the editor or agent as possible. Submission rules exist to keep their work days manageable as much as to make sure everyone submits the things they truly need. They don't want a lot of back and forth, and they don't want to have to reiterate anything already covered on their posted submission guidelines. Just follow the instructions to the best of your ability. If they aren't clear, ask friends to tell you what they think the instructions mean, and then do your best to follow them. It shocks me how many people don't follow simple instructions like "Don't embed your manuscript in the body of the e-mail." That leaves the recipient to wonder if you're lazy, careless, unprofessional, or just not very bright. You're definitely causing them more work; will you be equally troublesome during book production? That's all they know about you at that time, remember. Another tip: Don't send them to a million websites. Give them all they need to know in the e-mail. Provide the links as *extra* info if you want, but don't make them go to a website for the essential information. That's extra work—and believe it or not, sometimes the links don't work.

You can send your manuscript out to multiple agents and editors at the same time, though I recommend doing so in small batches. That way, you can stop submitting and revise your manuscript or your pitch materials should you hear similar criticism from all the editors. Just note in the final paragraph of your manuscript that this is a *multiple submission*. Editors and agents know that multiple submissions are the nature of publishing today; they just ask that you let them know and then follow up if there's interest so that they don't spend their time reading a project that was already snapped up by someone else.

INDUSTRY INSIGHT: WHAT IT MEANS TO LOOK FOR "FRESH"

BY KEVAN LYON, LITERARY AGENT

When I'm reading a query or synopsis for a debut New Adult novel, or even from someone who has had modest success possibly as a self-published author in the genre, I'm looking for a story that really grabs me from the shortest description. What does that mean? It really means that there has to be some unique element to the story that I haven't read from another author or read in another descriptive blurb from the many queries and descriptions I've received. Identify that element that is completely fresh in your story, something new about your character, the setting, or the conflict that they're facing that immediately makes you or a reader think, *Oh that sounds great.* That's what I'm looking for.

I realize this sounds nebulous, so here's an example of a book with a fresh take: I sold the debut NA *I See London* by Chanel Cleeton this past year. It features a heroine from South Carolina who has had much tragedy and disappointment in her life, and when she isn't accepted to her dream university (Harvard), she applies to an international university in London. The story tells the tale of a small-town Southern girl entering a London university full of kids of the rich, the famous, and the aristocratic. She falls for a hot Lebanese bad boy and dates the very proper British guy. You get the picture! Immediately there is intrigue in these uncommon details. It is something fresh and probably has a story arc that you haven't heard before. The author was able to draw from her own experiences at a London university to tell an amazing, page-turning story. What is in your background, or maybe that of someone you know, that's so "out there" that it will be new, fresh, and exciting to most readers? *That* is the element you are looking for.

When I see that an author has found that element, then for me it's all about voice and character: Is it a voice I love and a character or characters

I can care about? I want to really love the hero and heroine, even if they're full of conflict, turmoil, etc. I've seen heroes that dropped the f-bomb every sentence or two, or treated women badly. That would be an immediate turn-off for me—that's a character I couldn't care less about, even if you redeem him. There has to be something immediately evident to readers that makes them feel some level of empathy or understanding for the character. The reader needs to love these fictional people enough from the beginning to care about their redemption and, ultimately, their "happy ever after."

Kevan Lyon is a literary agent and partner with Marsal Lyon Literary Agency. www.marsallyonliteraryagency.com

Crafting Your Query

A *query letter*, or simply a *query*, is the pitch you submit to agents and editors. Its goal is to deliver the hook that'll make readers sit up and take notice, then to present the distinguishing themes, conflict, and characters or other details. This is the place to share your credentials as a writer or any other pertinent information, such as how your expertise at restoring WWII tanks led you to write that WWII historical NA thriller. All this will happen in three paragraphs, in this manner:

> **PARAGRAPH 1** leads with some form of the hook statement you crafted for your story in Chapter 2. You want to intrigue them with your concept in a nutshell. This is also a good time to work in why you think this editor or agent would be a particularly good match for you, an important detail that'll make you stand out for your thorough professionalism.

> **PARAGRAPH 2** is a brief and intriguing callout of distinguishing plot elements. There might be some mini-summary, but only so much as is necessary to set the stage for the statement of conflict and to convey the core themes. Stress the elements that make this appealing to the NA fiction reader and that fit into your genre of choice.

PARAGRAPH 3 is your time to toot your horn and cite your writing history or pertinent facts about why you're right to tell this particular tale. If you've self-published this or other books, this is the time to say so.

This should all fit on a single page and be as concise and clear as possible. The voice of the letter should be polite, well-spoken Professional You, laced with some of your story's tone (for example, a funny story gets a touch of lightheartedness in the query). Definitely steer clear of Used Car Salesman. These professionals are experts at evaluating concepts and craft; they don't need some big production.

If you've self-published prior to this submission, mention the book(s) in the third paragraph. The editor or agent will be Googling you very early in this process and doesn't need to discover you've held something back to talk about later. If you have positive reviews from notable reviewers, share those. There's not much you can say if your self-pub sales track record isn't overwhelmingly impressive yet; in that case, simply state that you have self-published titles for sale and now want to build your career with an established house. If they love your pitch and then first pages, the time for discussing your self-pub history in depth will come. (See the Chapter 13 section "Making Your Business Plan," for a full discussion of using self-publishing as a backdoor to traditional publishing.)

Editors and sometimes agents may ask for *exclusives* in their submission guidelines. That means you're supposed to cease submitting to others while the manuscript is under consideration with that editor or agent. You could offer exclusive submission as a way of letting the agent or editor know they're your top pick, using the words "This is an exclusive submission for four weeks" in the last paragraph of your query letter. Anything less than four weeks isn't helpful to the agent or editor who doesn't already respond quickly, and more than four weeks is tying your hands unnecessarily. If you don't hear back by the end of the time limit, you can send a nudge e-mail with another week, letting them know that at the end of that time you'll start submitting but will still leave the submission with them because you do really want to work with them.

Using this structure, I've fashioned a sample query for you using the book concept from my back-cover copy in Chapter 13. This shows you that you can adapt your selling copy for multiple uses, compressing or expanding as the need and space limitations require.

Dear Ms. Editor:

I saw in your Blog X interview that you love stories about strong women who defy gender stereotypes. I'm hoping you'll be interested in my NA contemporary thriller THE DARE CLUB, about a college girl who agrees to ocean dive from a car driven off a cliff in order to expose a secret thrill-betting network offering big payoffs to desperate students.

Sharia Santanillo is devastated by the senseless suicide of her best friend. Sure, Carlo was exhausted, working three jobs to put himself through school. But he loved life. He was invincible. Yet nothing he'd done that week made sense. He'd given her a wad of money and told her to meet him at the bank in three hours and if he didn't show up, to give the cash to his mom. He had shown up—shaking, bruised, with $90,000 more. Days later, sleepless, skittish, refusing to talk about the money, he'd jumped from the school clock tower. With Carlo's brother Victor, Sharia discovers her friend had been recruited by a thrill-betting ring that preys on desperate students. She and Victor blood-swear to find the scum who recruited Carlo. Dark, chiseled Victor is methodical, fierce, and passionate. She can't resist him any more than she can resist her yearning for revenge. Yet she's sure Victor is wasting precious time, that a desperate kid will take the next horrific dare so some rich bastards can get a power thrill. So Sharia hatches a plan: She'll take the next dare herself.

I've self-published two contemporary New Adult novels featuring strong females. I'd very much like to grow my career with a publisher and hope you see potential in THE DARE CLUB to do that. At 100,000 words, THE DARE CLUB can stand alone or be developed into a series. Thank you for your consideration.

All best,

Audrey Author

Writing Your Synopsis

Your synopsis can be a vital element in winning over an agent or editor. When an agent or editor likes your query and sample pages, they'll likely turn to your two- to three-page synopsis to see how you plan to work out the plot and character arcs. They're evaluating whether you can plot well and develop character growth without investing the time it takes to read a full manuscript. Some will skip the synopsis, though, preferring to be surprised all the way through the full manuscript reading.

It can be overwhelming to render your 80,000-word manuscript down to two or three pages of summary, but you can do it, I swear. The thing to remember is that you're not telling the story, you're telling *about* the story. You're scrapping my "Show, don't tell" la-di-da and instead utilizing direct statements and functional language to tell the agent/editor what your main character needs or wants to achieve, what threatens her enough to kick-start the story, what steps she takes to achieve her goal, and what challenges she overcomes to get there. Basically, it's that seven-step story structure worksheet I gave you in Chapter 7, just fleshed out into paragraph form that marches you through the chronology of the book. Make clear what important things happen, how you make them happen, and how those happenings make your characters' lives better or worse. Nobody has to come away from this synopsis feeling emotionally connected to the character or moved to tears. Rather, they should be moved to read the full manuscript.

Here are two ways to go about crafting a synopsis that showcases the main plotline and how it drives the character's internal arc.

- **SUMMARIZE EVERY CHAPTER, ONE BY ONE, THEN MERGE.** Starting where the story starts, the opening of your synopsis should start with a paragraph (perhaps two) that states who the main character is, what she wants, the reason this desire is in jeopardy, and the catalytic event. Then, moving through each chapter, write down the main event(s) of that chapter and how the main character reacts to it or what state she is in by the end. If you've got dual points of view, then you may summarize a few paragraphs about one character, then tackle a few of the other character's reactions to the plot events. Let clarity be your guide in how to interweave the character's threads in this summary, favoring bare-bones statements over wordy explanation. Be sure that we can plainly identify the points you've listed in your seven-step story structure (the character's need, the catalyst that spins her world, each new problem and how it worsens things, etc.). When you've done this first draft of chapter paragraphs, go back and merge them where appropriate, aiming for a smooth-flowing read.

- **BUILD IT FROM OUTLINE FORM.** If you're an outliner, this'll be a natural method for you. In list-like fashion, write down the character's wants and needs, then write down the problem that the character will have to deal with. That is, your chief obstacle, or conflict. Then write down the problems you throw at the main character, along with how the character reacts to that problem, how it affects the internal journey. When you get to the climax, make it clear that the character's internal journey has come to a head. Then list how the character solves the final big problem. In this option, too, you can use the Seven Steps of Structuring a Storyline worksheet in Chapter 7. Your next step is to turn this list into paragraphs.

When you're done laying it out, go back and smooth the flow into a natural read, making sure readers can easily trace the primary storyline and character arc. Then tweak the tone and tense, adding in details as you have space and as clarity allows. Don't bury the core threads as you add stuff. These details really are about creating a flavor with details and evocative verbs instead of generic phrases like, "Not one to give up" or "They have a fight." Your tone will get a boost if you change "They have a fight" to "Joe splits Tad's nose in a bare-fisted brawl." Also, be sure the synopsis is in present tense (the *literary present*, if you want to get technical). We always talk about stories as if they are happening now, even if they happen in the past tense within the covers of the book.

What You Need to Know About First Pages

When you get a request for a partial manuscript, send the opening pages, because that's what readers of your final book would start with. Agents and editors want to know you can start strong and reel in readers. They'll probably tell you how much to send for the partial, or their website's submissions guidelines will do so. Some want a huge chunk, like the first twenty or fifty pages. If they don't specify a page count, send the first ten pages. It's okay to go over the requested page count by a few paragraphs or even a whole page if that lets you finish a scene; no one will hold that against you. Their submission rules are meant to make their lives easy, not to be Draconian. In that spirit, don't go changing all your margins, single-spacing the manuscript, or eliminating the first page title and contact information in a Herculean and disruptive effort to send as much content as possible. Professionals can get a feel for your voice, characterization, and pacing in a very short time and will request the full manuscript based on their reaction to what they initially requested.

Following Up

Submission guidelines usually give you an approximate turnaround time for their response. If the end of that period comes and you haven't heard back, send a polite nudge, provided the agency or publisher guidelines don't prohibit that; publishers often limit your follow-up simply to cut down on their correspondence volume. Don't be afraid of this nudge contact, worrying that you'll offend. As long as you're professional and positive about further contact, you're fine. The recipient recognizes the emotions and hopes you have in this endeavor. Their lack of response is almost certainly an issue of time and workload, not callous disregard. Frame your nudge along these lines: You submitted on X date, X amount of time has passed so you're checking in, you are continuing to submit elsewhere but remain hopeful that the manuscript will strike a chord with him/her and that you'll get to work together. Use the same approach if your submission was an exclusive, adding that you're extending the exclusive period by another week or two and then you'll start submitting elsewhere, even as you continue to believe that they're the editor/agent for you and hope they'll feel the same.

If you don't hear back, resist any frustrated urge to fire off an e-mail telling them how unprofessional or insensitive they are. I've seen authors do that—in fact, one asked me last week if I thought he could unburn a bridge with an agent he'd torched. Nothing is served by putting out an unprofessional vibe. The publishing world is small, and your reputation important. It's entirely possible you'll run into that person at a future book event, such as a book convention or the ceremony for your award-winning bestseller. Instead, simply write off that agent or editor as not for you, and then move on. Publishing professionals are humans, too, and sometimes they blow a call. Set your sights on finding the teammate who will be aces for you from day one.

And if you get the e-mail that says, "This project isn't for me," then take that at face value: Your story isn't for that agent or editor, and so you don't want it there. It isn't a personal rejection—even though your writing is the most personal thing you can imagine. Your agent and your editor both need to be convinced they can sell your book, and they need to be excited enough about it to go to that effort and put their own reputations on the line with it. That's a lot to ask of someone, and it's all very subjective. People get excited about different things. Some will go the extra step and point out what they think stopped them from going nutso over it; you can use that to home in on potential revisions. Chapter 12 helps you process rejection commentary and know what's worth playing around with and what's to be shrugged off because it sounds like their personal taste rather than your storytelling weakness.

Because of that subjectivity and the money and reputations involved, you'd be the rare bird if you didn't get rejections. Bestsellers and lauded authors are known to pull out their rejection letter folders to show aspiring writers that it happens to everyone. J.K. Rowling's phenomenal Harry Potter series was famously rejected numerous times. That doesn't make the editors idiots. That speaks to the unpredictability of reader interests and the challenges of identifying things that will break out in a crowded marketplace. With hundreds of thousands of books published every year, publishing isn't for the faint of heart. On the flip side, millions of books are purchased every year. People want stories, and you're a storyteller. No matter the speed bumps you encounter on your path to publication, hang on to the joy of storytelling that drives your pursuit. Write your best book, lay your best plans, identify the people who you believe can best help you, then submit away. While you wait, continue submitting or set about writing your next book to keep your mind always on the storytelling. Before you know it, you'll have your next book ready for the world.

WHAT YOU SHOULD EXPECT FROM YOUR EDITOR AND AGENT

Your editor will share your vision for your book and will dedicate more to the book than anyone else but yourself. She'll help you develop the final text through her editorial guidance, and she will lead the in-house team of designers, production staff, marketing, and sales staff. She'll write the majority of the sales copy (the book cover, catalogue copy, etc.), feeding the key selling points to the marketing and sales staff through in-house documents called *tip sheets*. She'll read and edit the heck out of this book with you. To commit to all that work and hang her professional destiny on your book, the editor must feel passionate about your manuscript at the submission stage. That's why writers get so much of that frustrating "I love it but not enough" or "Someone else will probably snap it up, but it's not for me" phrasing in rejection letters. Those editors aren't blowing smoke—those manuscripts are good, they're just not pushing the editors' "Passion" buttons.

Your agent is your publishing partner and advisor. She has relationships with editors and knows their tastes, knows the marketplace, and must be a go-getter and advocate for your career. Big-name agents are well connected and respected—but they also often have a full client list and take on new clients only by referral from other clients. Be open to newer agents within established agencies because they're supported as they list-build. I'm all for the newbie with the newbie agency, but you need to scrutinize that agent's publishing past and feel confident in her ability to forge editorial relationships and know the business and contracts side of things. Does she have a gregarious personality? Does she demonstrate selectiveness instead of just signing up anybody she can find in an effort to build the agency? She needs to be cultivating her client list as carefully as you're cultivating your career. My children's book agent had a young agency when I signed with her, but her career in publishing was long, her sensibility synced with mine, and her relationships with editors were expanding rapidly and lucratively. My writing career has grown along with her agency.

Editorial sensibility in an agent is important. Agents need to understand what makes a project work and appeal to readers and editors. Some agents have a strong editorial hand and will work through revisions with you, others may refer you to trusted freelancers for editorial guidance. It's worth noting again that no agent should charge you to read and/or edit your manuscript—that's not kosher practice. They should make their money by selling your book, handling your business stuff, and guiding your career, not editing your writing. They edit if they are inclined and able; they refer it out or pass on your manuscript if they're not.

Experience in New Adult fiction isn't going to be deep right now for agents, since the NA category and marketplace is so new. Some will have that experience, and that's definitely an asset. But an agent who understands the general fiction marketplace for adults or for YA will be in a great position to deal with editors and identify those who are also branching out into NA. Agents already working with NA or interested in it will say so in their interviews and on their websites, and you'll see it in the books they've published.

You'll be working closely with your agent and editor on this project as well as your career, so you need strong communication, trust, and respect—all of which require you to give those same things. An agent or editor of experience has learned the importance of mutual professionalism and respect. If you're new to publishing, your ignorance can work against you in this regard, particularly if you have already self-published and are used to having total control of every aspect. Here's how to be a team player with your manuscript at stake:

- **COMMUNICATION.** If you have expectations, talk about them up front, before signing any contracts. Your agent and editor can give you their takes on those possibilities, and you can tell a lot from that.
- **RESPECT.** If there's an issue, don't complain about it, but rather work it out. Understand that everyone is working for the success of your book and of you. No one wants this to fail. Respect that they have experience, even as you demonstrate your own growing experience. Never bad-talk online—that will likely come back to bite you, and it makes you look unprofessional to future replacements.
- **TIMELINESS.** Produce what they ask for as soon as you can. Communicate delays promptly so they can rearrange their schedules.
- **INPUT.** Editors and agents expect to find a balance with you in terms of the production of the book, but they also expect you to maintain a professional web presence and a willingness to put in the legwork promoting the book. Self-promotion isn't just for self-publishing authors, it's for *all* authors.

When it comes to signing the final contract, listen to that little voice inside you. Acknowledge any misgivings you have and explore them with your prospective editor or agent. As tempting as it is to sign any contract just to have a book or representation deal, it's essential that you feel confident in this business relationship. That agent will get a cut of any book they sell for you for the duration of that book license. Any book you complete with that editor stays with that publisher unless they agree to revert your publication rights, which is a legal process requiring agreement by all parties and signatures on documents. Once you sign your book contract, you are legally obligated to deliver your materials or return your advance.

INDUSTRY INSIGHT: ON BEING A "HYBRID" AUTHOR

Hybrid authors publish with traditional houses but also self-publish some of their fiction. That can be a fine line to balance, though. Publishers aren't big fans of the hybrid author because (1) the author is seen as competing against himself, undercutting his efforts and the publisher's efforts, and (2) the publishers worry about the quality of the pieces he's self-publishing and how that might hurt the performance of his traditionally pubbed books. Is that hybrid author self-pubbing a story that his editor turned down because she felt it didn't match the quality of the rest of his work? No one wants him hurting his brand with less-than-stellar stuff on the side. If you want to exercise this option with your career, make these four points part of your business strategy:

1. Hire professionals for the self-published materials so that your house is happy that you aren't hurting yourself—and you're confident about that, too.
2. Create a positive professional environment for your hybrid efforts by being up front with your agent and editor about your goals with your self-published works and your reasons for doing so. Your agent can help you know if the work is maybe one that should be tucked into the drawer for later when you're in a better place to develop it further ... or for never. Your editor needs to know you're not undermining her efforts.
3. Consider self-pubbing short stories based on secondary characters in your book. Thus, you're offering your readers bonus material they couldn't get from your publisher. Often publishers of NA novels ask the authors to create such materials as part of the overall publishing/marketing strategy, feeding fans interim episodes and stories about secondary characters to keep their appetites whetted.

4. Look for ways to team your hybrid efforts with the marketing department's plans whenever that's possible. Your smaller pieces can be momentum builders and reader enticements.

5. Be brand conscious in your hybrid efforts. Recognize that not everything you write will or should be published. Maybe the fact that it's not up to par is the reason why your editor doesn't want to publish this one, not because she's mad at you or has lost faith in your muse.

Marketing Your NA Fiction ... and Yourself

egardless of whether you traditionally publish or self-publish, you have to hawk your books to sell your books. Readers are out there in droves and crave stories, but they have a lot to choose from—you have to help them discover *yours*. The good news is, you have the power to do that! You've got old-fashioned, tried-and-true tactics like personal appearances at your disposal, but even better, you've got scads of promotional opportunities available to you on the Internet and a target audience that looks for and buys books almost entirely online.

This empowerment can be intimidating. With so much to do, it's hard to know where to begin, and of course you want to put your efforts and funds behind the most efficient and successful marketing methods. In this chapter I guide you in creating a self-marketing strategy with an emphasis on social media and give you a host of promotional tools and actions that you can cherry-pick according to your budget, skills, time, and temperament.

START WITH YOUR BIGGEST STRENGTH—YOU

Your best chance for creating and stoking reader awareness of your book is a consistent, focused, maintainable strategy that's founded on your strengths and that taps into the NA fiction community. Here are four core elements of that strategy:

1. **LEVERAGE YOUR STRENGTHS.** You can't do it all, and you can't be everywhere. Figure out the things you're good at (public speaking, writing quick sound-bite articles, being an expert on something that others want to know about), and build a strategy around those. When you're good at something, you'll enjoy doing it and you'll do it well.

2. **MAKE TIME.** Marketing is an ongoing venture, so set aside windows of time daily or throughout the week to focus solely on marketing items. Be as accountable to that time as you are to your writing time, protecting it from yourself and your family. When you've got a book launch looming, block out a week for strategizing your marketing efforts a couple of months before you're ready to publish, then block out significant time after the launch to do nothing but enact your marketing plans.

3. **RECIPROCATE.** You may be selling yourself and your books, but you don't have to go it alone. Plenty of other authors are doing it, and you can work with them instead of competing against them. Reciprocity is a marketing philosophy that has you promoting others even as you promote yourself and getting that treatment in return. If you're re-Tweeting others' news and interesting links, they'll start re-Tweeting yours. That's how you build a social media network and following. Consider setting up formal team marketing arrangements, as with a group blog where each member only writes a couple of posts a month even as the blog gets updated twice a week or so. Do group blog tours, buy group ads, hold group signings at events, and rent booths at book festivals for the entire group, bringing each member's rental fee down to a pittance. When you team up with others, you get access to each other's networks and can cross-promote like crazy. Plus, it's just plain fun to have partners in crime. If you don't already have potential teammates, opportunities will arise as you form relationships with other authors online.

4. **BE AUTHENTIC.** Be yourself when you reach out, and your relationships will grow. Everything you do in service to your books is based in your core enthusiasm for stories and NA fiction and creative people, so push that outward and watch it connect with readers rather than trying to gather readers to you.

"My entire 'marketing strategy' is to interact with readers and know my audience. I want to know what's important to them, what they want to read about, what kind of stories touch them."
—**TAMMARA WEBBER**, *The New York Times* and *USA Today* best-selling author of *Easy* and the Between the Lines series

MAKE YOUR WEBSITE THE HOME BASE FOR YOUR BRAND

Leave your career room to grow by setting it up to revolve around you, not around your individual books. This means treating yourself as a brand—you are, after all, selling *your* writing, *your* storytelling, *your* books. The writing and the stories and the books will change; you are the constant.

Give your brand a home base with a website that revolves around you the author rather than any one book. Stay away from the static "billboard" site that just displays your book covers, story blurbs, and bio. Rather, think of your website as your command center, with links to all your social media, an active (even if basically so) blog, and "buy" links that send readers straight to the e-retailers selling your books. I recommend installing plug-ins (also called *widgets*) on your site that make your most recent social media site postings visible. Let visitors see how active you are so they know where to follow you. For example, a spot on your website would say, "[Your Name] on Twitter" then your latest Twitter post would be visible, next to which would be a "Follow Me" button that a reader could click to become your newest Twitter follower, easy-peasy. If you have someone design your website for you, she can easily plug in those widgets for you. If you're creating your own site using a web host's template, you'll have a bunch of plug-ins to pick from and can choose those that feed your Twitter posts onto your page, etc. The point is to make your website the place where your readers find anything they need to know about you.

You can easily set up your own author webpage using templates that your web host makes available to you, or you can hire someone to customize a WordPress site that you can then update yourself as easily as any free blog, adding pages at your discretion. You'll have to pay a monthly fee for your website, but it's usually just a few dollars. If you've got an active blog on a blogging site like LiveJournal or Blogger, consider importing all your blog entries over to a full, robust website that gives you more flexibility. Though blogger sites like those are free, they're extremely limited. Plus, you want a website that has your name as its URL (website address, or *domain name*): www.[yourname].com instead of www.[yourname].blogspot.com. You're branding yourself, remember. Plus, that makes your website address easy for your fans to remember. You'll be plastering this URL all over your promo material, in your byline for anything you write (even e-mails!), and in all your social media profiles.

There are oodles of website hosts to choose. The best way to pick one is to ask your writer friends who hosts their sites and if they're happy with the company. The host site will provide you with set-up directions, then you can choose a template and type in all your info and import over blog entries if you choose to do so. I can't cover all that here, but there are plenty of articles online about it.

You can sign up for your domain name through your host. There are many "kinds" of website addresses, but the most recognized one is ".com" so go for that. If it's taken, then try another domain name, perhaps using your first initials instead of your full name, staying as short as possible. You can go with ".net" if you have to, but people will look at the ".com" version belonging to someone else first and get confused.

If all that sounds intimidating, or if you want a customized look and functionality for your website, spend a few hundred dollars to hire a website designer. Again, the best way to do that is to ask around in your social media to see who other authors have hired. Authors are happy to recommend their web designers. Designers usually put their names at the bottom of the sites they design, so if you see a site you like, take note of the designer's name. The Authors Guild offers low-priced, full-featured author website hosting for its members at www.authorsguild.net. You can always create your own basic website for now and upgrade to a customized, designer-created site later when you know better how you'll be using it.

Once you have your website up and running, you've created your foundation for all your social media and marketing efforts. This is the place to post news about your career happenings, your book covers, blurbs, reviews, and excerpts. It's the full You, the author experience, something no fan can get from brief updates in social media.

MINING NA FICTION'S SOCIAL MEDIA OPPORTUNITIES

The writer-reader relationship was the core of the initial New Adult fiction boom, with social media being the connector. As the category evolves, writers continue to cultivate their relationships with readers through social media, along with their relationships with fellow writers, book bloggers, and publishing professionals. Your marketing strategy must incorporate social media as a gateway to readers and networking opportunities.

"Social media is the reason NA is where it is now: the communication and sharing."—**L.G. KELSO**, member of the NA Alley blog and writer of speculative NA fiction

That said, you must walk a fine line when promoting yourself online so as not to turn off followers. People don't want you waving your book in their faces and tweeting, "Buy my book!" all the time, even though they know you have books to sell. That's a social media faux pas. Even with e-mails and personal interactions, people don't like being directly solicited. Think about the authors and entertainers you follow. Likely the ones you enjoy following tell you about their new projects even as they share news about the books and songs and movies they like, the adventures they have in going about their careers, etc. Keep your followers' attention with interesting tidbits that give them insights into you as an individual. Impress them with the way you promote others' work and good news, and inform them with links to news you want to know about the industry and art. When something happens with your book or career, such as revealing your new cover or getting a great review or gathering your fun swag for your book signing tonight, share your excitement about that, which is much more inviting than "Buy my book!" Your followers' pleasure then translates into a book sale for you and, in the best-case scenario, into good reviews and recommendations to their followers.

Other principles to keep in mind as you develop and stoke your social media presence:

- **LURK BEFORE YOU LEAP.** Before you engage people on a social media site, spend time reading and watching the interactions so that you can get that community's philosophy and unspoken rules of engagement down first.
- **LEAP BEFORE YOU PITCH.** Establish a presence on the site well before your book launches. Then, when your pub date arrives, you'll know how to go about promoting the launch in each site and will have relationships to tap.
- **DON'T TRY TO DO IT ALL.** No one has the time to be truly present on every social media site they find. Pick a few main sites in which you'll maintain a strong, fruitful presence.

What is an "active" presence? Social media marketing for authors requires responding to others' posts, giving them the thumbs up, and sharing their good news and interesting links, etc., on your timelines or feeds. It requires time and constant effort, but that's the basic etiquette in the social media realm. That's what NA readers expect from their NA writers. And it's the very thing that may make extensive social media participation palatable to you, as many writers prefer not to be hard sellers anyway.

"You need to give value back to the reader or you're just shouting into the void." —**CARRIE BUTLER**, author of the Mark of Nexus series and member of the NA Alley blog

---

There are many social media sites, but below are the most frequently used by NA authors. Keep your eye out for new ones, but wait to see if they develop a big enough audience to warrant your time before you join. You'll most likely develop your favorites based on what's most comfortable for you to use and where you get the most useful interactions.

- **FACEBOOK.** One of the most popular social media sites. Sixty-seven percent of all Internet users in the U.S. were on Facebook going into 2014, with 83 percent of the eighteen- to twenty-nine-year-olds who use the Internet on it, making it prime NA discoverability ground. The site shows steady growth in the thirty-five- to fifty-four-year-old age range, so they've got the crossover readers there, and anecdotal evidence tells NA authors, agents, and editors that their primary readership is comprised of the crossover readers who sent the YA fiction category to the top of the publishing heap.

- **TWITTER.** Limited to 140-character posts, Twitter is great for quick back-and-forth chatting about common points of interest. Many NA writers point to Twitter as the site they get the most dynamic interaction with the greatest number of readers, reviewers, publishing professionals, and other NA writers.

- **PINTEREST.** This social network works like a virtual bulletin board. Everyone is able to see what you've pinned and are able to re-pin the things they like, too. NA authors post book covers, photos from book events or of models who look like their characters, book trailers, fan art, lists related to their stories or writing, reviews, news, giveaways… just about anything.

- **GOODREADS.** This community of readers finding, discussing, ranking, and reviewing books is another prime place for NA authors to maintain a presence. Many NA-focused "bookshelves" exist on Goodreads, and its review sections are active and passionate. You can maintain an original blog on your profile or set your profile to automatically pick up your blog posts from your regular blog site whenever you post something new.

- **TUMBLR.** This site has posts that are richer and longer than Twitter but not as developed as full blog posts. NA authors post photos, videos, music, and status updates related to their books.

- **INSTAGRAM.** A social networking service for sharing photos and videos. You can take photos or shoot video with your smartphone using the Instagram app, then modify the photos and video before you share it on the site. Authors feed those photos and videos to other social networking services like Facebook, Tumblr, and Twitter.

- **VINE.** Vine is a video-sharing site owned by Twitter, making several-second looping videos viewable on your Twitter timeline. Authors and readers post super-brief book reviews, make short book-related videos, or post quickie updates about their books, appearances, and career.

- **GOOGLE+.** This is Google's attempt to compete directly with Facebook, but it has failed to meet the challenge. There are users there, though, including some modest NA fiction group pages, so many NA authors feel it's useful to maintain a presence there.

Consider using a social media management service to handle all your social media pages from a single dashboard. Many of these services are totally free or have free basic accounts, and all let you upgrade to a monthly fee account with more options. A popular service is HootSuite, which has a free basic account. Another big service is TweetDeck, which is free and associated with Twitter, although you can manage Facebook, LinkedIn (a professional networking site), Foursquare (a location app), and the photo managing site Flickr from it, too, and new features are regularly worked in. Another way to keep a handle on social media is to link sites whenever possible so that one post can feed into others, as happens when you link your regular blog to your Goodreads profile blog. Automatic updates rock, although you do have to remain aware that some posts may be appropriate only for particular audiences. For instance, if you blog about your family as well as your books on your regular blog, you might not auto-feed into your Goodreads blog if you want only book-related stuff in that community.

Facebook and Google+ allow you to have personal pages or fan pages. The line can be blurry between the two, so consider how you'd use the site. Do you want to keep things separate with two pages, or does your writing and personal life overlap so strongly that one page is best? Many authors establish a middle ground by maintaining a personal account where they update as normal, including both personal and book stuff because book stuff is personal to them (being aware, of course, that they are now public figures and should post accordingly). Those authors keep their entries on their fan page to book and writing-/reading-related topics. *Do not* open pages for specific books, though—you don't want to have to maintain that many pages, and you surely don't want to have to get people to like a whole new page every time you publish.

Always sign up for your social media accounts with your author name. Catchy theme names like @bookkisser may be fun, but they don't sell *you*. Your name is now your brand; keep it out there. Some writers want to keep a line between public and private and so adopt a pen name. This is helpful for keeping things separate, although you do have other issues like awkwardness during in-person introductions at events and one-on-one professional relationships when it comes to a pen name. Perhaps because of the often steamier content of NA fiction, many NA authors use pen names to keep their writing life separate from their personal life and their nonwriting careers.

A last point on building your social media presence: Don't get too focused on collecting followers or on increasing traffic to your website. You want quality followers, not just high numbers. Some authors will do big giveaways with prizes like e-reading devices in an effort to build numbers, but that just draws in people who want to win the device. They'll stop following after the contest, and they won't buy your books. Take the time to build quality followers through sincere interaction. You're working mighty hard—make sure what you get in return is sincere readers and well-wishers, not just people who want free stuff.

THINGS YOU CAN DO TO MARKET YOURSELF AND YOUR BOOK

Writers are forever coming up with new ways to market their books. Here are a couple dozen to get you started. You can't do them all—but you won't want to. Pick those that suit your personality, your skill set, your budget, and your books, and that seem most likely to lead to sales in your particular campaign. Trying to do too much will spread you thin and wear you out. For your next book, stick with what worked and add other things, building on your strengths. As with writing or any other endeavor, you have a learning curve. Do set a marketing budget and stick to it. All that excitement for your book and its potential needs to be tempered with the reality of your time and finances. Remember that marketing is constant and you've got to make the budget stretch.

- **BOOKMARKS, POSTCARDS, AND BUSINESS CARDS.** Basic author promo items. Bookmarks can double as your business cards. Book-specific bookmarks and postcards should show off your cover and give a teasing tagline along with your website and contact information for your major social media. Consider being creative with the back of your card. For example, if your character is a list-maker, include "Sara's Top 10 Whatevers" on the back. Does she love music? List her favorite songs, then provide the link to your playlist on SoundCloud or on your website. There are many printers and swag sites online, including www.printplace.com, www.gotprint.com, and www.vistaprint.com.
- **GIVEAWAYS.** These are an author promo mainstay. The NA social network likes to share news about giveaways. You can give away your book, swag,

naming rights for minor characters in your next story ... anything you can think of that's related to your fiction. Use www.rafflecopter.com to help you manage entries. If you're going to mail a physical giveaway item to a winner, limit the contest to U.S. residents only because international shipping costs are high.

- **SWAG.** Common swag items include pens, mugs, T-shirts, fridge magnets, bookmarks, jewelry related to your story, reusable bags or totes, nail files, notepads, candy with promo wrappers, key chains, temporary tattoos, guitar picks, trading cards, stickers, buttons, tumblers, and fortune cookies with your book title inside them or quotes from your book. You can use theme swag, such as poker chips for a book set in Vegas. Consider cost, logistics, and likely effectiveness when picking swag. Mugs can be fun, for example, but they can also cost a lot to make and ship, and then you may have to lug them around to events. Would a smaller item work just as well?

- **FREEMIUM AND PROMO PRICING.** I talked in the self-publishing chapter about giving away your books for free or $.99 as a way to get them out there and create buzz. You can publicize these deals on BookBub and BookGorilla, as well as in your social media. Authors usually make these deals time sensitive, prompting people to buy immediately.

- **REVEALS.** Reveals give you great reason to talk about your book on social media, and readers love them. Cover reveals are the most flashy, but you can also reveal snippets of the story, perhaps your first chapter, or anything that is distinct and tantalizing. Reveals let you celebrate your book even before it's ready, building buzz. You can tie a giveaway to the reveal or use it as reason to send out celebratory e-mail blasts that nudge your friends to spread the word. Your author friends can fête you and your new cover on their sites and in their social media.

- **SIGNINGS.** Book signings are fun ... if people come. They can easily end up being a waste of time and money and leave you embarrassed when you're sitting at a table with no one but your family showing up. Be strategic about where and when you sign in order to increase your chances of success. Local bookstores are easier to deal with than chains and can give more customized publicity. That said, some bookstores won't let independent authors do book signings unless their warehouse already stocks the books; if you provide the books yourself, they can work out a profit split with them. You can set up signings at the cafés where you write, or at events related to your book topic, such as the local art museum if your book features an art heist. Thematic signings can intrigue people. Don't count on your venue to do all the promoting; spread the word through your local networks, and contact your local paper if they have a Happenings Around Town section. Use your e-mail list and social media to ask people in the area to spread word of the event through their social media.

- **CONVENTIONS.** You can sign at category- and genre-specific conventions, but do consider that those will have many other authors there, too. They will likely cost you money to travel to, and they may charge you signing or table fees. Can you sell enough books to make those opportunities worth it? There is the added usefulness of networking at the event to consider.

- **NICHE MARKETING.** As with signings in places that are related to your book's themes or topics, reach out to blogs or publications outside regular NA fiction channels that might be interested in your book. Of course, if your book contains explicit sexual material, do consider the appropriateness for each niche audience.

- **PRESS RELEASE.** This may seem old fashioned, but press releases are useful for local publications and radio shows if your book is appropriate for those outlets. Pitch an angle for an article or guest spot that is more than "Local writer publishes book!" The TV stations and radio hosts don't care about you, they care about what you can offer their watchers or listeners. Perhaps you can offer them something like, "Local author has five tips for self-publishing like a pro" since everyone is interested in that these days. Or "NA fiction is more than sex … though it has that, too!" and you can then talk about this fun category.

- **CHAPTER SAMPLERS.** You can produce a small printed sampler with several chapters of your book to give away at events. You should certainly post sample material on your website. Use the first chapters so that you don't have to give context for the sample.

- **GROUP SAMPLERS AND ANTHOLOGIES.** This is a great thing to do with other authors in a marketing team-up. Each of you contributes the first chapters of your book to a single e-sampler that you make available for free through e-retailers. You can also print them up to give away at events. You all promote it heavily. Or you can pick a theme and all write original material for it, gathering it together in a self-published anthology.

- **BLOG.** Writing a blog lets you personalize yourself to readers. Maintaining it takes time, though, and depending on how serious you get about it, you can find yourself spending as much time writing your blog posts and building your blog following as you did writing your book. I recommend maintaining at least a basic blog to keep your site dynamic and to post all your news. You don't have to wax poetic on a topic twice a week. Reveal your covers. Show off your new bookmarks, talk about that movie you saw that had a hot actor who could so totally be the hot guy in your book. Talk about the book you just read by your favorite author. Post pictures from your events. Treat the blog as your all-things-writing-related diary. That keeps it fun for you, and it gives your website a personal touch that endears you to readers. I suggest steering clear of expressing opinions on controversial issues or politics. Set your blog to send you alerts when someone leaves a comment, and respond to all your commenters in a timely manner. Relationship building!

- **BLOG TOURS.** This is a lot of work, but it's a fun way to launch your book. Before your book launches, ask strategically selected bloggers to host you as a guest blogger or to interview you the week or month your book pubs. Do this with enough lead time to coordinate the dates and provide the bloggers with the things they need, like interview answers and giveaway items. You and the bloggers promote your tour in social media. You can manage your own tour or hire a blog tour specialist.

- **AUTHOR BLURBS.** If you've got the connections, reach out to authors who are known by NA readers and ask them if they'd be willing to read your book and, if they like it, provide a cover blurb. Give them as much lead time as you can to read your book and blurb it. If they take the time to blurb it, you need to follow through and use that blurb, so don't ask a ton of authors for blurbs hoping to pick the best one or trying to increase your chances that at least one will say yes. These blurbs are best on the front cover, short and sweet, crediting the author's name and their big book or series. If it's wordy, you can excerpt it for the front cover and put the whole long blurb on the back cover or on your website.

- **BOOK COMMUNITIES.** Goodreads, LibraryThing, Shelfari, and Book Blogs are online communities for readers to talk books, reading, and writing. Check them out and establish a presence—at the very least, a basic profile—in one or more. I recommend Goodreads if nothing else, as it has a lot of NA readers.

- **STREET TEAMS.** Street team marketing harnesses the enthusiasm of your fans. You offer a handpicked group of readers exclusive promo and author access in return for them promoting your events or latest releases. Publishers use them on a larger scale to promote entire lines of books or author groups. Some authors love street teams; others feel they cross a line of trust with the public since these folks are being incentivized to rave about you.

- **AWARDS.** Winning an award adds to your book's appeal and gives you something to announce on social media, in e-mail blasts, etc.—making it a fabulous marketing tool. Your publisher will enter some award contests for you, applying and paying the fees, while you can enter others, such as local author awards. Self-published books can qualify for awards, too, such as the Amazon Breakthrough Novel Award, which includes a publishing deal for the winner. Research "independent book awards" for lists of current opportunities.

- **BOOK TRAILERS.** You can hire a book trailer company or make your own trailer using basic free software like Windows Movie Maker, which is a free program on most PC computers with Windows; Mac's iMovie; Photo Story 3, a free Windows program; QuickTime; or Adobe Elements. Or you can invest in software that has more features. Ask other authors for the companies they used to produce the trailers you like. The Coalition for Independent Authors maintains a book trailer production company listing at www. coalition-independent-authors.com/book-trailer-production.html. Darcy Pattison, author and blogger at the popular site Fiction Notes, has a great primer in her book *The Book Trailer Manual*, at www.booktrailermanual. com. You can buy stock footage just like you would stock photos, picking free footage or paying for higher-quality selections at these sites:

  - archive.org
  - www.artbeats.com
  - www.artzooks.com
  - www.bottledvideo.com
  - www.budgetfilms.com
  - www.gettyimages.com/footage

- www.globalimageworks.com
- www.ignitemotion.com
- www.istockphoto.com
- www.omnimovi.com
- www.pond5.com
- www.shutterstock.com
- www.stockclipsnow.com
- www.stockshop.com
- www.virtual-studio-set.com

If you film your own footage, be sure to have your actors or models sign a release. Sample releases are found easily online. You can get royalty-free music at The BeatSuite, Digital Juice, Music 2 Hues, and Stockmusic.net.

- **VIDEO BLOGS.** If you're a public speaker, consider doing video blogs, or vlogs, instead of blog posts or in addition to them. You can post them on your own YouTube Channel, make them accessible on your website with widgets, and spread the link for each new vlog post through your social media.
- **PLAYLISTS.** NA authors frequently make playlists to go with their novels, posting them on their websites (see Gayle Forman's playlist for *If I Stay* on her website at www.gayleforman.com/books/if-i-stay/playlist), pinning them on Pinterest, or hosting them on SoundCloud. The playlist can be songs inspired by the book, songs that appear in the story or that the characters would like, or perhaps songs that you played while you wrote the book to get you into the right mood for particular themes. While a playlist isn't likely to sell many books for you, it is a fun way to add depth to your website and your other social media posts.

ROLLING OUT THE MARKETING CAMPAIGN

Your marketing efforts start long before you upload your book for publication. On pub day, you should already have a plan in place and be ready to start executing it. Set aside one or two blocks of time a month or more before your book is done to do nothing but marketing preparation and planning. Here's what you should be doing pre-launch:

- stoking social media and blogger relationships
- planning your launch strategy and schedule
- reaching out to others who can be a part of your campaign
- creating or updating your promo materials

Once you upload your book and officially launch it, you'll be acting on your plans. At this point, you'll tap your network. Send e-mail blasts asking those contacts to share your good news—people like to help out friends and family. Give them everything they need to do so: Describe the book using your hook, include the cover image, and give them any info they could share about your upcoming events. Keep the message clear and the materials and links spare.

This is also a good time to encourage honest positive reviews. Let them know that positive reviews on retail sites and in book communities are important to the success of a book, so if they read your book and love it, you'd be grateful if they could take the time to review it. Supply the book to a number of people so they can post their reviews online as soon as your book is released (pick your beta readers since you know they'll like it). Obviously you don't want fake reviews or anything that smells insincere, but there's nothing wrong with a friend loving your book and saying so in a review.

BRINGING IN PUBLICITY PROS

If you have the budget to hire a publicist, he can help you strategize your campaign and decide what's best for your particular book. Tasks he can take off your plate include identifying bloggers, review sites, and publications; niche marketing; placing ads; creating website content and promo copy; navigating social media; coordinating events; and applying for awards. If you only want a publicist for a blog tour, you can hire a blog tour management company.

You can find a freelance publicist through www.odesk.com or elance.com, or you can ask your writer friends, your agent, or your in-house marketing contact for references. Read the publicists' websites to determine their experience—general fiction with experience in NA fiction is perfect, but knowledge of YA or Romance markets helps, too. Be up front with the publicist about your expectations so that you know what he can do and what you're better off handling yourself.

If you're traditionally published, you'll have access to a member of the marketing department who is in charge of your book. She can help you strategize your personal campaign to complement the house's efforts, although she can't plan your campaign for you. Even with a marketing department on your team, you're going to be doing a lot of work on your own. Publishers recognize the value of writers cultivating their relationships with readers. Let this chapter be your guide in working out a self-marketing plan that is consistent, focused, and achievable with your unique time commitments and resources.

INDUSTRY INSIGHT: USEFUL NA SITES TO KEEP CURRENT AND CONNECTED

As a business person in the New Adult marketplace and just a fan of the fiction, you should stay abreast of events and developments in the category. I recommend you follow NA Alley. The main website (www.naalley.com) has resources including an NA book blogger directory; a Publishing guide listing publishers, agents, independent cover designers and editors; a forum for readers to share their news; and contests. The blog (naalley.blogspot.com; also accessible through the main site) features news, guests posts, interviews, cover reveals, and giveaways and other events. Editors and agents regularly stop by the site for guest posts and interviews as well as to announce contests and new imprints. NA Alley is a group blog founded by NA authors Jaycee DeLorenzo, Victoria H. Smith, and Bailey Kelsey in May 2012, when NA fiction was just getting off the ground. Now authors Carrie Butler, Juliana Haygert, Diana Long, L.G. Kelso, E.J. Wesley, and Reese Monroe (a.k.a. Lynn Rush) are on the NA Alley team. They all watch the industry as well as publish into it as self-publishers, traditionally published authors, and hybrid authors, writing across genres and story formats. Their diversity keeps the blog a lively meeting ground, and an active reader base adds to the conversation through the comments section.

The weekly #NaLitChat on Twitter is also a useful place to take part in or simply follow discussions about the literature itself as well as the marketplace. Host E.J. Wesley archives the discussions on the website New Adult Authors (www.newadultauthors.com), which has many great resources for NA authors. The site's Camp NA podcast series, affiliated with #NaLitChat, is also archived at that website and has some intriguing discussion about the craft of writing NA fiction.

You can also follow New Adult Authors on Google+ and the various New Adult groups on Facebook. Postings on those pages can range from authors promoting their books to discussions about pricing strategies and page count in NA fiction.

A great place to mix it up with NA fans and bloggers as well as writer peers is New Adult Book Club on Goodreads (www.goodreads.com/group/show/85934-new-adult-book-club).

I urge you to keep abreast of developments in the publishing industry as a whole, too, by subscribing to these free e-newsletters:

- **PW DAILY NEWSLETTER.** From *Publishers Weekly*, the authoritative international news website for book publishing and bookselling. (www.publishersweekly.com/paper-copy/email-subscriptions/index.html)
- **THE PW SELECT REPORT.** A monthly e-newsletter covering self-publishing from *Publishers Weekly*. (www.publishersweekly.com/pw/email-subscriptions/index.html)
- **PUBLISHERS LUNCH.** A daily digest of book publishing news and original commentary and analysis, produced by Publishers Marketplace. (lunch.publishersmarketplace.com)
- **DBW DAILY.** Follows e-book and digital publishing developments, from Digital Book World. (www.digitalbookworld.com/newsletter-registration)

Index

actions, 89, 133–34, 196

active voice, 51–52

advances, 236, 238, 243

adverbs, 51, 102

agents, 229, 242–60

Albertson, Alana, 233–34

ambivalence, 42–43

angst, 177–78

arcs
character, 58–59, 145, 194
completing, 141, 142
external, 59, 65, 121, 124, 127
internal, 58–59, 60, 65, 77, 121, 127, 143, 172
series, 34

Armentrout, Jennifer L., 7, 11, 20, 45, 115, 116, 188

audio books, 233–34

author services company, 211–13

back matter, 221

backstory, 77–78, 136–38

barcodes, 228–29

Bergeron, Amanda, 33, 47, 88, 193

beta readers, 189, 191–92

blogs, 20, 247, 264

blurb, 28, 227–28

books
building, 217–29
interior design, 220–21

production costs, 216–17

Bowker, 228

branding, 224, 225, 263–64

breather moments, 148, 149

budget, 214–15

business plan, 213–17

Butler, Carrie, 18, 276

Card, Melanie, 133, 147, 148

catalyst, 124, 133, 136

challenges, 121–22

change, 15, 58–60, 72, 133, 167

characterization, 69, 195, 197, 206
and dialogue, 92–93
elements of, 61–66
and plot, 111–19
and setting, 179–80

characters, 14, 28, 29, 57–87
and challenges, 121–22
and decision-making, 111
discovery exercise, 68–69, 73, 81
evaluating and revising, 194–98
foundational knowledge about, 66–68
and money, 112–13
physical attributes of, 69–73
profile worksheet, 85–87
realistic responses, 160–61
romantic, 157–62
secondary, 78–84, 144
and series, 33–34

and setting, 177–81
  techniques for revealing, 74–78
Clayton, Alice, 119
Cleeton, Chanel, 249
clichés, 51, 110, 132, 158, 172, 204
cliff-hangers, 139, 168
climax, 123, 125, 128, 141, 165
comparisons, 77
conflict, 16, 26, 27, 28, 30–31, 42, 114, 122,
  123, 124, 126–27
  escalating, 111, 145–52
  evaluating, 206
  in openings, 146–47
  and setting, 165
  and subtext, 150–52
context, 31–32
contradiction, 151
copyright, 220, 221, 223, 229–32
covers, book, 222–26, 240
credibility, 64
critiquing, 189–92, 218
crossover readers, 5, 19–20
Day, Sylvia, 11, 17, 20–21, 34, 114, 124, 155,
  188, 208
decision-making, 40–41, 111
defiance, 42
DeLorenzo, Jaycee, 41, 203, 276
denouement, 127
depth, 158, 159
descriptions, 76–77, 184
dialogue, 76, 88–107, 135
  and characterization, 92–93, 195
  crafting authentic, 99–106
  and emotions, 97–99
  evaluating, 203, 206
  internal, 49–50, 106–7, 204
  and plot, 95–97
  and sensibility, 90–91
  and sentence construction, 102–6
  and setting, 93–95
  sexual, 173
dialogue tag, 102, 185, 204
Dionne, Aubrie, 124, 137–38
direct thoughts, 106–7
Donaghy, Stacey, 66, 112, 243

ebb-and-flow strategy, 164, 165, 166, 201
e-books, 10, 208–10, 237–38
editing, deep, 192–204
editors, 193, 205, 218–20, 240, 245–60
emotions, 53–55, 72, 89, 97–99, 117, 153,
  201
empowerment, 119, 126–27, 139
endings, 141–44, 200
epilogue, 144
epiphany, 126, 127
escalation, 121, 122–27, 138, 145–52, 199
exclusives, 251, 255
Exley, A. W., 179–80
expectations, high, 15–16, 40, 63, 111–12,
  113–14, 122, 146
experiences, universal, 16, 29, 35, 74, 109
experimentation, 4, 10, 16, 37, 39, 41, 55,
  178
exposition, 134
failure, 122
fair use, 230
fear, 66, 122, 125, 158
feedback, 192
first drafts, 182, 189, 197, 203, 219
first pages, 254–56
first person POV, 45
flashbacks, 140–41
flaws, 60, 61, 62–63, 64, 83, 126, 127, 158,
  162, 195
foreshadowing, 143, 200
Forman, Gayle, 208, 274
format, 215–16
forward movement, 30, 33, 34, 41, 75, 76,
  96, 104, 119, 138, 139, 140, 149, 159, 199–
  200
front matter, 221
genres, 17–19
Glines, Abbi, 17, 208, 235
goal, 30–31, 65–66, 72, 123, 146
Grove, Karen, 13, 38, 241–42
Hocking, Amanda, 240
hook statement, 24–35, 123, 224, 227
Hoover, Colleen, 188, 208
hybrid authors, 235, 259–60, 276
idealization, 113–14

immediacy, 204
independence, 15
indirect thoughts, 204
info dump, 137, 140, 200, 203
in media res, 132–33
interior design, 220–21
ISBNs, 228–29
Lane, Summer, 18, 114
language mechanics, 204, 207
legal considerations, 229–32
libel, 232
love, 118, 153–72. *See also* sex
Ludwig, Robin, 225
Lynn, J., 7, 11, 17, 20, 45, 115, 116. See Ar-
    mentrout, Jennifer L.
Lyon, Kevan, 249–50
marketing, 217, 261–77
marriage, 156–57. *See also* sex
maturity, 44, 115–16, 203
McAdams, Molly, 10, 20, 55–56, 168–69,
    209
McGuire, Jamie, 10, 17, 208
middles, 138–41
mirroring technique, 143
Moggy, Dianne, 25–26
money, 112–13
multiple points of view, 46–48
multiple submissions, 248
narrative beats, 54, 89, 100–102, 184–85,
    195, 197, 203
narrative statement, 134
new adult (NA) fiction
    conflict and tension, 146–48
    differences from YA fiction, 37–38
    ingredients, 14–17
    market, 8–23
    overview, 3–7
    useful sites to stay current, 276–27
openings, 132–38, 146–47, 199
optimism, 40
pacing, 54, 104, 138, 140, 145, 148–50, 199,
    204, 206
paragraphs, 199–200
parents, 16, 39–40, 79–80, 114
Park, Jessica, 11, 17, 208, 235
passive voice, 51–52

Peck, Richard, 199
peers, 16, 79, 116–17
permissions, 230–32
personality, 37, 50, 72
perspective, 15, 22
pitch, 25, 27, 248–56
plagiarism, 229, 230
plot, 59, 108–19
    beginnings, middles, and endings, 131–
        44
    and dialogue, 95–97
    evaluating, 198–200, 206
    structuring, 120–30
point of view, 33, 45–49, 168–69, 206
price point, 215–16
print on demand, 211
priorities, 77
problem-solving, 119, 127
production costs, 216–17
promotion, book, 225
proofreading, 205, 219
props, 76, 93–94, 185
protagonist, 58–68, 124–25, 139. *See also*
    characters
public domain material, 231
publicity, 275–76
publishers/publishing, 21. *See also* self-
    publishing
    and agents, 242–45
    digital (*See* e-books)
    traditional, 235–60
punctuation, 53–54, 89, 104, 106
query letters, 226, 248, 250–52
reaction, 133–34
reality, 15–16, 17–18, 111–12
rejections, 256, 257
relationships, 16, 93, 153, 163–64, 167–68,
    200
request for partial/full, 248
resolution, 128, 141, 142
responsibilities, adult, 42–43
returns policy, 241
revising, 182, 187–207, 218
rhythm, 121, 125, 148, 196
risk-taking, 41, 43, 63, 116–17, 122
romance, 16, 17, 118, 153. *See also* love; sex

evaluating and revising storyline, 200–201

making it matter, 155–57

through a series, 167–69

rough drafts. *See first drafts*

royalties, 212, 215, 216, 229, 236, 237–38, 240–41, 243

self-awareness, 44, 45, 91

self-critiquing, 190–91

self-focus, 15, 39, 90–91, 202

self-marketing, 262–63

self-publishing, 10, 208–34, 259

self-reliance, 113

senses, 76, 171, 182–83, 202

sensibility, 36–56, 90–91, 202–3

sentences, 52–53, 102–6, 150, 204

sequels, 128–29, 143–44

series, 32–34, 143–44, 167–69, 200

setting, 110, 139, 176–86, 201

and characters, 177–81

and conflict, 165

describing, 183–84

and dialogue, 93–95

evaluating, 202, 206

exercise, 181, 185–86

making it feel real, 181–85

and narrative beats, 197

sex/sexuality, 5, 16, 23, 118, 153–72

Shepard, Aaron, 211

show, don't tell technique, 45, 51, 75–76, 82, 127, 137, 181, 182

social circles, 16, 79–81, 118

social media, 247, 262, 263–64, 265–69

Steinhaus, Nicole, 241–42

stereotypes, 73–74

St. Martin's Press, 22–23

Stop Looking Test, 194, 195–97, 202, 203, 204

story evaluation, 205–7

Story Evaluation Questions, 192

storyline. *See plot*

strengths, character, 64–65, 126, 158

stress, 39, 58, 111, 113, 117, 133, 146, 198

structure, 42, 129–30

submission guidelines, 255

submission lists, 243, 246–47

subplot, 125, 127–29, 161, 200

subsidiary rights, 244

subtext, 97, 145, 150–52, 203

survival, 44, 141–42

suspense, 148

swearing, 105–6

synopsis, 248, 253–54

tagline, 27–28

temporary state, 142

tense, 49–50

tension, 16, 30–31, 54, 63, 66, 117, 122, 123, 125, 138, 139, 140, 146–48

emotional, 162

increasing, 199, 200

romantic, 162–66

sexual, 153, 161, 163–64, 166, 171, 173

and subtext, 150–52

themes, 14, 16–17, 29–30

third person POV, 46

thoughts, direct, 106–7

time, 139, 178

tip sheets, 257

transitions, 138–41, 204

trends, market, 34–35

twist ending, 143

Twitter, 263, 267, 268

uncertainty, 146

Vaughn, Carrie, 19, 114, 133

verbs, 51

vocabulary. *See* dialogue

voice, 36–56, 202–3, 207

vulnerabilities, 43, 63

wants and needs, 65–66

Webber, Tammara, 4, 10, 11, 62, 155, 169, 208, 209, 210, 235, 263

websites, 263–64

Weiss, Dan, 9, 21–23

wisdom, 36, 65, 115–16

word choice, 50–55, 102–6, 207

world-building, 135

worldview, 38, 154, 177

young adult (YA) fiction, 11–12, 37–38

Zusak, Markus, 18, 65–66, 136

WRITER'S DIGEST

Is Your Manuscript Ready?

Trust 2nd Draft Critique Service to prepare your writing to catch the eye of agents and editors. You can expect:

- Expert evaluation from a hand-selected, professional critiquer
- Know-how on reaching your target audience
- Red flags for consistency, mechanics, and grammar
- Tips on revising your work to increase your odds of publication

Visit WritersDigestShop.com/2nd-draft for more information.

CRAFT POWERFUL STORIES BY BREAKING THE RULES

Story Trumps Structure

BY STEVEN JAMES

All too often, following the "rules" of writing can constrict rather than inspire you. With *Story Trumps Structure*, you can shed those rules—about three-act structure, rising action, outlining, and more—to craft your most powerful, emotional, and gripping stories. Award-winning novelist Steven James explains how to trust the narrative process to make your story believable, compelling, and engaging, and debunks the common myths that hold writers back from creating their best work.

Available from WritersDigestShop.com and your favorite book retailers.

To get started join our mailing list: WritersDigest.com/enews

FOLLOW US ON:

 Find more great tips, networking and advice by following **@writersdigest**

 And become a fan of our Facebook page: **facebook.com/writersdigest**